SARAH

—FROM—

ALASKA

SARAH
—FROM—
ALASKA

★ ★ ★

THE SUDDEN RISE
AND BRUTAL EDUCATION
OF A NEW CONSERVATIVE
SUPERSTAR

Scott Conroy
and Shushannah Walshe

PublicAffairs
New York

Book Design by Pauline Brown

Library of Congress Cataloging-in-Publication Data

Conroy, Scott.
     Sarah from Alaska : the sudden rise and brutal education of a new
conservative superstar / Scott Conroy and Shushannah Walshe.
          p.   cm.
     Includes index.
     ISBN 978-1-58648-788-1 (hardcover)
     1. Palin, Sarah, 1964-2. Women governors—Alaska—Biography. 3. Women
politicians—Alaska—Biography. 4. Vice-Presidential candidates—Alaska—
Biography. 5. Presidents—United States—Election—2008. I. Walshe,
Shushannah. II. Title.
F910.7.P35C66 2009

                                                            973.931092—dc22
                                                                        [B]

                                    2009032659

                                   First Edition

                            10 9 8 7 6 5 4 3 2 1

★ ★ ★

A constant source of love and support:
our parents, Mick, Estelle, Jim, and Lynn;
sisters, Dalia and Erin;
and all of our grandparents

Contents

✳ ✳ ✳

Introduction: Lights Out 1

1. Frozen Paths   23
2. Seeing Red   41
3. Honeymoon in Juneau   59
4. Sharp Elbows   77
5. Plucked   91
6. The Iron Curtain   123
7. Taking the Reins   145
8. The Final Limp   169
9. Can't Let Go   193
10. Only in Alaska   217
11. Alaska Outgrown   233
12. The Next Chapter   259

Acknowledgments 281
Sources 285
Index 293

SARAH

—FROM—

ALASKA

Introduction: Lights Out

IN A CONDOMINIUM SUITE at the Arizona Biltmore Hotel, Republican vice presidential nominee Sarah Palin read over the election night victory speech that she would never have the chance to deliver. *Thank you all so much. And thank you, America, for the great responsibility that you have given to President-elect John S. McCain.*

It was just minutes before the stirring moment when the official results would begin to trickle in, but as the sun descended toward the desert horizon, her fatigue must have been crushing. Palin's two months on the trail had been not just physically exhausting but mentally draining. This short, strange trip had tested her in ways that might have broken even the most hardened political pro, and she had suffered more than her fair share of setbacks and embarrassments. Still, it was Palin's gripping story and alluring personality

1

that had breathed life into a once flatlining campaign. Her addition to the ticket had sparked a flood of donations, standing-room only crowds at rallies, and a surge in the polls for the Republican ticket. But along with Palin's many positive contributions to the campaign had come as many ruinous malfunctions. In the final hours of this frenzied voyage, she would discover just how expendable she had become, as the McCain campaign was literally about to turn the lights out on her.

How had she skyrocketed so quickly into the stratosphere of American politics? Who had really been at fault for her many public stumbles? And what was it about Sarah Palin that drew such passion from both her fans and her foes? Even with the benefit of the thousands of hours of media attention that had been devoted to her candidacy, the heat of the moment did not afford the perspective for anyone to answer these questions adequately, least of all the candidate herself. On this last night of the campaign, Palin remained focused on the momentous judgment that the American people were about to deliver.

Even by presidential-campaign standards, Palin's last two days had been borderline inhumane. She had started her Monday morning outside Cleveland, Ohio, and made her way across the Lower 48 to rallies in Missouri, Iowa, and Colorado, stopping twice in Nevada, before catching an overnight flight to Anchorage. Then she staggered to the finish line here in Phoenix. While mapping out the final days, Palin's aides had suggested it might be more practical for the governor to vote absentee, rather than make the sixteen-hour Alaska detour, but she insisted on casting her ballot in her home state.

A few paragraphs down, the victory speech became more personal, adding a touch of humor about her famously low-key husband. *We were ready, in defeat, to return to a place and a life we love. And I said to my husband Todd that it's not a step down when he's no longer*

Alaska's "First Dude." He will now be the first guy ever to become the "Second Dude."

Palin and more than a few of her aides had earnestly believed all fall that they could come from behind to win the thing, even though McCain's top advisers knew the near collapse of the financial system in October likely foretold the Republican ticket's doom. Yes, the crowds that had greeted her were enormous and passionate, and, yes, there was always hope that God would answer her prayers and grant her just one more miracle in what had been a string of unlikely successes in her short political career. But the recent polls were uniformly grim.

She turned her attention to the other set of remarks that had been penned for her, the concession speech. Like the victory address, its very existence would remain a secret after McCain and his inner circle denied her the opportunity to deliver it later in the night.

I wish Barack Obama well as the 44th president of the United States. If he governs America with the skill and grace we have often seen in him, and the greatness of which he is capable, we're gonna be just fine. And when a black citizen prepares to fill the office of Washington and Lincoln, that is a shining moment in our history that can be lost on no one.

It was a poignant passage in the far less triumphant of the two speeches that Matthew Scully, a former speechwriter for President George W. Bush, had written in advance of either outcome. A cerebral animal-protection activist, Scully was an unlikely wordsmith for the governor who could field-dress a moose. He had also penned Palin's game-changing address at the Republican National Convention, field-dressing Obama with charges of arrogance, elitism, and inexperience. This time, however, he was exceedingly cordial in a manner appropriate for the occasion. Palin scribbled in another line with her black pen, dropping a cherry atop the hot fudge sundae: *God bless you and your beautiful family, President-elect Obama.*

She had first discussed her victory and concession speeches with Scully two days earlier, when they spoke in Room 719 of the McKinley Grand Hotel in Canton, Ohio. Like Scully's former boss and many of his predecessors in the Oval Office, Palin was the kind of Christian who felt comfortable expressing her faith in public, which the speech reflected: *I will remember all the people who said they were praying for me.* She squeezed another handwritten line in the margin, perhaps in an attempt to get the last word in against some of the McCain aides who thought it was better for her to tone down the God talk: *You prayer warriors have been my strength and my shield.*

The last few weeks had been particularly trying ones for Palin, as public missteps and allegations of selfish motives had accumulated one after another and threatened to define her. But tonight's speech was her chance to launch the next stage of her political career, and surely her fellow Republicans had seen the excitement she had inspired among the voters; surely they perceived the promise she held for the Republican Party's future. Still, she knew how important it was to avoid any perception that her own ambitions were anywhere near the forefront of her mind. She had done most of the things she had been asked to do in order to get John McCain elected, but she had only come on board for a small piece of the ten-year odyssey he had begun when he launched his first presidential campaign in 1999. This night was about him. Palin's antagonists in Washington, in Juneau, and especially in the media would be paying close attention to whether or not she played the good soldier in this final battle of the war.

The concession speech included a paragraph about Todd and how his schedule would now be clear to win a fifth Iron Dog snowmachine race back home in Alaska. She was glad to see that it also allowed her to give one of her characteristic shout-outs to Charlie, the boy with Down syndrome whom she'd met in Florida and had been corresponding with ever since. *Charlie and I swapped email addresses, and the last time he replied he said, "By the way, please don't call me 'sweetie'—it's not tough enough." So tonight, a special shout-out to you, Charlie . . . sweetie.* But actually, she had referred to Charlie as "darling" in her last e-mail, not "sweetie," as Scully had written. She crossed it out and scribbled in "darlin'," though she hardly needed to remind herself to drop the *g.* She then took out the second "Charlie" and wrote in "Chuck"—just a little something extra to make him sound like the resilient kid she knew he was. Even at this climactic moment in her career, Palin was still immersed in the details.

But perhaps the most important part of the concession speech lavished further praise upon her running mate. *It would be a happier night if elections were a test of valor and merit alone, but that is not for us to question now. Enough to say it has been the honor of a lifetime to fight at the side of John S. McCain.* She scribbled in just one more line: *To the Senator, Cindy, and your amazing family—thank you. I honor you. I love you.*

Palin always devoted significant time and effort to honing her speeches, to making sure that they reflected her own voice. Back in Alaska, she had often written her own remarks, and it had taken some time on the trail to get used to the concept of giving a repetitive stump speech. But she had come to admire the work that Scully and his speechwriting partner, Lindsay Hayes, did for her, and this was one of their better efforts. Now she handed both the victory and concession speeches to her personal assistant, Bexie Nobles, to give back to the writers, who were waiting outside the condominium to update them with Palin's changes. Little did they know how complicated—and painfully tense—this matter of her speech was about to become.

Earlier in the day, Scully had run into longtime McCain speechwriter and confidante Mark Salter in a hallway of the Biltmore.

Salter told Scully that he was writing McCain's victory and concession speeches, and Scully said that he was doing the same for Palin.
There had been no official confirmation that the vice presidential
nominee would speak at all on election night, but a lack of communication had become the norm on this campaign, and why else
would aides have dispatched Scully to Phoenix if not to draft remarks for Palin? Before they parted, Scully asked Salter if he thought
there was a chance the Republican nominees would end up delivering the victory speeches rather than the concessions.

"It's gonna be tough," was the somber answer.

Scully later crossed paths with McCain's campaign manager,
Rick Davis, who expressed some surprise when told there was a vice
presidential speech in the works.

"We certainly don't have to," Scully said, "but it's been my assumption that she would speak briefly, and we have some four or
five minutes of remarks there."

Davis thought about it for a moment. "Okay, I see how it would
work. She would introduce him."

Scully nodded. "Exactly. For either outcome, she would say
some appropriate things, express her gratitude and admiration for
Senator McCain, and that would be that."

Davis agreed with Scully that it was a fine plan.

Shortly before 5:30 P.M., Bexie Nobles delivered the folder containing Palin's edited speeches to Scully and Hayes. The writers retreated to Hayes's room, where they worked furiously to insert the
governor's changes in both versions, knowing the results at the polls
would start trickling in at any moment. When they finished, they
went down to the lobby to find a printer. A staffer they encountered
on the way told them Pennsylvania had just been called for Obama.
This first bad news of the night was pretty close to devastating.
Most polls had shown the Democratic ticket enjoying a double-digit

lead in Pennsylvania, but Palin had spent more time there than in any other state during the previous two months, and the Republicans were banking on an upset win with help from those white, working-class voters everyone talked so much about.

On this last night of the campaign, the McCain and Palin camps would ostensibly see their fates sealed together, but in practice, the two sides had long viewed themselves as distinctly separate operations. In striking contrast to the unity and cohesiveness that propelled the Obama campaign, staffers assigned to the top and bottom of the Republican ticket had spent as much time fighting each other as they had their shared opponent. When Palin's plane had landed in Phoenix earlier in the day, for instance, the governor had decided to turn down a dinner invitation from John and Cindy McCain, knowing she had almost no time to get ready before the polls closed on the East Coast. Word of perceived slights from the McCain side always spread like a virus, and several of Palin's staffers now speculated that the senator's dinner invitation had been an empty one. "I think that if he really wanted her there, he would have scheduled the dinner for a later time," one Palin aide said. "She was literally taking feet off the plane right when the dinner started."

But the lingering tension between the two factions must have been far from her mind as Palin waited for the election results to come in. Just a few hours earlier, she had cast her own ballot along with her closest friends and family in her frigid hometown. Wearing a deliberately Wasillan ensemble of sneakers, blue jeans, and a Carhartt sweatshirt with her name embroidered below the left shoulder, she had swept into Wasilla City Hall behind her closest aide, Kris Perry, and her husband, Todd, who wore a navy-blue zip-down fleece with an oversized "Iron Dog" patch. After the First Couple of Alaska voted, bright lights from a half dozen television cameras provided the only glow in the predawn air. The temperature outside the polling station hovered around fourteen degrees, but Palin was the kind of Alaskan who took inordinate pride in never admitting the effects of cold weather and wore no hat or gloves. Reporters wiggled numb fingers as they extended small digital tape recorders upward toward the candidate, and icy clouds hung in the freezing air after each breath.

"So, we have a very optimistic, very confident view of what's gonna happen today, and again, so glad to get to be home in Wasilla to cast this vote," Palin had said, as her shadow danced on the pavement. "Because forever I'm gonna be Sarah from Alaska."

She had tried to project optimism then, but now that Pennsylvania had gone the other way, the outlook was incontrovertibly grim. The television set in her suite was tuned to *Fox News* as usual, but Palin wasn't paying much attention as her husband and young daughters, Piper and Willow, shuffled in and out. She was worried about the members of her extended family who had flown in with her from Alaska and were still scrambling to find their respective rooms after someone lost the lodging assignments list.

"When can I see my family?" she asked. "These people traveled with me. I want to see them."

A few minutes later, Karl Rove's voice drifted from the television into the bathroom where Palin's second personal assistant, Jeannie Etchart, knelt in front of her, pinning the governor's skirt.

"If he loses Ohio, he goes from 286, which the Republicans carried in 2004, down to 266," Rove said of McCain. "And that puts him below the 270 threshold needed to win the White House." As if on cue, *Fox News* anchor Brit Hume interjected, "Guess what Karl? I've just received word that the state of Ohio has gone for Barack Obama."

Palin swallowed a mouthful of air. "Oh, well, that's it," she said.

Her young aide struggled to find the right words as she fought back tears, surprised by how calm and stoic her boss seemed.

Etchart came up with something about how it had been a great ride, but Palin wasn't quite ready to reflect just yet. As she added some final touches to her outfit, she asked for an edited copy of her concession speech but was told her remarks were not finished yet.

Now that defeat was no longer in doubt, Palin, her husband, and their Secret Service entourage made their way to McCain's suite to prepare for the candidates' final appearance together. The Secret Service agent guarding McCain's door allowed the Palins inside, where the senator was in the bedroom watching the still-menacing returns come in. Chief campaign strategist Steve Schmidt, Mark Salter, Rick Davis, and McCain's two closest friends in the Senate, Joe Lieberman and Lindsay Graham, chatted somberly in the suite's living room. While Cindy McCain stood just inside the doorway and made sure that no one else entered the suite reserved for the inner circle, the First Couple of Alaska joined McCain in the bedroom.

Once Sarah and Todd Palin were out of earshot, Schmidt, Davis, and Salter huddled together. Each of these men had been through it all with McCain over the course of the two-year campaign (or many years longer, in Davis's and Salter's case), and the night's emotions weighed heavily. Though they all knew a speech had been written for Palin, they agreed now that it seemed like a bad idea for her to deliver it. If they let her go forward with her speech, they ran the risk that she might upstage John McCain during what should be his moment. At least one senior aide worried that she might go off script, as she had done to negative effect several times during the campaign.

Schmidt entered the bedroom and asked McCain for a moment of his time. The senator excused himself and retreated to a corner of the living room with the top campaign aides, who told their boss that Palin intended to give a speech.

"We don't think it's a good idea," one of them said. "It's kind of unprecedented." Except that it wasn't. Democratic vice presidential nominee John Edwards had given his own concession speech in 2004 and incumbent vice president Dan Quayle had done likewise for the Republicans in 1992.

"Do you think Governor Palin should speak before you?" another senior aide asked.

"No, no," McCain said.

McCain took Schmidt up on the chief strategist's offer to break the news to Palin. As poised and direct as ever, Schmidt wasted no time in telling the Alaska governor that since this night was really about the peaceful transfer of power, it would be appropriate for only the presidential nominee himself to speak and concede the election. Palin showed little emotion as she appeared to accept the campaign's decision. Unbeknownst to Schmidt, she was not about to give up that easily.

McCain and Palin reconvened to watch the returns together with their spouses at their sides. Their fates as also-rans were sealed at 11 P.M., Eastern time, when the networks declared that Barack Obama would become the nation's forty-fourth president. Palin then left McCain's suite and headed back to her own quarters with her husband and a small contingent of aides.

Though McCain's decision that Palin would not deliver her speech had been conveyed to the governor with an air of finality, she didn't treat it as settled doctrine. She did not, for example, inform her staff or do anything to clarify the confusion that would soon beset the night's events. The first sign of a major problem came when Jason Recher, a Palin senior adviser, ran into McCain aide Davis White. White's job as director of advance was to make sure that logistics ran smoothly. Recher, one of the many staffers in Palin's inner circle who was a veteran of both of the Bush-Cheney campaigns, was more used to organizing morning victory speeches than nighttime concessions. He wanted a walk-through with White to make sure everyone was on the same page.

"How is this going to work?" Recher recalls asking White. "She'll speak first and then McCain?"

White stopped in his tracks. "I'm not sure she's going to speak. Rick Davis said it may not happen."

Recher couldn't believe it. Like everyone else in Palin's sphere, he had assumed she would introduce McCain to the disappointed crowd. His personal opinion aside, it was a rather important logistical matter to clear up quickly, and Recher asked if he should call Rick Davis in order to do so.

"No, I'll figure it out," White said.

Meanwhile, as word began to spread that prospects for Palin's speaking were looking dim, some on her team began to lobby on her behalf. Scully fired off an e-mail to members of McCain's senior staff emphasizing the positive, pro-McCain message of the speech he had drafted for Palin and making it clear that he thought it unfair to block her from having a modest final moment in the spotlight.

Jason Recher had just rejoined Palin in her suite when he received a frantic call on his radio set from McCain's trip director, Mike Dew, who demanded to know where Palin was. The senator was ready to go on stage, anxious to get the unenviable task of conceding the race over and done with.

"We need a minute," Recher said.

"Get her back here," Dew replied. "He is waiting outside. We are going on."

"Okay, go for it," Recher said, though he doubted Dew would. McCain's team knew there would be negative fallout if the candidate left his dynamic running mate behind in his final public appearance of the campaign. Recher's challenge was a way of calling Dew's bluff.

Palin still had not told Recher about McCain's decision to veto her speech. Instead, she gave him some curt instructions. "I'm speaking," she told him. "I've got the remarks. Figure it out."

Recher acknowledged the direct order from his boss, whom he admired deeply. He said through the radio set, "Recher for White. We're coming down with remarks."

As confusion continued to mount, Palin's deputy chief of staff Chris Edwards, another Bush veteran, sprinted across the stage toward the teleprompter with a flash drive containing the governor's speech. There, he ran into Steve Schmidt, who reiterated the decision he had already relayed to Palin. No, Schmidt told Edwards, Palin would not be allowed to speak. Not realizing that the governor had already been informed of McCain's decision, Edwards concluded that the game had gone on long enough and that he should be the one to break the news to his boss. He caught up with Palin on her way to the holding area backstage and told her what Schmidt had just relayed to him. She again did not let on that she had already heard the news from Schmidt. Perhaps she was hoping that if she could prolong the uncertainty for long enough, she would be able to go ahead with the speech. After all, in this campaign, it had always seemed that no decision was ever really "final."

Palin was still holding her prepared remarks when another of her staffers gave her some hope by contradicting Edwards's report and sharing what he had heard: she *would* be allowed to speak. The governor asked rhetorically what the big issue was. "This speech is great," she said in frustration. "It's all about how John McCain's an American hero."

After she finally located her parents, Palin and her small entourage met up with McCain outside his villa with top aides, including White, Schmidt, Salter, Davis, and communications guru Nicolle Wallace and her husband, Mark, who had run Palin's debate-prep operation. In a last-ditch attempt to come to the governor's rescue, Jason Recher decided to try to end the confusion about Palin's speech by acting as if none existed. "She's got remarks," he told White loudly enough for everyone present, including McCain, to hear.

The McCain side stood its ground, and Mark Salter decided enough was enough. He removed his trademark sunglasses and approached Palin. "You're not speaking," he told her. "John has decided it's unprecedented."

The caravan of family, staff, and Secret Service moved as a group to get into position backstage. Meanwhile, Palin was still shuffling through her notes, and Schmidt picked up on some chatter that led him to believe the issue *still* had not been resolved. He approached Palin again to reiterate what he had told her in the suite. "Apparently there is some confusion over the speech," he said. "There is just going to be one speech tonight. Only the senator is going to speak."

Davis White was there to greet the entourage, and Salter asked him to announce the procedure to everyone in the group. "So we're going to announce y'all, and Senator McCain's going to speak, and then y'all are going to depart," White said in his thick Alabama drawl, becoming the fourth staffer of the night to pass on the official word to Palin that she would not be speaking. Mike Dew chimed in immediately in order to preclude any opportunity for arguments. "We're walking, we're walking, we're walking," he said, giving his best tour-guide imitation.

John and Cindy McCain continued to lead the procession toward the stage with the Palin team trailing behind. Later that night, Salter would send Scully an e-mail apologizing for the confusion. But now, as the governor prepared to walk onto the stage to stand, wave, and applaud in silence, she was visibly dazed.

Recher leaned into her ear. "Do you want me to try again?" he asked.

"No, I think it's dead."

"I will try one more time."

"I think it's dead," Palin repeated, finally admitting defeat.

McCain turned around to speak to his downcast running mate in a well-meaning, yet nonetheless absurd, attempt to lift the mood. "It's a nice night out, isn't it?"

She agreed that it was.

"Look at the stars," McCain continued. "Ah, Sarah, wasn't this fun? Are you staying here tonight? Go to the pool with the kids."

The running mates and their spouses ascended the stairs and waved dutifully to the crowd of supporters, volunteers, and staff that stretched across the Biltmore lawn. The audience interrupted McCain's speech several times to applaud and chant his name, but it wasn't until the senator thanked his running mate that the throng let out its most boisterous cheer of the night. Palin managed a smile, but her face betrayed the sting she felt. She had been a team player most of the time, but there was no doubt that she resented the decision to deprive her of the chance to soak up the crowd's adoration and jump-start her future success.

After he concluded his humble speech, perhaps his best and most widely admired of the entire campaign, McCain left the stage promptly, but Palin, having nothing to do for the first time in over two months, lingered a little longer and walked off in another direction with her family and staff. "What are we doing now?" she asked. "Are we going back to the suite? Are we gonna say good-bye?"

No one was sure whether Senator McCain and his wife intended to stay longer at the Biltmore or return to their Phoenix home, so Palin and her entourage made their way across the parking lot back toward their condominium where they expected to receive word of their late-night plans. As they walked past the rows of cars, they stopped suddenly, surprised by the sight of some familiar faces getting into a Chevy Suburban.

"John? Is that you?" Palin asked.

Cindy was already in the car, and the senator had just given a final hug to his press secretary and personal aide, Brooke Buchanan. He spun around.

"Oh, hey. How are you, Sarah?"

"Are you leaving?"

"Yup, we're out of here."

Palin paused. "Okay, well, good night."

"Yes, good night. We're headed back to the house."

The now former running mates exchanged final pat-on-the-back hugs and a muffled thank you or two. There was no discussion about the shared experience they had just completed and no photograph to memorialize the gloomy occasion, as there had been on that buoyant day in Arizona nine weeks earlier when he had asked her to be his running mate. As some of Palin's staffers gazed at the scene, they marveled at its awkwardness. McCain was never one for overwrought sappiness, but this was a strikingly anticlimactic way to end his partnership with Palin.

Back in the suite, Todd broke out a bottle of champagne and poured a glass for everyone in the room. After excusing herself to change clothes, the governor reemerged to toast the "friendships and memories made" on the campaign trail. But after everyone took a sip, she couldn't help but wonder aloud, "What just happened?"

She asked the Bush campaign veterans if election night was always so dysfunctional. They reminded her that on election night in 2000 and 2004, the outcome had still been in doubt when most Americans had gone to bed, so they didn't have anything with which to compare it.

"There was no closure," Palin said.

As Todd Palin and Recher began to plan the trip back home the next day, the governor retired to another room in the suite to call in to an election night party in Alaska. When she returned, Recher told her he was going to attend the party that members of the campaign advance staff were throwing in the courtyard.

"Should I go with you?" Palin asked. Recher explained that it was probably best that she didn't. The booze had been flowing for a while now, and the alcohol combined with the intense emotions of the day gave the event the potential to get a little rowdy.

Recher had been at the party for all of five minutes when Piper, the governor's precocious seven-year-old daughter, snuck up behind him. "My mom is looking for you," she said. "She wants to go on stage and take a picture."

Recher didn't have time to think twice about how the governor had ignored his advice. Palin was following not far behind Piper with two or three dozen members of her extended family in tow. Traveling staffers would soon receive messages on their BlackBerries about the group photo plan and make their way to the outdoor stage. Recher's instincts still told him it was not a good idea. There were still a lot of TV cameras in the area. Even though McCain had already left, his aides were likely to see this as an attempt by Palin to have the last word.

"Let's find another area not on the stage," Recher suggested. "The press is still set up, and there are a ton of cameras. They'll likely turn live to cover this."

The group assembled backstage as a kind of compromise. But that didn't feel festive enough to Palin. "I want to go on stage and take a picture with my family," she said.

"All the press is there," Recher recalls reminding her.

"My loyalty is to my family at this point, and I want to do it."

Kris Perry stepped in to try to convince her boss and close friend that Recher was right, but Palin had made up her mind. "I flew them all the way out here," she said. "It's the least I can do."

Recher surrendered and began to assemble the family and some staffers on stage. As startled members of the media looked on, the now former candidate joined the group and began to smile and wave. But the press weren't the only ones who were surprised. Some of McCain's aides could barely believe their eyes as they saw the young rock star of the Republican ticket apparently trying to upstage the venerable senator one last time.

Senior McCain aide Carla Eudy had already left the Biltmore to attend a downcast late dinner at Morton's steakhouse. She received a frantic phone call from Davis White, who told her that it looked as though Palin was about to give her speech after all. Eudy told him in no uncertain terms that Palin's apparent final act of rebellion was unacceptable.

She immediately called Steve Schmidt, who did not hesitate to issue his last order of the campaign. "Take the set down," he told Eudy. "Unplug it."

Eudy forwarded the message back to Davis White.

"What is going on?" White demanded of Recher. "Is she going to give remarks?"

Recher explained that Palin merely wanted to take pictures with her family, but to White, it sounded like a dubious cover story. Acting on the instructions that had filtered down from Schmidt, White put in a call to the soundboard operator and told him to bring the lights down and cut the sound.

"Come on, this is ridiculous," Recher remembers saying to White.

"We pay for this stuff," White replied.

The lights went down, but the effect was minimal, and no one seemed to notice that the stage had become dimmer as Palin waved and posed for pictures with her family.

When she found out what was happening, an incensed Carla Eudy called Recher to express her displeasure. "You never had control of her," she said, according to Recher. "Get control of her! Get her ass off stage!"

Recher was not in the mood for yet another argument with the McCain team. "The campaign ended tonight, and so did you," he said before hanging up the phone.

Palin did not give a speech as she continued to pose for pictures with her family. Nonetheless, she had succeeded in punctuating the night on her own terms. She would save her next big move for another day.

★ ★ ★

"WHAT JUST HAPPENED?"

That was the question that Sarah Palin blurted out in exasperation on the night of November 4, 2008, after her running mate hightailed it out of the Arizona Biltmore and her role in his campaign dissolved into history. And it is the very same question that always seems to be asked about the woman who rose from obscurity to celebrity in near record time.

Alaskans asked it when a young mother from Wasilla trounced an incumbent Republican to claim the governor's seat and did more in a year and a half to change the way state business was done than many governors manage in two terms.

The media asked it when John McCain made one of the most stunning moves in American political history by selecting a first-term governor from the nation's most isolated state as his choice for vice president.

Democrats asked it when Palin floored the nation with a gritty, self-confident speech at the Republican National Convention and suddenly eclipsed Barack Obama as the biggest political force of the moment.

Her campaign aides asked it when she fumbled critical plays and stopped listening to their advice, becoming something akin to an unguided missile every time she handled a microphone.

After her election day defeat, we, the authors of this book, asked it when Palin dispatched her press secretary to accuse us of "stalking" her when we were simply reporting from Alaska and of "cornering" her daughter Piper after we had exchanged pleasantries during a chance encounter on a street in downtown Juneau.

And in the aftermath of Palin's staggering resignation from the governorship of Alaska in July 2009, the question resounded everywhere—not just on op-ed pages and in political media but even in the private conversations of some of Palin's most fervent supporters.

Her ascent to the national stage had been so unexpected that even her own campaign's communications team was left entirely unprepared to answer questions about her record. She remains so polarizing that her very name elicits visceral emotions ranging from adoration to abhorrence, with little room in the middle. Americans tend to project their ideals and fears onto Sarah Palin and define themselves politically by how they react to her every move.

Contrary to the simple judgments that both her admirers and detractors have settled on, Palin's character is marked by complexity and paradox. She is outwardly confident but frequently shows signs of profound insecurity. Her convictions are deep, yet her greatest successes have been products of compromise. She is the daughter of educators, though she sometimes comes across as proud to be incurious. She is unafraid to take on entrenched power but is hypersensitive to criticism and naysayers. She is quick to push aside people who stand in her way, yet her compassionate nature is sincere. She likes to assert control of her own fate but declines to fire in person aides who have fallen out of favor. She is proud of her humble background but unflinching in her quest for superstardom. She can be refreshingly blunt but is prone to contorting the truth in ways that range from dubious to flat-out deceitful.

While traveling the country as embedded reporters on her vice presidential campaign plane for two months, we were struck by Palin's magnetic qualities and innate political shrewdness, just as we were taken aback by how disastrous her mishaps became. True believers by the tens of thousands waited in line for hours just to catch a glimpse of her, while swarms of protesters hounded her just as ardently. She was so polarizing that she inspired a civil war within her own campaign during the precious final days before the election.

We spent several weeks in Alaska after election day and watched as the glitz and glamour that Palin had reveled in on the campaign trail evaporated into the suddenly unappealing slog of governing on a small stage, under constant assault from critics large and small. While we cannot claim to have predicted her sudden resignation (or, as she so acrobatically described it, her decision "to avoid putting Alaskans through the typical, 'politics-as-usual, lame duck' status"), it was certainly clear to us then that she had in her own mind outgrown the job she had begun just two and a half years earlier. For Palin, the appeal of the bright lights under which she had once glowed and her longing to escape the ugly reality to which she had returned were too strong to deny.

On the campaign trail, we witnessed some of the proudest and most embarrassing moments of Palin's political career and have spent the better part of a year gaining insights and behind-the-scenes stories from scores of her friends, foes, family members, and former staffers. We have synthesized all of this information with the intention of providing a thorough account of "what just happened." Despite the too-easy caricatures, Palin is neither an unblemished victim of fiendish, unpatriotic forces nor a preposterous dolt worthy only of a smirk. This book is designed to chronicle one of the unlikeliest, most fascinating and turbulent political ascents in recent history. It is a story rooted in a small town nestled in the American frontier, which takes a dramatic turn when Sarah from Alaska is suddenly called up to the major leagues.

It is easy to forget just how rapid Palin's political ascent has been. When she took office as governor in December 2006, John McCain had already launched an exploratory committee for his presidential campaign. She has benefited from an incredible streak of being in the right place at the right time, but whatever one thinks about her politics, anyone who can, in just six years, rise from the mayor's office in a city of fewer than ten thousand people to become the biggest draw in the Republican Party must be doing something right.

What is Sarah Palin really like? It is a question that anyone who has spent time around her is asked frequently. Honest answers may vary, but no one can doubt her drive to spread the tenets of her worldview or her determination to take advantage of her critics' tendency to underestimate her profoundly. Palin's small-town experience fine-tuned her innate ability to connect with people on a personal level, and the sincerity of her common touch is often striking to those who expect anyone in her position to be a prima donna. Campaign staffers marveled at how deeply she appreciated the lengths the Secret Service went to treat her like royalty and keep her safe. Lisa A. Kline, the New York City stylist brought in to make the now infamous high-end wardrobe purchases, still remembers the moment just before she parted with the governor at the Republican convention in St. Paul on the biggest night of Palin's career. "The woman is going to make her acceptance speech, and she had the whole family stop and say, 'Thank you,'" Kline recalls. "I appreciated it so much."

But as genuine as her warmth and kindness can be, Palin's ruthless streak is just as real. It has led her to engage in bullying tactics and to toss aside old friends and close aides who have crossed her personally, even in minor ways. She is rigidly certain that she is right, and they are wrong—a characteristic common to human nature but one that in her case is amplified and rarely second-guessed. This conviction allows her to confidently maintain cognitively dissonant positions, such as declaring her family off-limits to media, while simultaneously using her son's military service as a frequent talking point and demeaning the teenaged father of her own grandson through a political spokesperson.

Now that she has abandoned the constraints once imposed on her by the governorship of Alaska, Palin is free to attempt to recapture the national adulation that she first enjoyed after a stunning speech on a warm August night in St. Paul, Minnesota. It will not be an easy quest, but her intense experience in the political spotlight has only deepened the determination that helped catapult her to such heights. The story of Sarah Palin has an uncertain ending, but it is guaranteed to be intrinsically interwoven with that of the Republican Party as it struggles to redefine itself and recapture the necessary margin for national political victory in the next decade.

⋆ ⋆ ⋆

1. Frozen Paths

IN A WAY, SARAH PALIN'S political career began on a driveway in a small town tucked away in the Alaskan backwoods where her parents had set up a basketball hoop for their four children. Whether it was a cold fall morning with the season's first snowfall on the way or a warm summer night illuminated by endless sunlight, Sarah could often be found on the makeshift court, honing her skills and developing her aggressiveness.

With her short-cropped hair and tomboy instincts, she was always the most competitive of the Heath kids. Her sister Heather was older and her brother Chuck Jr. was older, taller, and stronger, but that just made Sarah more determined to keep up with them during family games. From a young age, it was clear to anyone who saw her play her favorite sport that she was a natural competitor.

It was long before the days when promising young athletes were expected to participate in formal camps and summer leagues, and the kids in Wasilla were on their own. Even before they started playing organized sports, young children in that pre-Nintendo era were left with nothing but the outdoors and their imaginations. Sarah joined her first organized town-league team in elementary school at a time when Wasilla was enjoying rapid population growth, and basketball had become the sport of choice for girls and boys who wanted something to do in the ice hockey off-season. Though the basketball culture in Alaska during the 1970s may not have been as deeply rooted as it was in the cornfields of Indiana or on the playgrounds of the Bronx, the sport enjoyed surprising popularity considering the climatic limitations that challenged year-round practice time.

It can be easy to overstate the importance of youth athletics in providing the foundation for a career, but time and again, Palin has pointed to basketball as instrumental to her development as a politician. At least as critical, though, were the frontier setting in which she was raised and the community in which she achieved her modest athletic stardom. Wasilla in those days would have seemed like a foreign country to someone hailing from an urban environment, and although it has since become more of an Anchorage suburb than an isolated outpost, it retains its unique character.

Chuck and Sally Heath's current home is bigger than the one they raised Sarah in, but the ten-foot pyramid of antlers next to the driveway is the first sign that they are still hanging on to the rustic lifestyle that brought them to Alaska in the first place. A vintage "Sarah Palin for Governor" yard sign leans against the staircase leading up to the side entrance, but "Vegans Beware" might be more appropriate. Though her typical childhood weekend away from the driveway basketball court might have involved hunting caribou and maybe a little trapping, even Sarah concedes that the wood-paneled home that her parents purchased during her college years might better be described as a taxidermy museum.

On a cold Sunday morning in January, Chuck stands outside on the porch wearing blue jeans and a sweatshirt proclaiming, "We

Are All Joe the Plumber." Were it not for the genuinely warm greeting that he and his wife, Sally, offer, their home might be somewhat disquieting even to the heartiest of carnivores. The reptile and amphibian collection sits just inside the doorway on the staircase leading up to the balcony, accented by the snake skins dangling over the banister. A cougar perched on a rock by the living room window is the king of this indoor jungle, though he was shot in Utah and cannot compete in sentimental value with his neighbor, the mountain goat, who happens to have been the largest of his kind ever shot in Alaska when Chuck took him out in 1965. Next to the cougar hangs an Alaskan king crab and a few stuffed birds, while a pack of foxes adorn the far corner. There is also a stuffed elephant sitting comfortably on the carpeted floor next to Chuck's favorite easy chair, but it is the kind that can be found at a Republican National Convention souvenir stand rather than in the depths of the jungle.

Chuck begins the conversation emphatically. "Even though Tina Fey made a big joke about being able to see Russia from my house, you actually can see Russia from Alaska."

In case we don't believe him, he points to a photograph of himself standing proudly on Little Diomede Island in the Bering Sea. He was there many years ago to work on an oil spill cleanup, and sure enough, Russia's Big Diomede Island is visible across the water. To drive the point home, Chuck makes his way to the kitchen to show off a wall map of Alaska and to demonstrate that there are in fact two places in which coastal Siberia can be seen from the fortyninth state.

The derision of his daughter by the *Saturday Night Live* skit clearly remains a touchy issue in this house, but he does not come across as exasperated when he makes his point. Instead, he is quietly selfassured and methodical. Decades as a public school science teacher have reinforced his belief that physical evidence is the cornerstone of any argument. And Chuck Heath does not back down from an argument.

Still, the barrel-chested manly man with thin, gray wisps of hair would rather share a drink and a bawdy joke than quarrel without good reason. The vanity license plate on the basement wall reads "OLD-FART" and empty beer cans are lined up on top of his refrigerator. Chuck is careful not to embellish his famous daughter's accomplishments, confident that the truth is good enough. You get the sense that his easygoing nature did not fully blossom until the years after his children left home. And it is apparent that Sarah inherited his straightforwardness and skepticism toward the powers that be.

Chuck's frankness and mildly gruff exterior are balanced by Sally's warmth and courtesy. A tall, fit woman nearing seventy, she wears blue jeans and a red sweater with a small gold cross around her neck. She sips nervously on a cup of coffee as she sits perched on the corner of one of the two living room couches, periodically trying, in vain, to keep her husband's bluntness in check. Sally passed down to Sarah her ability to make other people feel comfortable and good about themselves. She worked for many years as a secretary in the same school where her husband taught science.

Chuck and Sally are not ones to slow down in retirement. Besides their continued expeditions into the Alaskan wilderness, they try to visit one or two foreign countries a year—and not just the usual tourist destinations. Their travels have ranged from Africa to Asia. "What a change we've seen in China," Chuck says. "Shanghai—we were there in the eighties and [there were] nine million bikes in Shanghai. Now there's nine million cars. I'm guessing at that number."

Their palpable curiosity about experiencing life in foreign countries has not rubbed off on Sarah, who did not leave North America until 2007 and has not expressed to her parents any desire to see some of the places they have visited. "Well, she hasn't talked about it," Chuck says when asked, before hedging a bit. "I'm sure she does. Right now when she travels, she catches hell because [people say], 'Oh, you're trying to make a name for yourself.'"

Chuck may have been born in Los Angeles, but his heart could not be further from Hollywood Boulevard. He and Sally started their family in Sandpoint, Idaho, and had their son Chuck Jr. and daughter Heather before Sarah made her debut on February 11, 1964. On that day, Beatlemania in America was at its peak. The four young lads from Liverpool had played *The Ed Sullivan Show* just two nights earlier and were set to take the stage in Washington, D.C., that night. But in Sandpoint, the date was marked by searing flames rather than screaming girls.

Chuck was driving Sally to the hospital when they came upon thick black smoke towering over the local Chevrolet dealership. As they pulled up alongside the building, Chuck's inquisitiveness got the better of him. He parked on the side of the road to watch for a few minutes as his friends at the dealership hurried to remove cars from the burning showroom. After three or four vehicles had been rescued, Sally observed to her husband that while the demolition derby at the Chevy dealership was certainly interesting, she did have a baby to bring into the world. She laughs at the memory now. "So that was how the day started, and then it was very easy."

Because of the state's reputation for some of the best hunting and fishing in North America, Chuck had dreamed about relocating the family to Alaska for years. The expense of moving precluded it until later that same year when he found a teaching job in Skagway that paid an annual salary of $6,000. It was just enough to pack the family up and begin his Alaskan adventure.

As Chuck combs through his basement treasure trove of sheep horns, fishing lures, rifles, and photographs, he takes special pleasure in showing off his facility for remembering details of the basketball team he coached forty-five years ago and delights in reciting facts about moose hoofs and whale hearts.

"You've probably seen pictures of rams getting back and fighting," he says. "If you and I were to butt heads, we'd have all kinds of problems, but look inside of a ram's skull. . . . It's corrugated honeycomb and acts like a shock absorber." Though she would be criticized later on for lacking facility with facts and figures, Sarah shares her father's extraordinary memory. Her ability to recall details about constituents and people she meets is one of her most valuable political skills.

The Heath parents took turns coaching the kids' teams, but it was Chuck who focused intently on encouraging Sarah's athletic development. He took note of her persistent work ethic, and he did not have to point out the weaknesses in her game. Sarah was naturally relentless in her drive to improve her skills. When she reached high school, her focus remained squarely on sports. She was social and attended parties but did not generally engage in activities that could get her into trouble, like underage drinking. She joined the track-and-field team that her father coached, in part to improve her stamina for basketball season. When she started out as a distance runner, her limited natural abilities kept her squarely in the middle of the pack. But by her senior year, her sheer determination had put her in the upper echelon of runners in the state.

Sarah and several of her basketball friends were just as competitive in running cross-country, even though it was decidedly less glamorous to trudge alone through miles of cold rain and snow than to play for cheering crowds of friends and classmates in a packed gym. Chuck recalled one trip to Kenai, Alaska, when he drove the school bus and Sally came along to assist him. The Heaths took with them a two-quart coffee thermos to help them stay awake on the five-hour drive. As they pulled into Kenai, Chuck was generous enough to offer his wife the last cup. As he tilted the thermos to let the coffee pour out, a dead mouse dropped out with the last drips of warm liquid. "Don't know how that mouse got in there," Chuck recalls. "He fell in and couldn't get out."

The track-and-field conditioning helped Sarah develop on the basketball court. She compensated for her lack of natural athletic skills by becoming a specialist on the defensive end, where heart mattered more than ability. As a sophomore and junior, she was one of the stars on the junior varsity squad and suited up occasionally on the varsity team in her junior year. By then, Sarah was a strong enough player to fill a role on almost any other varsity team in the state, but the 1980–1981 Warriors were loaded at the guard position. As one of the smallest schools in the state's "big school" division, Wasilla's players liked to think of their team as a perennial underdog, and their achievement of so much success at the state level was a testament to the skills of Coach Don Teeguarden and his assistants.

Teeguarden, who taught various subjects at Wasilla High, was in his mid-thirties, with light, blow-dried hair and a bushy mustache. His coaching philosophy was in the Bobby Knight mold, without the temper tantrums. He stressed fundamentals and physical fitness above all else, and his athletes still look back fondly on the "tough love" he gave them on the court. During practice, Teeguarden ran the team through a gauntlet of wind sprints that involved running both forward and backward, which the players dubbed "crushers." If they didn't throw up after the first couple of practices, he knew they weren't working hard enough.

Sarah may not have been the quickest girl ever to put on the Wasilla uniform, but she was mentally tough and willing to play to the team's strengths. At the start of her senior year, she earned a starting spot on the varsity team and was named cocaptain. Though Sarah would refer to being a point guard in later years, the Warriors lacked a natural talent for that position and instead relied on a three-guard set, which shared ball-handling responsibilities. She was far from a flashy player but a good passer who avoided silly errors. In most situations, she and her backcourt teammates had two primary responsibilities on the offensive end: don't turn the ball over to the other team and get it inside to Wanda or Heyde.

A sprinter and shot-putter during track season, 5' 9" sophomore Wanda Strutko was by far the best pure athlete on the team. It was a futile proposition for opposing defenses to try to stop her in the low post. Around school, a handful of athletes proudly wore their "200-Pound Club" T-shirts, which memorialized the weight they had conquered on the bench and leg presses. Wanda was the only girl in Wasilla who had earned the right to wear the shirt. Senior Heyde Kohring was listed at 6' 2", and even if the media guide exaggerated by an inch or so, her height was an overpowering factor at a level of play in which opposing teams routinely fielded players who were more than a foot shorter than her.

Every team Wasilla played would zero in on Wanda and Heyde, each of whom threatened to score over twenty points per game. On occasion, opponents' relentless double-teaming afforded Sarah and the other guards opportunities to step up and play a bigger role on the offensive end than the game plan called for. In an early-season game against Barrow, Sarah scored fifteen points to lead the Warriors, and in a loss to Bartlett High, she stepped up with eleven.

Though the team had a winning record, Wasilla was not playing up to its potential early in the season and suffered a couple of close losses. When their arch rivals from next-door Palmer came to town for the Wasilla Christmas Tournament, the Warriors were thought to have too much firepower for the Palmer Moose to handle. But Palmer surprised everyone and took control of the game, building a seventeen-point lead as students, family, and fans from both schools rocked the rafters in a packed Wasilla High School gym. Though her team was struggling, Sarah was having one of the best games of her career on her way to a fourteen-point performance. Wasilla closed the gap until, with just over two minutes remaining in the fourth quarter, they trailed 55–54. The Warriors put the ball in Sarah's steady hands, and the senior leader was fouled. Her free throw in the state championship game two months later would be the defining shot of her high school career, but here in December, she faced an even more pressure-packed moment. Her team was trailing rather than maintaining a fairly comfortable lead as it did in the final game. Sarah stepped to the line with the home crowd's eyes upon her, facing the pressure only rivalries like this one can generate. The Wasilla players on the bench joined hands as they leaned forward in their seats. "Okay, Sarah, come on," they pleaded. She calmly made both free throws, which proved to be the difference in the game.

One of the most exciting parts of playing high school basketball in Alaska were the road trips to away games, often days-long expeditions rather than quick jaunts down the road. Six-hour bus rides to Fairbanks and North Pole were common, and the team sometimes took chartered flights to play seven hundred miles north in Barrow or three hundred miles southwest on Kodiak Island. For girls like Sarah who grew up rarely leaving Southcentral Alaska, these were opportunities to see the vastness and diverse geography of their state. When the Warriors played rival Cordova High School, they drove six hours to Valdez, where the oil pipeline ends, and took a ferry across the majestic Prince William Sound to play a game in the tiny fishing village of Cordova. On one trip to Fairbanks, the temperature dropped to forty-five degrees below, forcing Sarah and her teammates on the school bus to don gloves, hats, and down jackets and burrow into their sleeping bags. The game was nearly canceled since Fairbanks followed the sensible policy of closing its schools when the temperature hit fifty below. Only then would the arctic city authorities consider it too dangerous to play basketball.

A typical road trip required an early-morning departure, and after several hours of travel time, the team would play a game that evening and spend the night sprawled in sleeping bags on a classroom floor at the opposing team's school. They would then travel to a nearby town on Saturday morning, play an afternoon game there, and return to Wasilla on Saturday night.

"The longest trip we ever took, I remember, we left at seven or seven-thirty Friday morning, and we played two games in Delta Junction and three games in Fairbanks," Teeguarden recalls. "And we got home at about three on Thursday afternoon, so we were gone just short of a week and played five games."

The road trips caused Sarah to miss a significant amount of class time, but the girls on Coach Teeguarden's team had to be serious about their studies if they wanted to play, and a 1982 *Mat-Su Valley Frontiersman* profile piece extolled Sarah's 3.7 grade point average. To this day, Chuck Heath's proudest boast about the team is that every one of the girls graduated from college. Not that there wasn't time for some fun too. On one particularly long excursion, Sarah and her teammates got hooked on the song "I Love Rock and Roll," which Joan Jett turned into a 1981 hit. "We would take my Walkman until the batteries ran out, and we would play the song over and over again," Susan Oakley, then a junior forward, recalls.

During her senior season, Sarah began dating Todd Palin, a senior transfer student from Glennallen High School, 150 miles to the east. The new kid was soft-spoken, handsome, and one of the best players on the boys' basketball team to boot. Before his daughter started dating Todd seriously, Chuck heard about the new hotshot athlete while coaching the track team and caught up with him one day when he was shooting around in the school gym. One of the two alpha males challenged the other to a game of HORSE, and to Todd's embarrassment, the old man won the shooting contest. "I didn't rub it in [then], but I do now!" Chuck said before adding quickly, "He's a good kid. He's the type of son-in-law that all guys should have."

One night, Todd brought his younger brother J.D. to the Heath's house for a double date with Sarah and her little sister Molly. Chuck still laughs when he recalls how the younger siblings, in eighth grade at the time, broke some of the adolescent tension by applying makeup to each other's faces. Things moved quickly from there for Todd and Sarah, and he soon became her first serious boyfriend. During basketball season, the two spent hours together on the bus that the boys and girls teams shared for road trips.

At nighttime, Teeguarden would retire to the teacher's lounge or the nursing office, where he enjoyed the luxury of a couch or a pullout bed. There he would prepare for the next day's game and leave the girls in the hands of their chaperone. "When you get twenty women in a room together, you don't want to hear the conversation," he says. "I just never felt like I had to worry about anything."

Though Teeguarden may not have faulted Sarah and his other young players for spending a little time gossiping before calling it a night, the team took the call for lights out even more earnestly than he expected of them. They were serious players.

Before each game, Teeguarden would leave the girls alone for a few minutes, and they would say a prayer together. "The whole team basically shared the Christian faith," Susan Oakley recalls. "There wasn't anybody that didn't agree with that philosophy of Christianity, so it was really easy for us to talk about that and share in that aspect because of the community we were in."

Indeed, the Mat-Su Valley was a rather homogenous place. Its residents were overwhelmingly white, middle-class, and politically conservative to libertarian. Palin would never lose sight of the values that pervaded her surroundings. The merit of working with your hands, unbridled patriotism, and devout Christianity were the ideals that would define her belief system. Sarah attended church regularly with Sally, her siblings, and on occasion her father. "I mean they weren't radical or anything like that because I was there," Chuck says. He still attends services from time to time with his wife, "but not religiously," as he adds with a chuckle.

Chuck's guarded attitude about matters of faith has not rubbed off on Sarah. The fervent brand of Christianity that her mother instilled in her played a critical role throughout her teenage years and continues to do so in her adulthood. Though Sally Heath had been a practicing Catholic, she moved the family to the Wasilla Assembly of God when Sarah was young. A Pentecostal church in which many believers stand with their arms outstretched and speak in tongues when the spirit moves them, Assembly of God advances an End Times theology that implores adherents to prepare for the biblical apocalypse. It actively promotes Republican politicians and socially conservative causes. In 2002, the year she first ran for statewide office, Palin and her family switched to the nondenominational Wasilla Bible Church, citing their preference for the children's ministries there. Both churches are evangelical, but unlike Wasilla Assembly of God, Wasilla Bible Church does not preach about politics.

"There are things the Bible teaches that this or that may be wrong, but it's not my job to force that down other people's throats," says pastor Ashley Brown, Wasilla Bible's executive director. "It's my job to share and extend God's grace."

During the vice presidential campaign, Palin would pause backstage, close her eyes, and say a quiet prayer before every speech she delivered. She deeply believes (and says so publicly) that God guides her through every decision she makes.

Sarah and about half of the other players on the varsity basketball team were members of the Fellowship of Christian Athletes, which provided a forum for Wasilla students from all athletic back-grounds to meet in church weekly. "They learned a lot of history of other athletes or other people that had done very well, kept Christ in their life, and still enjoyed their sports and their school and nor-mal activities," Sally recalls. "It was real important to them, and in those days they were able to have these groups in school after school hours."

As Sarah's senior season wore on, the Wasilla Warriors started racking up an impressive string of victories. When they won the North Region III tournament in neighboring Palmer, they earned a spot in the eight-team state tournament. When Sarah and her team-mates arrived at Anchorage's West High School for the first game of the tournament, four or five hundred Wasilla fans were waiting in the stands to greet them—not a bad turnout for a town with a population of about two thousand people at the time. Before taking the floor against powerhouse East High, Sarah donned her home-game white tank top and mid-calf-length shorts with red trim and pulled up her white knee socks with the letters "WHS" stitched on the sides. She knew that if she and her teammates didn't win, it would be the last game of her high school career.

Even though Wasilla had beaten East early in the season, their second game against that team was an embarrassing showing for the Warriors, who were handed an unceremonious fifteen-point defeat. Public wisdom made Wasilla the heavy underdogs in the state-tournament game. One of the coaches from a different An-chorage school was even quoted in a local paper as saying that East High would have a cakewalk to the finals. But Teeguarden remem-bered a sense of quiet confidence pervading the locker room be-fore the game began. Sarah only scored three points but lived up to her "Sarah Barracuda" on-court persona by making life exceed-ingly difficult for East's point guard. Wasilla held on for the win in a back-and-forth game after East's Stephanie Begich, sister of

Alaska's future Democratic senator Mark Begich, missed a critical free throw.

There was little time for celebrating, as the next night the Warriors faced off against their semifinal opponent, Lathrop. Wasilla led throughout and shrugged off a few questionable calls against them, defeating the purple-and-gold-clad Malemut 62–51 in a game that wasn't as close as the score indicated.

The culmination of a brilliant run for Wasilla and Sarah's uniformed athletic career came in the form of the championship game against Service High. Wasilla's opponent was another team featuring an aggressive defense, which the Warriors felt they could exploit with effective passing. With three minutes left to go in Wasilla's attempt to capture its first state title, Service had chipped a fourteen-point deficit down to six. Benefiting from the absence of a shot clock, Wasilla went into stall mode, passing the ball around the perimeter without even attempting to shoot. In desperation, Service began fouling Wasilla's players, and a string of missed free throws narrowed the Warriors' lead to four.

Sarah had sat on the bench for much of the game, having suffered a stress fracture in her leg, and was only at about 75 percent capacity when Teeguarden pointed to her and sent her back in for the final seconds. Sarah was the best free throw shooter on the team, and despite her inability to cut to the ball as she usually could, the coach needed girls in the game who could handle the pressure.

Hanging on to a 57–53 lead with fewer than twenty seconds remaining, Sarah Heath was fouled in the backcourt. She ignored the screaming crowd as she walked painfully to the free throw line at the opposite end of the court and focused on the task at hand. Wasilla needed Sarah to make just one foul shot to secure the win. The referee handed her the ball, which must have seemed twice as big in her small hands. She pounded it against the floor five times, then spun it slightly in her hands to line up the seams. Then she paused for a long two seconds and aimed her shot before releasing it, needing the strength from both hands and a little bit of a jump to get it all the way to the hoop. Her form was less than perfect. She even committed the free throw shooter's cardinal sin of taking a step back from the line while the ball was in the air. The ball danced off the front of the rim, ricocheted off the back, then grazed the backboard before taking an improbable fall through the net.

Few recall that Sarah missed her second shot, as the Wasilla fans' celebration had already begun. The final seconds of the game remain the most vivid memory of then sophomore Katy Allers's basketball career: "Sarah and I are standing, because we're the guards, and we're standing at the very back of the court because Coach Teeguarden is yelling, 'No fouls! No fouls!' So Sarah and I, since we were both pretty intense, he backed us way up, so we wouldn't jump in and hurt anybody or foul anybody. . . . I have a picture of her and I standing there, and it's her senior year, and she is sobbing because we are going to win this. And she's sobbing, and I'm standing there with my hand on her back, and I've got my hand over my mouth. And I will never forget that."

Coach Teeguarden hugged his assistant Dan Wales and joined his players on the court to celebrate with the crowd. On being handed the championship trophy, he turned toward the Wasilla students who had gathered near courtside and held the prize up high. A beaming Sarah Heath accepted her individual medal, soaked in the glory of having made the critical shot. If she had never entered politics, she would have enjoyed a year or two of local celebrity status in sports-crazed Wasilla. But Sarah had bigger plans.

She surprised both of her parents by declaring her intention to attend college in Hawaii. Chuck and Sally never could pin her down on why she wanted to make such a dramatic move, but they figured it had something to do with the glamour of the Aloha State. Either way, the girl who had grown up in homogenous Wasilla did not last long at the University of Hawaii at Hilo. According to Chuck, Sarah's decision to join her high school friend in transferring out of the school had to do with being outside her comfort zone for the first time in her life in an environment dominated by Asians and Pacific Islanders. "It just wasn't exactly what they expected," he says. "They were a minority type thing and it wasn't glamorous, so she came home."

At the age of twenty, Sarah entered the 1984 Miss Alaska competition in the hope of winning some scholarship money. As a teenager, she had never had any interest in modeling (or, for that matter, any extracurricular pursuits not athletic or spiritual in nature), but Sarah looked surprisingly comfortable in her one-piece red bathing suit as she twirled in front of the judges. The mere mention of her second-runner-up finish and Miss Congeniality prize in the beauty contest has sometimes elicited charges of sexism, but to ignore her physical attractiveness would be to leave out an important part of her story. Just as John F. Kennedy and Barack Obama harnessed youthful good looks to their advantage, Palin has not shied from using her beauty to help her get noticed along each step of her political career.

She attended four colleges in all, not including classes she took at a local community college, before earning her degree in journalism from the University of Idaho. Despite her academic odyssey, Sarah seemed well on her way to success in sportscasting after she landed a job as an anchor at KTUU in Anchorage. But a career at that time in her life became unfeasible since she had to be home in Wasilla to care for her newborn son, Track, while her new husband, Todd, was off starting his career on the North Slope.

When Sarah announced that she would run for the Wasilla City Council in 1992, her parents greeted the news with a shrug of the shoulders. "I'm sure I wasn't doing cartwheels or anything," Chuck says. It was a surprise to them that she wanted to be involved in government since theirs was a decidedly nonpolitical family, and Sarah had never expressed a desire to hold elected office. But the Wasilla City Council was not considered a springboard to political stardom, and there is nothing to indicate that the goal of statewide office was at the forefront of her mind at this time. She truly seems to have been just a gritty young mother who wanted to become more involved in her community and was worried about how a new sales tax would be spent.

The first sign that she really enjoyed the power and influence that came with public service came when she decided to run for mayor in 1996. Frustrated by how the city council was run like an old boys' club, Palin thought she could do better. She won the race on a platform stressing her antiabortion and pro-gun stances, which had little to do with the usual local concerns, like paving roads and reducing crime. Even her own father was concerned that she was doing too much too quickly. "When she first signed up for mayor, I said, 'Uh oh,'" Chuck recalls. "I thought she was over her head initially, but I could see a need for her because she was progressive."

Palin was indeed "progressive" in that her heavily engaged agenda dramatically counteracted the way business had always been done in Wasilla. Her most lasting accomplishment in her six years as mayor was the construction of the Wasilla Multi-Use Sports Complex, funded by a sales tax increase. Though the tax hike and her active pursuit of federal earmarks raise questions about her purity as a fiscal conservative, Palin did cut property taxes and eliminated personal-property and business-inventory taxes, as she would happily remind rally goers by the tens of thousands in the fall of 2008.

Those taxes were not the only things that Palin got rid of in Wasilla government. The young mayor created controversy by unceremoniously firing the city's museum director, the city attorney, and the chief of police. It was a kind of political shakeup that the small community had never before experienced.

Irl Stambaugh had become Wasilla's first ever police chief when he took the job in the new department in 1992. As a sign of loyalty to the new administration, Mayor Palin had asked him to resign and then reapply for his job along with all the other department heads. But Stambaugh balked at that idea, citing his contract, which stated that he could only be fired for cause (he later lost a wrongful-termination lawsuit). Stambaugh says that after her initial decree, Palin seemed to acknowledge his view on the matter and twice assured him that he would not be fired.

"Just a couple of days before I was terminated, I was in the hallway of city hall, and we were just passing in the hallway," Stambaugh recalls. "And she again said, 'You don't need to worry about it. I'm not going to get rid of you.'"

Just a couple of days later, he arrived at his desk to find a letter from the mayor notifying him that his services were no longer needed. He could scarcely believe the passive manner in which he had been fired, but in letting Stambaugh go, Palin had come through on her campaign promise to shake up city hall. Her take-no-prisoners attitude may have facilitated her rapid rise to power, but her reluctance to get her hands dirty proved a recurring trait that would deliver increasingly severe consequences.

$$\star \quad \star \quad \star$$

2. Seeing Red

THE ANNUAL ALASKA REPUBLICAN Party picnic had always been a rather cordial affair, but that changed on an August afternoon in 2006 when the chalet at Anchorage's Kincaid Park was filled to capacity. The signal was given at the most highly anticipated moment of the day: the instant the buffet line opened. Without warning, campaign volunteers spread out like vendors at a baseball game and dispersed one hundred T-shirts, custom-made for the occasion. As each member of Team Palin put on his or her bright red "Sarah Palin for Governor" shirt with the campaign slogan "Take a Stand" printed prominently on the back, the impact became more jolting. The picnic was supposed to foster unity among the party faithful. There were three Republican candidates for governor, and this was not traditionally an occasion to campaign for any one of them in particular.

One of the shirt hawkers made his way to the corner of the room where the three-piece rock band Spank the Dog was taking a break between songs. The drummer wasn't in on it, but slide guitarist John Bitney and lead singer and rhythm guitarist Paul Fuhs put down their instruments as planned and donned their shirts in solidarity with the ninety-eight other Palin supporters packed inside the building.

In her short political career, Palin had already demonstrated an ability to achieve far more than was expected of her. Both in ushering out the three-term mayor of Wasilla in 1996 and in finishing a close second in the lieutenant governor's race in 2002, she had benefited from her opponents' tendency to underestimate her visceral appeal to voters. After her impressive showing in the lieutenant governor's race, Palin's status as a major statewide player had been secured, and as incumbent governor Frank Murkowski's popularity plunged, she started hearing from experienced statewide operatives who told her that the political winds might next sweep her into the governor's mansion, if she wanted it. And, yes, she did want it. She had accomplished a great deal at the local level, and now she hoped to transform Alaska in the way she had changed her hometown.

With just two weeks to go, she found herself surging ahead of her two opponents in the Republican gubernatorial primary, Murkowski and former state senator John Binkley. Still, the outcome of the race was very much in doubt, and Palin was not going to abandon her insurgent tactics just because she was no longer the underdog. She had signed off on the T-shirt stunt when a clever young volunteer named Matt Peters proposed it in an e-mail. As she handed out slices of watermelon to the more than four hundred people gathered in the chalet, she could sense that this was a big moment. Her campaign had, from its inception, been an outsiders' movement, and here she was in the lion's den, looking on as her supporters flipped a sartorial middle finger to the establishment that Murkowski and, to a lesser extent, Binkley represented.

Though the rules prevented them from saying so out loud, the leaders of the state Republican Party were almost all lined up against the ambitious former mayor who already had a reputation for planting her toes firmly across the party line. She had earned her rebel status by taking on Alaska Republican Party chairman Randy Ruedrich, the very man who was now incensed by the T-shirt stunt. Ruedrich, who had organized the picnic every year since 2002, had recognized Palin's uncanny ability to connect with voters during her days in the Wasilla mayor's office and had helped nurture her career. In fact, he had appealed to her personally to run for lieutenant governor in 2002, calling her into a meeting at a downtown Anchorage law office to persuade her to cast aside her most serious concern about running—that the campaign would cause her to desert her post as mayor of Wasilla. Palin's decision to take Ruedrich's advice and run had been a turning point in her career, and her second-place finish in that race was the best possible outcome. It allowed her to build name recognition without having to join a Murkowski administration that quickly floundered. After that race, both Ruedrich and Palin accepted Murkowski's offer to join the Alaska Oil and Gas Conservation Commission, which they both left two years later after Palin turned on her colleague and reported Ruedrich for ethics violations. The infractions were on the order of conducting political business from his state computer and leaking confidential information to a company he had been tasked to regulate. Ruedrich admitted wrongdoing and paid a record $12,000 fine.

Many of Palin's detractors maintain to this day that her ethics crusading was a self-serving ploy to boost her own reputation as a reformer. But that view ignores the real courage it took for her to come forward in a manner that jeopardized her standing in the Republican Party just as she was trying to elevate it. Her whistle-blowing turned out to be a boon to her political career, but at the time, it seemed more likely to imperil it. Even if her critics are right that she was not thrilled with her job on the commission and the hour-long commute it required, it could not have been easy for her to give up a six-figure salary when she resigned over what she said were her concerns about the way in which state law prevented her from speaking out about the Ruedrich saga.

For his part, Ruedrich remained at the helm of the Alaska Republican Party and kept his focus on the great fun of beating Democrats. But it was no secret that he was now leery of the woman who, in his view, had capitalized on his lapses in judgment to make a name for herself. The Palin campaign's T-shirt spectacle infuriated him, but he could not claim it to be technically against the rules. Politicking had always been allowed inside the chalet's walls. But the musical act was another story altogether. The performers were there to entertain everyone in attendance, not to promote one candidate, even though Palin had "donated" the band for the event.

Ruedrich fumed as he made his way to the corner of the room where Spank the Dog had restarted its upbeat set of rock, country western, and folk songs, two of its three members proudly wearing their Palin regalia. He approached the guitarist, Bitney, a former lobbyist and current Palin campaign volunteer who would go on to become one of the chief architects of her general election campaign, and whispered in his ear.

"Hey, you guys are the band, and you are on stage," Ruedrich said, according to Bitney. "I'm trying to manage this as a multicandidate Republican event, and you guys are wearing those shirts. It looks like this is a Sarah Palin event. Here goes. Your options are lose the shirts, or get off the stage."

Bitney was a bit perplexed since the band's drummer, Tom Anderson, had not been asked to remove his T-shirt promoting the state senate candidacy of his wife, Lesil McGuire, but he decided not to argue the point. Instead, he turned to lead singer Paul Fuhs and relayed the party chairman's demand. The bandmates exchanged glances before picking their button-down shirts up off the floor and putting them back on over their Palin T-shirts. Bitney derived a small sense of satisfaction from opening one of his buttons and allowing a rebellious patch of red to poke through, but that minor gesture of disobedience was nothing compared to what Fuhs was about to do.

As the crowd lined up for the fried chicken, hot dogs, and cookies, Fuhs stepped to the microphone. "Ladies and Gentlemen," he began as he waited for everyone's attention. "Randy Ruedrich was just up here, and he gave us a special request."

Certain that Fuhs was about to pick a fight with the chairman by publicly revealing Ruedrich's T-shirt edict, Bitney looked for the nearest hole to climb into. Finding none, he felt his heart kick into overdrive as he waited for his bandmate to dig their collective grave. But Fuhs had a surprise in store.

"He wanted us to play some Elvis Presley," Fuhs said. "So this next one is for Randy Ruedrich!" Without skipping a beat, Fuhs belted out the opening words to "Blue Suede Shoes," and Bitney collected himself sufficiently to strum the chords to the song, feeling the relief flow into his nerves.

As Ruedrich was left to seethe over having his authority mocked, the band played two more numbers before breaking into one of their popular standards: Ben E. King's "Stand by Me." Halfway through the song, Fuhs's confidence had grown to the point where he felt obliged to give voice to another inspiration. As the song segued into its familiar chorus, he made a slight adjustment to the lyrics, incorporating the Palin campaign's tagline: "So darling, darling, stand by me . . . oh, stand by me . . . take a stand . . . take a stand."

At that point, Ruedrich's special assistant Dave Moreno decided to take a stand of his own. He walked up to the band and made a declaration, "You guys are done!"

Fuhs reacted as if he would not put up a fight. "Well, all right," he said.

But the setup had been too perfect, the opportunity for the last word too inviting. Fuhs and Bitney led the band through one more song before taking their final bows and packing up their equipment. Palin had been oblivious to the scene as she worked the other side of the room, but when Fuhs rushed over to tell her and Todd what had happened, the incident became a call to arms. Palin was visibly upset over what she saw as Ruedrich's strong-arm tactics, especially considering that stacks of Binkley campaign literature had been allowed to remain in place next to the front door. She lamented that her folks were being "pushed around" by Ruedrich and his minions.

When a small group of particularly outraged Palin supporters decided to organize something of an insurrection, collecting "Palin for Governor" yard signs and assembling just outside the chalet, the candidate did not try to dissuade them. Over the course of the next half hour, as people walked in and out of the building, her boisterous fans waved their signs and shouted, "Vote for Sarah!"

When the party leaders caught wind of this latest breach of authority, they knew that the high ground had shifted back to their side. This time, it was Republican Party attorney Bill Large's turn to act. "Our permit to use a city building was that we were not allowed to have any political signs on the building or in front of the building," Ruedrich recalls. "Now these folks were on the curb in front of the building, so [Large] just wanted to make sure that these folks complied with the permit."

Large, the burly lawyer with a Dickensian name, stormed outside to confront the group. He told the Palin supporters that they were violating the rules and needed to disband. But the outraged rabble-rousers began to argue with Large, encircling him like a school of sharks as the confrontation grew more heated.

"It's a free country!" one Palin supporter shouted.

To Large, the scene was more reminiscent of a different country in another era. "You're all a bunch of brownshirts," he said.

The comparison to Nazi storm troopers had the effect of escalating the outrage among some of the Palin supporters while confusing others. "What do you mean brownshirts?" one of them demanded. "We're wearing red shirts!"

"Well, alright then, you're Communists!" Large shot back.

This slander had a far greater impact. Any chance of diffusing the tension was lost the moment the *C* word left Large's lips. "This is America, and we're showing support for our candidate!" one of the increasingly livid Palin supporters said.

Still alone and determined to face down the swarming hive of Palin supporters, Large stood his ground. "The rules are you can't be out here."

Just then, a robust man in his late sixties with a penchant for inserting himself into situations where trouble was brewing accosted Large. It was Chuck Heath, a fellow whose sunny demeanor belied his confrontational side, and he was there to stand up for his daughter. He had stared down enough grizzly bears and mountain lions in over fifty years of hunting them to know when to move in for the kill.

Heath challenged Large to produce evidence that the policy he was referring to actually existed. Accepting the test, the attorney tore a piece of paper from a folder he was carrying and took out a pen. He scribbled, "No signs outside," and handed it to a Palin supporter.

"Here is your policy," he declared with monarchal authority.

Unsurprisingly, the crowd wasn't swayed, and a shoving match ensued. Accounts of what exactly transpired next vary, but one way or another, Large came into contact with an older woman wielding a Palin yard sign, who was convinced he had pushed her. Now that the war of words had crossed the line into a physical battle, the woman gripped her makeshift weapon and swung it like an axe in the lawyer's direction. Though still convinced that he was in the right, Large thought better of getting into an all-out brawl with a member of the opposite sex and marched back inside the chalet. There, he and Ruedrich confronted Palin about her supporters' behavior, demanding that she order them to disperse. Instead, she defended their right to speak out against unfair treatment. Meanwhile, embellished stories of the atrocities that had just taken place were already spreading quickly via phone calls and e-mails.

The local NBC affiliate and the *Anchorage Daily News* gossip column "The Ear" relayed snippets of the firsthand reports about the picnic fracas, which quickly became the stuff of legend. Palin, already widely known for taking tough stands against her party, was now the candidate whose supporters the Republican big shots were intimidating physically. Though she had already climbed ahead in the primary race, this was the moment that turned Palin's relatively barebones campaign for the governorship into an unstoppable force. "She became the front-running underdog at that point and never looked back," John Bitney recalls.

Bitney knew they were truly in good shape the following weekend when he helped organize a group of Palin supporters to gather in Anchorage outside the Sears Mall on the corner of Northern Lights Boulevard and Seward Highway—one of the busiest intersections in the city. Murkowski and Binkley supporters had assembled on two other corners of the intersection, with only tepid reactions from passing motorists. But the Palin signs generated a response on an entirely different level. Driver after driver laid on their horns and waved and cheered at the Palin group.

"I've waved signs in political races before," Bitney says. "You get a couple of honks, a couple of birds, [but] people were going nuts. There were rolling down their windows. . . . They would pull in sometimes and go, 'Do you got a sign for me to wave with you for a while?'"

The scene so heartened Bitney that he called the candidate on her cell phone and told her he had found the perfect remedy to relieve some stress as they entered the last week of the primary campaign. Palin arrived in minutes. "Wow," was her most frequent utterance as she joined her supporters and waved to passing motorists, letting the adulation sink in.

On primary day, Bitney drove to Palmer, the town neighboring Wasilla where he lived. Just as he arrived at the polling station, a voice on the radio announced that there had been a drive-by shooting near the exact corner where he had been helping out with some more sign waving less than an hour before. Realizing that there were still Palin supporters on the corner, Bitney panicked and dialed a campaign volunteer, who assured him that no one in the Palin crowd had been hurt. The opponents' ranks had not been so fortunate, however, and it was soon reported that a Murkowski volunteer had got caught in the crossfire between passing gang members and was shot in the chest outside the Murkowski campaign headquarters.

Though a police spokesman said that the shooting had nothing to do with the election, Governor Murkowski was soon on the radio relaying a dramatic account of the incident. Seizing the opportunity to score political points, he began reminding the audience of the crime bills he had sponsored and his commitment to public safety.

Bitney could barely believe what he was hearing. His months of hard work on behalf of Sarah Palin could be lost with even a small swing of votes in Murkowski's direction. Just then, he drove past a serious four-car accident on the other side of the Glenn Highway that was blocking traffic from Anchorage to the Mat-Su Valley. "By now it was about three-thirty P.M.," Bitney recalls. "And it looked like the highway was going to soon be officially closed, just in time to slow down all the Mat-Su [Valley] commuters who would be heading home to the polls in about two hours. Those were our voters!"

Bitney called into the local radio station to report details of the spectacular accident, and the producers interrupted Murkowski to let him on the air, unaware of his connection to the Palin campaign. By the time he was done talking, the news channel had lost Murkowski. "Right after I hung up on the radio, the stress of the whole thing caused me to have to pull over my truck and cry," recalls Bitney. "That was how committed I was to Sarah Palin."

Palin won the primary with 51 percent of the vote, a remarkable number for a race that featured three serious candidates. Murkowski, the incumbent who never seemed to recover from charges of nepotism and self-indulgence, finished third, at 19 percent.

As Palin began gearing up for another three-way contest in the general election against former Democratic governor Tony Knowles and Republican state representative turned independent gubernatorial candidate Andrew Halcro, she quickly became the beneficiary of another stroke of good fortune in her quest to become the state's youngest and first female chief executive. On August 31 and September 1, city residents and summer cruise ship tourists were treated to the jarring spectacle of a parade of FBI agents descending upon the capitol building in downtown Juneau and carting away evidence in the form of state legislators' files. The subsequent indictments in the corruption scandal, related to political payouts from the oil-field-services company VECO, confirmed the sorry state of what many Alaskans had already considered a hopelessly corrupt system of state government. Palin, already well-known for her role as an ethical watchdog from her days on the oil and gas commission, needed only to sit back and watch. Her reputation as a reformer did the talking for her.

As the tides kept moving in her favor, Palin began to believe more deeply what others who had watched her career from the beginning already knew: She had remarkably good political instincts. "She was her own campaign manager," says Republican Bill Stoltze, one of only three state representatives who openly backed her primary campaign. "You couldn't micromanage her to say something."

As Palin traveled throughout the state to chamber of commerce forums, town hall meetings, and debates, she sharpened her already considerable communication skills. Perhaps no one in Alaska had a better seat from which to observe her uncanny ability to connect with voters than her independent opponent, Halcro, who was something of a rebel in his own right. Often called the "smartest kid in the class" by his supporters and detractors alike, Halcro could cite government statistics the way an avid baseball fan throws out batting averages, and in his own way, he could match Palin's youth and enthusiasm. But with his white-collar background, he had a difficult time passing the "Alaska test."

"There is sort of a rule in Alaska," longtime state government official and 2010 Democratic gubernatorial candidate Bob Poe says. "You've got to look good in Carhartts, and the Carhartts have to have holes that you put in them, right? If you are hanging out with hunters, your gun ought to look a little scraped up because you've actually been out there hunting with it. I don't think Andrew passed those kinds of tests."

Halcro, who remains a vocal Palin critic, spent all nine months of the campaign crossing paths with her as an independent candidate and was continually stymied by her ability to deflect the verbal grenades that he and Knowles threw at her. Palin always seemed able to remain above the fray in debates by sticking to the same talking points that she knew would resonate in a climate of disillusionment with state government. "Her message never matured, and the reason was that it didn't have to," Halcro says, still smarting from his inability to pierce her armor. "She got popular so fast just by the glittering generalities and just by the broad brush strokes that nobody cared."

Palin may not have been able to offer up the policy details that Halcro and Knowles handled deftly, but she knew how to hit just the right notes, and she did it again and again. At an Alaska Conservation Voters forum a month before the election, Halcro tried to pounce on Palin's stance on abortion. Though Alaska has long been a red state, its fierce libertarian streak makes many voters deeply suspicious of any government involvement in private affairs. Halcro thought he could use the abortion issue to siphon off pro-choice voters drawn to Palin's charisma and message of reform.

"My question for you," Halcro said as he stood in front of a seated Palin, avoiding eye contact with his rival, "is, if you're [in] support of equality and equal access and support the foundation of the Constitution, will you as governor give equal weight to the right to privacy in protecting a woman's right to choose?"

Halcro's challenge elicited a hearty round of applause from some in the audience, but Palin was unfazed. What came next was reminiscent of Ronald Reagan's "there you go again" routine, in which he directed a patronizing sense of pity toward an opposing candidate struggling to gain traction.

"Here, again, abortion—a sensitive, private issue—being used to divide both sides in a forum like this where I just think, you know, there are conservation issues that we're gonna be talking about to-day," Palin said.

It was a remarkably cautious handling of the abortion issue for a woman who would later become the epitome of a pro-life evange-lizer. Having completed the setup, it was time to move in for the kill. "But in answer to Andrew's question—and Andrew, bless your heart, you know my position on abortion. I'm pro-life. For years, even when you asked me how many times to run as your running mate, you knew what my position was then."

Social conservatives had comprised Palin's base since her days as a candidate for mayor of Wasilla, but it was her success in wooing moderate Democrats and independent, college-educated women that flummoxed her opponents. Knowles and Halcro could not come close to matching Palin's ability to charm nearly everyone who came into contact with her, including the local media.

Dani Carlson, the University of Alaska at Fairbanks (UAF) stu-dent body vice president in 2006, recalls how Palin won her over during the spring of that year at a resources debate. The event took place a month before Carlson graduated and four months before she took her first job as a reporter at KTVF-TV Fairbanks. "She made you feel like you were part of the discussion, and she didn't throw [around] these statistics," Carlson says. "She spoke very, very well, so I was very impressed with her."

After the debate, Carlson approached Palin to introduce herself and tell her she had done a good job breaking down complex sub-jects into simple terms so that the college students who were watch-ing could understand them. Palin surprised Carlson by engaging her in conversation, and when the student told the candidate that she was a broadcasting major, Palin beamed. "Oh my goodness, I stud-ied broadcasting in college and I did sportscasting for a little bit," she said. "Oh, it's so much fun! What are you going to do with it? Are you going to stay in Alaska?"

Carlson couldn't believe that *she* was the one getting her ear talked off. "She was legitimately interested in what was going on, and I felt really special," Carlson recalls.

The candidate offered a prediction to the aspiring TV reporter before parting ways with her. "I think you are going to be a journalist," Palin said. "I think the next time I see you, you're going to have a camera and be a reporter."

After Carlson graduated, she landed a reporting job at the Fairbanks NBC affiliate that August. Within a month, she was assigned to cover a major announcement. Former Alaska natural resources commissioner Tom Irwin, a casualty of the Murkowski administration's intolerance for dissent, was going to endorse Palin's candidacy. As Palin was shaking hands after the event, Carlson approached her. The candidate's reaction was instantaneous. "Hey, I remember you," Palin said. "You're Dani. You're the broadcasting major from UAF. So you graduated and you're in news? I told you! I told you this was going to happen."

Carlson glowed. "I just was like, 'You're cool,'" she recalls. "That to me is who she is."

Through the rest of the campaign, Carlson was continually flattered whenever she ran into Palin on the stump. "She always said, 'Hey, Dani. How's it going?' . . . or 'Hey, your dad just retired from the army. That's awesome, how's he doing?'"

Palin's positive relationship with the media was manifested in the generally favorable coverage her campaign received as she continued to maintain her lead in the polls. She and her small team of advisers began election night at the Captain Cook Hotel in downtown Anchorage where a single computer terminal in the lobby displayed incoming results. There were only a few career politicians and lobbyists among the cheering supporters inside the hotel. Instead, the crowd was packed with Alaskans who might never have even set foot in Juneau. They did not have to wait long to see that their candidate had scored a solid victory, triumphing by about 7 percent with most precincts reporting.

With the outcome appearing certain, Palin and her family and staff made the four-block trek across Fifth Avenue to the Egan Civic and Convention Center, which served as a central location for candidates making their media rounds. As she shuttled from TV interviews to radio booths, she was careful not to declare victory until Knowles conceded. In one episode that tainted the night for some, a small group of overzealous Palin stalwarts began to taunt the soon to be former governor Frank Murkowski when he made a brief appearance. His daughter, Senator Lisa Murkowski, confronted the group. "Could you have some dignity for my dad?" she implored them.

Republican state representative Nancy Dahlstrom, one of the three Alaska House members who had backed Palin early in her primary battle, stood beside the candidate's husband, Todd, as the results became official.

"Did she do it? Did she do it?" Todd shouted, his winner's instinct kicking into overdrive.

"She did it! She did it!" Dahlstrom confirmed.

Palin had won 48 percent of the vote to Knowles's 41 percent, with Halcro coming in a distant third at 9 percent. During the primary campaign, Murkowski's last-minute decision to run for reelection had been a decisive factor. It split the party establishment vote and highlighted Palin's ability to offer an even more dramatic break from Murkowski than Binkley did. Here again, in the general election, Palin benefited from having two opponents, as Halcro picked off a not insignificant tally of independent and pro-choice Republican votes. Governor Murkowski took the high road and congratulated the governor-elect.

John Bitney, the guitarist and volunteer turned senior campaign adviser, tried to push his way through the media scrum at the

convention center to offer the new governor his own congratulations. At the same time, Palin was asking others about Bitney's
whereabouts. She knew how crucial he had been to the victory. In
fact, many observers credited Bitney with developing the folksy
touch that worked so well for her on the stump. But the fortress of
well-wishers was too thick as the governor-elect went from interviews to victory speech, and Bitney gave up. He had been outside in
the cold all day holding yard signs, and he just wanted to go home.
He would get in touch with Palin the next morning.

As he made his way through the Captain Cook Hotel toward
the back parking lot, Bitney came upon a half dozen people gathered in a hallway next to the lobby. They were surrounding Palin,
who had just finally arrived to crash after a long night. When the
governor-elect caught Bitney's eye, she smiled broadly, relieved that
they had been able to connect in the end.

"There you are!" she said to her top strategist.

"Congratulations, Governor," he replied.

Despite the monumental fatigue and head-spinning chaos, Palin
didn't miss a beat. "Everybody, it's John's birthday!" she said.

As the governor-elect led the small group through the "Happy
Birthday" chorus, Bitney was reminded of something he had known
all along. As much as he had taught her how to take her campaigning skills to the next level, her God-given gift for remembering
details about people's lives and making them feel good about themselves had carried the day.

Palin chose to hold her swearing-in ceremony in Fairbanks to
signal a break from tradition and mark the fiftieth anniversary of
Alaska's constitutional convention there. It was a month and a half
into her term before her inaugural ball was held at Centennial Hall
in Juneau. But grand social functions were not really Palin's thing,
and two days before the event, her new deputy press secretary,
Sharon Leighow, told the *Anchorage Daily News* that the governor

still hadn't picked out a dress. On the night of the ball, Palin showed up in an eye-catching bright-fuchsia-and-black gown accompanied by a jeweled broach. Her hair, which she usually wore pulled up, cascaded in curls past her shoulders.

When a reporter from the *Juneau Empire* caught up with Palin and inquired about her outfit, the new governor remarked that she had bought her shoes two hours earlier and could not remember who her dress designer was. "You'd have to look at the tag to find out," she said.

More than eight hundred people paid the $35 general admission price or $50 for a reserved seat at one of the tables set up in front of the stage where the Thunder Mountain Big Band played old hits for the partygoers to dance to. The spread was decidedly Alaskan. Sautéed reindeer sausage, smoked sable, poached salmon, and bacon-wrapped sea scallops filled the room with the aromas of Denali National Park and the Bering Sea. Among the crowd gathered for the rare Saturday night Alaska society event were several state lawmakers and a cadre of lobbyists and business leaders. Before taking to the dance floor with her tuxedoed First Dude, Palin took time to mingle with many of the political bigwigs already competing for her ear.

As the new governor made the rounds among the champagne-glass-clinking set, she stopped to say hello to a well-known Juneau lobbyist, whom she would go on to work with throughout her governorship. His presence conjured up a memory of a meeting they'd had a few months back, when her chance of winning the race for governor had seemed like a long shot.

Among the lobbyist's many friends in Juneau was John Binkley, the former state senator who had run against Palin in the Republican primary. In the early days of that battle, Binkley had asked the lobbyist to meet with Palin and offer a proposal. Binkley recognized Palin's political shrewdness and valued the small but passionate band of supporters she had already won over, but he simply did not think she had the level of statewide experience required to be an effective governor. The two candidates were on the same ideological wavelength, so why not run as a team? Rather than waste a lot of money and energy in a primary fight, a Binkley/Palin ticket could focus on the general election right away, with the perfect combination of experience and change.

Palin loved the idea when Binkley's lobbyist friend proposed it to her. She had a quibble with just one detail: Palin/Binkley had a much nicer ring than Binkley/Palin.

The lobbyist knew that swapping positions on the ticket was a nonstarter for Binkley, but he could not persuade the determined former mayor of Wasilla that her quest for the governorship would be quixotic. The meeting ended amicably but without a deal, and the primary battle went on. Palin had had several other meetings with prominent Alaskans and had even traveled to Juneau to gain state legislators' support while deciding whether to run for governor, but in the midst of the excitement of the inaugural ball, the meeting with the lobbyist who now appeared before her stood out. They exchanged hugs, and the lobbyist offered his congratulations.

"If I'd listened to you, I wouldn't be here," Palin said.

According to the lobbyist, she added an expletive to hammer her point home, which caused him to laugh at the uncharacteristically blunt, yet good-natured jab. Palin was well aware of the lobbyist's penchant for friendly ribbing laced with four-letter words. "I hope you don't take my political advice in the future," he said.

The gubernatorial campaign had taught Palin the importance of trusting her instincts rather than others' advice. It was a critical lesson, but one that she would apply to a fault in later years. Just as importantly, she had discovered the power of taking people by surprise.

$\star \quad \star \quad \star$

3. Honeymoon in Juneau

THE BRICK-FACED CONCRETE SLAB of a building on Main Street looks more like a Soviet-era administrative complex than a state capitol, but Alaskans value beauty and elegance in their natural wonders and practicality in their man-made structures. There are no walking grounds, and the four marble columns that support the carved legend "ALASKA STATE CAPITOL" appear to be an architectural afterthought—a halfhearted reminder to the part-time employees here that this is indeed the home of their government.

The building perches on a hill overlooking the port city, and some of the prized fourth-floor legislative offices that sit above the governor's third-floor headquarters are just high enough to offer views of the glistening harbor. But the only decorative indulgences in the hallways are a few understated busts of famous Alaskans and a series of framed newspapers and photographs documenting the former territory's colorful history.

No roads lead to Juneau. Tucked in the southeast corner of the state, the capital is accessible only by plane or boat, almost as if Alaskans wanted to quarantine their politicians when they moved the capital here from Sitka in the first decade of the twentieth century. Lying in the shadow of Mount Juneau, the tiny downtown consists of a few winding streets scattered with tourist traps for the cruise ship patrons who flood the town each summer, several book shops, and bars where grizzled fisherman and eager young legislative aides relax together. Everything is within a short walking distance in this city of thirty thousand (approximately one-tenth the size of Anchorage), where several homes boast signs reading, "A House of Peace," and fliers posted on city walls promote local folk and rock bands.

The capitol is less than a one-minute walk from Calhoun Street, where visitors can find the understated governor's mansion. The pristine white home stands in the middle of an ordinary neighborhood just a few feet from the road, and the only hints that the governor occupies it are the Alaskan state flag flapping in the wind and the three-story totem pole springing up from the bushes in front. Visitors are not greeted by a security guard. They simply walk up to the front door and knock.

For as long as any legislators can remember, there has been talk of relocating the capital to a more practical location around the state's population center in Southcentral Alaska, but many who live in less densely populated areas of the state are suspicious of concentrating even more power there. Juneau residents have also been fiercely protective of their capital status and the economic benefits that come with it. In 2001, Sarah Palin had joined two other mayors in the Matanuska-Susitna Valley area and signed a petition to move the legislative session to her home borough, which left the capital's voters skeptical five years later during her gubernatorial campaign when she insisted that she now favored keeping a "star on the map" in Juneau. Some of them worried that the reference meant that Juneau would just be left with a star while the state's business moved elsewhere.

"It was a quote that was used a lot in her campaign, and it did more to really concern the people here than anything that she really ever said," Juneau Republican representative Cathy Munoz says. "We were thinking that means that everything is going to move out of here."

Those concerns proved unfounded, and talk of moving the capital soon died down. When Palin arrived in Juneau in advance of the first legislative session of her governorship on December 8, 2006, she told the local media how she had decided to explore the town that weekend. "I thought, 'Nobody's going to recognize me,'" she said.

The new governor's astonishment when people spotted her on the street and extended warm welcomes demonstrated just how foreign Juneau seemed to her. Publicly, at least, Palin had taken it as a compliment when former state senator Ben Stevens derided her Wasilla brethren as "valley trash." She felt out of place in a city where legislative aides far outnumbered oil-field workers and trendy coffee shops featuring local artwork replaced her favorite early-morning destination in Wasilla—the Mocha Moose drive-in espresso hut.

Palin's first year in Juneau was the last in which the legislature met for a full 120 days before moving to a cost-saving, voter-mandated 90-day session in 2008. The smallest state governing body in the country, Alaska's House of Representatives seats forty members, and just twenty lawmakers make up the Senate. The legislators are in regular session for less than a quarter of the year, leaving them free—and, in general, financially compelled—to find private-sector employment for most of the months on the calendar. Their variety of life experiences makes for a lively dynamic in what is truly a citizen legislature. They also put Palin's formidable people skills to the test, as she worked through the challenge of dealing with an array of characters from diverse backgrounds.

Democratic representative David Guttenberg, for example, was born in the Bronx and came to Alaska to fight forest fires after barely graduating high school. During his first eight years in the state, he lived without running water and electricity.

Jay Ramras, a House Republican with a flair for the dramatic, first found fame when *New York* magazine ran a series of stories about his five-month jaunt to New York City in search of a suitable Jewish girlfriend to bring home to largely gentile Fairbanks. He later made headlines as one of Palin's harshest and most frequent critics.

Harry Crawford, who became the second-most powerful Democrat in the House, left the oppressive heat of Louisiana's oil fields to work in the extreme cold of the North Slope. His molasses-rich accent brings a taste of the bayou whenever he introduces a bill on the floor of the Alaska House.

The intimidating workload that would greet any incoming governor was all the more arduous for Palin since the legislature had held a lame-duck special session in November and passed a bill to deny state benefits to same-sex couples. Attorney General Talis Colberg advised her that the bill was unconstitutional. After weeks of deliberation, she put aside her own view on the matter and brought out her veto pen. Palin then signed a separate bill calling for a nonbinding public vote on whether a constitutional amendment should be enacted to achieve the same end. This approach endeared her to Democrats and independents, who saw a pragmatic governor more interested in finding consensus than she was in making a political point.

Despite the goodwill she was generating, a cost-cutting measure Palin undertook at the governor's mansion led some of the locals to worry about her commitment to Juneau. "People around here were pretty concerned when she fired her cook because that meant that basically she wasn't going to live here, and she hasn't," says Democratic representative Bob Buch.

Sure enough, Palin announced that she and her family would break the precedent set by previous governors and continue to reside at her secluded lakeside home in Wasilla when the legislature was out of session. She would return to Juneau frequently, she promised, whenever she needed to be there.

Despite the Juneau delegation's reservations about the capital issue, the new face that Palin immediately put on the executive branch by taking high-profile steps to change the tone in the capital impressed lawmakers. When she shunned the private jet that Governor Murkowski had purchased—a symbol of waste and abuse of power in the eyes of many—she sent a clear signal that she intended to make good on her campaign rhetoric. Republican senator Fred Dyson from Eagle River still recalls with admiration the day he first saw the new governor at the Juneau airport. "Here comes the Dodge pickup, [it] pulls up, Sarah's packing her own bag, comes in there and checks through the security just like me and goes and sits in the [coach] cabin."

Because of Alaska's unique cultural heritage born of its unforgiving and isolated terrain, the legislature's ideological divide between Democrats and Republicans has generally been narrower than in most states. Palin was pleased to find a receptive audience among pro-gun, pro-oil Democrats who went on to become some of her strongest allies in the early going of her governorship. Near the beginning of her term, she invited all sixteen members of the Democratic caucus to the governor's mansion. "We actually had one message," Guttenberg, the firefighter turned Fairbanks Democrat, recalls. "If you want to succeed in this, you have to engage. You have to play the politics of how the building works."

Guttenberg was not convinced that the message got through, and several lawmakers found Palin to be overly apprehensive about immersing herself in the details of the legislative process. But although the governor might not have engaged with lawmakers early in her term at the level they would have liked, she was generally accessible and willing to reach for compromise. Many Democrats were impressed with the team that Palin brought in and the level of contact with the legislature that they established.

"I think one of the first things that she did that was very important and showed me what kind of person she was going to be, was she hired some really good key people," says Democratic representative Scott Kawasaki from Fairbanks, who was elected to his first term in the legislature the same year Palin assumed the governorship.

Palin's appointment to her cabinet of Democrat Pat Galvin to run the Department of Revenue bolstered her bipartisan credibility. Kawasaki and his colleagues were particularly heartened when Palin rehired Tom Irwin, whom Frank Murkowski had fired for opposing his gas-pipeline proposal on the premise that it conceded too much to the oil companies.

"I had concerns that she wasn't a roll up your sleeves governor back then," recalls Democratic representative Les Gara from Anchorage. "But to me, she was so much better than the prior Republican governor, Frank Murkowski, and I spent a lot of time trying to find common ground."

Palin also continued to find a sympathetic audience among the journalists who covered her. The overriding sense among the Alaska press corps was that Palin's ascendance signaled a much needed rebirth in a state in which corruption had led to widespread public cynicism. And the new governor's personal touch had an undeniable and immediate effect.

"She has this very natural magnetism, I think, and I was really drawn to her," Rebecca Braun of the influential *Alaska Budget Report* recalls. "And especially after Murkowski was so sort of arrogant and prickly, and he would almost do everything in his power to turn people off, and she's sort of the opposite. She just smiles very warmly, makes you comfortable, so I don't know if she was purposely trying to manipulate us, but I do think that her sort of natural magnetism and comfort in talking to people had an effect."

During the early days of Palin's term, Braun shared her favorable impressions about the new governor with some friends, which led them to tease her about being in the tank. "And I said, 'No, no. Just because I personally find her appealing doesn't mean that I don't go as hard on her as everyone else in my writing.'"

Murkowski's relationship with the press had fallen somewhere on the spectrum between apprehensive caution and overt hostility. But initially, Palin signaled that her governorship would embrace, rather than pick fights with, the media. Her staff organized frequent press conferences early in her term, one of which was held in the dining room of the governor's new part-time home. Palin sat at the head of a long table flanked by several of her commissioners, with reporters occupying the middle. When the press conference began, no one balked when the governor referred reporters' inquiries to her commissioners. They were just pleased to get this kind of access. At one point, Palin's then five-year-old daughter, Piper, entered the room and began hopping around in the background, trying to drum up some attention. No stranger to juggling work and family, the governor tried to stay focused, but her daughter quickly grew tired of her mom's refusal to pay her enough attention and crawled up onto her lap. "I love you, Mommy," she said loudly enough for everyone to hear.

Christopher Clark, a reporter and debate moderator during the gubernatorial campaign who had switched careers to join the Palin administration as deputy legislative director, noticed that even the most hard-nosed reporters had melted. The affectionate moment between the young mother and her cute daughter was irresistible. "It was natural—it was not feigned, it was not forced," Clark says. "I know I found it endearing, and I would assume other reporters who have a human heart might have found it endearing as well."

When a reporter put a call into the governor's office with a question or an interview request, he or she would often get a call back the same day with a familiar voice on the line: "Hi, this is Sarah." Palin was a familiar presence to the media and would occasionally deliver baked goods to journalists hard at work on the story of the day. More often than not, that story was about the legislative corruption scandals that continued to make state and national news, revealing an engrained culture of corruption in Juneau with tentacles extending to Washington, D.C.

The *Anchorage Daily News*, by far the largest and most influential paper in the state, assigned the full weight of its investigative reporting staff to pursuing the ethical questions that had been raised against Congressman Don Young and Senator Ted Stevens. The latter was indicted in July 2007 after the *Daily News* reported in May that FBI agents were investigating extensive remodeling to his home in the ski resort town of Girdwood, which involved indicted executive Bill Allen of the oil-services company VECO. It seemed there could be no bigger story than the charges against Stevens, who had represented Alaska since before it achieved statehood. Before the corruption scandal, his reputation in the state was nearly on par with George Washington's.

Meanwhile, the *Daily News* suffered from the same financial strains affecting print media nationwide. At times, it could not afford a single reporter in Juneau. Throughout most of Palin's first term, its editors discussed closing the paper's capital bureau entirely. They often relied on the Associated Press, while doing what they could to cover the legislature day to day. The relationship between the new governor and the *Daily News* was helped by her having worked closely with one of its investigative reporters less than three years earlier to help bring to light details of the oil and gas commission ethics scandal that led to her break with Ruedrich and solidified her reputation as a reformer.

John Tracy—the longtime news director at Alaska's highest-rated television news station, NBC affiliate KTUU, Channel 2 in Anchorage—noted that Palin's reputation as an ethical stalwart helped account for her extended honeymoon with the press. "I do give Sarah very early in her career credit for being the maverick that she claims to be," Tracy says. "I think she did take on the establishment. I think she put her political career at great risk, and I think she showed great political instincts for doing that. And so I don't think she's ever really gotten enough real credit for that."

The positive relationship was solidified when she recruited several journalists to begin making the news rather than reporting it. No less than seven former Alaska reporters took prominent roles in the Palin administration on both the communications and policy sides.

After thirty years in journalism, Rhonda McBride departed KTUU after eight years to become Palin's rural adviser. After a twenty-year journalism career, including a stint heading the *Anchorage Daily News* op-ed page during Palin's gubernatorial campaign, Larry Persily moved to Washington, D.C., in May 2007 to run the governor's office there. Christopher Clark ended a nearly decade-long career in media to become Palin's deputy legislative director. Former KTUU executive editor Charles Fedullo, a veteran of the Tony Knowles administration, left his position as a journalism professor at the University of Alaska at Fairbanks to become deputy press secretary. Meg Stapleton, known to most Alaskans as a popular Channel 2 reporter, became Palin's press secretary. When Sharon Leighow ended a two-decade radio career to become the new governor's deputy communications director, KTUU's Juneau reporter, Bill McAllister, wrote an article on the station's website about her career change. Within six months, McAllister himself would become the most prominent Alaska reporter to switch careers when he became the governor's communications director.

McAllister was known for his hard-charging stance both on the tennis court and in the newsroom, and his aggressive reporting had earned him a string of journalism awards, not to mention the ire of Frank Murkowski. McAllister had certainly been up to the challenge of pushing back against Murkowski's combative style, but when Palin took over the reigns, some Alaskans noticed a change in the tone of McAllister's reporting. Charles Fedullo, whose stint in the Palin administration lasted less than a month, said the new governor's press office quickly recognized that the influential NBC affiliate's Juneau correspondent was sympathetic to their cause.

"Bill McAllister loved the governor so much," Fedullo says. "When I was the press secretary, we knew we could touch base with Bill McAllister, and he would say whatever we wanted. It was like from her mouth to his lips."

The criticism of McAllister's Palin coverage was not universal. John Tracy, his boss at KTUU, said that McAllister was unfairly denounced by ideologues on both ends of the spectrum and chalked up any difference in the tone and substance of his coverage to the access that everyone in the media was getting from Palin, which helped her to promote her side of the story.

Either way, McAllister joined the Palin team in August 2008. The symbiotic relationship the governor enjoyed with the Alaskan press at this point in her career is notable in light of how negative her view of the "mainstream media" later became.

Though he left the governor's office in early 2009 at Palin's request, media colleagues have described McAllister as a true believer in her and her agenda. It was a sentiment shared by many in the governor's inner circle, where personal loyalty was one of the most valued commodities upon which the boss judged them. Palin relied on her cabinet members to formulate much of her policy, and this "big-picture" style of governing lent itself well to bureaucrats who thought executive micromanaging did more harm than good.

"I think she does have an innate ability to cut to the chase [to determine] what is the primary issue she needs to be involved in for the topic at hand," says Pat Galvin, who served as her revenue commissioner. "It works well with her responsibilities that she doesn't get bogged down in extraneous issues. She's able to see her role and the decisions that she needs to make, gather the information that she needs for that decision, and then use that information to provide a clear direction."

But Palin's hands-off style challenged other administrators who felt that she often ignored their concerns. As the Washington liaison, Larry Persily says that his interactions with Palin were "very periodic." He recalls that during her trip to the National Governors Association conference in February 2008, the Alaska governor did not take the time to meet with the state's three-member congressional delegation and only stopped by her D.C. office for less than half an hour on her way back to the airport. Persily resigned in June 2008 after concluding that his position did not afford him regular opportunities to make the productive contributions that he had enjoyed in the newsroom.

Charles Fedullo says he never got the chance to speak to Palin during the short time he represented her to the media. He was particularly struck by the unofficial working hours he says she kept. "Everything stopped at three o'clock so she could go pick up her kids," he says. "That was pretty clear at my time there, and I respected that."

Fedullo resigned as deputy press secretary after less than a month on the job. Since he had worked hard to try to get Palin's opponent Tony Knowles elected during the campaign, the governor had initially been attracted to his ability to act as a liaison to his Democratic contacts and afford the governor's press office a bipartisan feel. But Fedullo's Democratic ties also raised eyebrows with others in the administration, who wondered whether he was really on board with his boss's agenda. Upon being encouraged to step down, he did just that.

But the intramural drama was relatively minor during Palin's first few months in office. Her policy challenges, on the other hand, were many and daunting. Palin set to work determined to tackle major ethics reforms and two separate initiatives on energy policy. Her wildly successful results would be difficult to overstate and helped drive her approval rating into the stratosphere.

When Palin took office, she set aside her immediate oil and gas goals to make it clear that nothing could move forward until Juneau did something about its reputation as an ethical cesspool. The new ethics rules that she ushered in marked a dramatic departure from the standard way of doing business in Alaska. One of the most talked about changes was a stipulation requiring lobbyists to report meals or drinks bought for legislators that cost more than $15. The new rule changed Juneau's social atmosphere overnight. Other restrictions prohibited lawmakers from being paid for legislative, administrative, or political work outside the official session and required them to complete ethics training.

The reforms Palin and the legislature achieved had obvious populist appeal, but the old guard in Juneau did not take too kindly to them. Republican establishment figures like Senate President Lyda Green, who had once supported Palin's political rise in Wasilla, came to see her as a sanctimonious do-gooder who refused to listen to experienced legislators when they tried to disabuse her of some preconceived notions about how state business was done. Green knew that Frank Murkowski may not have been Mr. Popularity, but at least he understood the process everyone was used to and believed in taking incremental steps instead of risking radical change. Green retired from public service in 2008 after Palin backed a family friend's designs on her seat.

"All the stars aligned to say, 'Oh, Alaska is totally corrupt,' which I happen to know is not true at all," Green says. "There are a lot of good people who sacrifice time, careers, and family, who've done a lot of great things in Alaska."

But Green's argument that the corruption in Juneau was not really so bad was a tough one to sell to the public. It was politically hazardous for any lawmaker to be seen as standing in the way of the popular new governor's sweeping reforms. Palin quickly became used to getting what she wanted from the legislature.

Though she was not steeped in economic theory, the governor's natural instincts favored fiscal conservatism—the sort that Green and Palin's old Republican Party nemesis Randy Ruedrich shared. In June 2007, she vetoed $231 million in local capital projects that had been inserted into the state budget, aggravating some legislators who said that she had not adequately communicated to them her budget priorities. Riding high on her popularity, Palin twisted the knife further by adding publicly that she had made the cuts because there needed to be "an adult in the room." Lawmakers took the comment as the patronizing reprimand she intended it to be, and though they were powerless to act against a governor with an approval rating as high as Palin's, they would remember the remark later in her term after her popularity had faded.

"Once you insult somebody publicly, trying to get back from that is very difficult," says Republican representative John Coghill.

"And not only that, I think she saw that as more of a cute statement, and [lawmakers] did not think it was very cute."

Palin believed in lower taxes and personal freedom, but at the same time, she was no free market fundamentalist, especially when issues of fairness arose. Oil was, and always will be, the fuel that propels the Alaskan economy. With no state income or sales tax, it funds about 90 percent of the state's budget. Alaska's energy reserves, Palin understood, belonged to its residents, not to the big oil companies. She became convinced that the people deserved a bigger share of the profits.

The idea of a sitting governor taking on Alaska's oil companies at first seemed even more ludicrous than if the governor of Nevada were to go after the casinos. But as oil prices soared to new heights, the timing was right for Palin to act. On September 4, 2007, she unveiled a new oil-profits tax proposal, calling on legislators to replace Murkowski's plan of the previous year, which Palin's administration thought gave too many concessions to the energy companies and was possibly tainted by scandal, given the recent high-profile indictments of lawmakers and lobbyists heavily tied to the oil and gas industry.

After assigning her own plan the sunny acronym of ACES (Alaska's Clear and Equitable Share), Palin called a special legislative session for the following month to debate it. The cornerstone of ACES was a proposal to increase the oil companies' tax burden to the state from 22.5 to 25 percent, a small hike at first glance, but one that would soon add billions to Alaska's coffers with an assist from sky-high oil prices.

"Most governors would not do anything that really fundamentally threatened their interests, and suddenly we had a governor who was willing to look at Alaska's public interest differently," Gregg Erickson of the *Alaska Budget Report* says. "And it was such a wrenching change from what had happened . . . that it stunned everybody."

Palin's initiative ran into a wall erected by some of the most prominent members of her own party, including Lyda Green, who found her proposal to raise a corporate tax "very liberal." Republican representative Jay Ramras, who cochaired the Alaska House Resources Committee during Murkowski's final two years in office, was particularly miffed by what he considered an effort to penalize the oil companies—a move he thought would threaten future exploration and long-term profits. "I think she divorced herself from Republican, free market principals up here—just tax, tax, tax, attack industry, plays to populist crowds," he says, adding, "She professes all these right-wing principles, but she seems to govern left of center, and I find it disingenuous."

After conceding to Democrats' demands for an even more aggressive tax that would be raised progressively as the price of oil increased, the ACES bill passed with bipartisan support in both houses, and Palin signed it into law in December 2007. ACES paid tangible dividends the next year, when every state resident received an energy rebate check for $1,200, in addition to the standard sum from the Permanent Fund Dividend, a constitutionally mandated payout drawn from oil profits. As she crisscrossed the country on the vice presidential campaign trail less than a year later, Palin quickly took credit, much of it well deserved, though Democrats point out that they had actually turned her proposal into reality.

"If it hadn't been for the House Democrats, it would never have happened. She didn't have the wherewithal. She didn't have the horsepower to get it done," Anchorage representative Bob Buch says. "We were the ones that had the voting block."

Nevertheless, Palin had continued to prove eager to work with, rather than antagonize, Democrats. Her success on ACES came in the midst of negotiations over an even more ambitious energy initiative: her proposal to begin work on a 1,715-mile natural gas pipeline that would run from Alaska's North Slope all the way down to the Lower 48, with an estimated price tag close to $30 billion. Much like proposals to move the capital out of Juneau that had come and gone over the years, the pipeline had been a recurring dream for many Alaskans over three decades. Palin was determined to use her ever-growing political capital to pass the Alaska Gasline Inducement Act (AGIA), which would initiate a competitive bidding process with the goal of awarding a license and public contribution to a private company. The winner would proceed with the pipeline project within the government's framework.

Palin and her commissioners knew that the key to getting AGIA passed was to secure the backing of the sixteen members of the House Democratic minority caucus, the largest unified voting bloc in either governing body (House Republicans were a more disjointed group). On the Senate side, one of Palin's closest allies on AGIA was Anchorage Democrat Hollis French, an ambitious former assistant district attorney. Palin added a personal touch to her working relationship with French by attending with her husband the state senator's constituent pizza party, which he held with Democratic representatives Lindsay Holmes and Mike Doogan. It was a show of good faith typical of Palin's congenial style of the time. A year later, there would be no more pizza parties after French helped run the investigation into the circumstances surrounding Palin's firing of Public Safety Commissioner Walt Monegan. Palin and French's previous partnership was then quickly forgotten.

After she had secured enough Democratic votes on AGIA, it was time for the hard part: reaching out to the Republicans, many of whom were skittish after the governor announced that Trans-Canada was the only compliant bidder on the license that fulfilled the AGIA requirements. They knew the government's license would not be a construction contract but an agreement to take steps toward the ultimate goal of manufacturing a natural gas pipeline by late 2018. But TransCanada did not own any natural gas itself, and without guarantees of cooperation from the companies that did, some Republicans thought it risky to put all of the state's eggs in TransCanada's basket. "I even struggled with it because I'm really pretty much a free market conservative," recalls John Coghill, who ended up voting in favor of passing AGIA.

Legislators who still opposed the project were convinced that paying $500 million out to TransCanada was akin to throwing money into the Bristol Bay. They thought it unlikely that a pipeline would actually be built. But they were outnumbered by lawmakers like Coghill, who were swayed by Palin's argument that the time to act had come. The historic vote passed in the Senate 14–5 on August 1, after only two hours of debate.

AGIA was signed into law on August 27. Later that day, Palin hopped on a private jet to attend a secret meeting in Sedona, Arizona. When she arrived at John McCain's ranch for her job interview, she had a brand-new accomplishment to mention to the Republican nominee who was looking to light a fire under his lagging campaign. As had often been the case in her political rise, her timing could not have been better.

$$\star \quad \star \quad \star$$

4. Sharp Elbows

SARAH PALIN'S FIRST YEAR AND A HALF in office was most remembered for the impressive accomplishments she and the legislature ushered in and the new tone she brought to Juneau, but a troubling undercurrent also manifested itself in the new governor's leadership style. She had difficulty separating her personal from her public life and demonstrated callousness in firing close aides who had fallen out of favor.

In early July 2007, John Bitney knew that his time in Palin's office was nearing its end. That much had been made clear to him. Bitney may have been Palin's former junior high school bandmate, the chief architect of her gubernatorial campaign triumph, and her legislative director, and he may have worked tirelessly to negotiate the details of her stunning successes in office, but he had made one major mistake. He had begun an affair with the wife of an old friend of Sarah and Todd Palin, and the governor had found out about it.

Bitney had not been up-front with the governor about the relationship, and he agreed that his continued employment in her office was no longer an option. But he was not exactly independently wealthy. He had to have a job, which Palin's chief of staff, Mike Tibbles, seemed to understand. Along with Deputy Legislative Director Christopher Clark, Tibbles and Bitney were the heart of the batting order on Team Palin—the power hitters who worked behind the scenes to turn the hands-off governor's ambitious goals into reality. Any staffer who had a question about policy or process could always ask Tibbles 'n' Bits—the joint nickname the pair had earned.

Bitney tried not to think much of it when his state-issued Black-Berry suddenly stopped working late one Saturday night on the eve of a trip to Juneau to meet with Tibbles. The two colleagues had planned to get together in the capital to figure out how to reassign Bitney to another department in which he would not have direct contact with the governor. His BlackBerry still not functioning, Bitney woke up early the next morning and packed his car for the long trip from his home in Anchorage to Juneau, an odyssey that could make anyone feel like a contestant on an episode of *The Amazing Race*. He would be on the highway for about sixteen hours, a drive that would include a border crossing into Canada and back, before capping the trip off with a four-and-a-half-hour ferry ride to Juneau. He planned to break up the journey by staying overnight in Tok—a small frontier town east of Fairbanks on the looping AK-1 highway—and then continuing on to the capital early Monday morning.

As he pulled out of his driveway, Bitney remembered that he had left some items in his Anchorage office, so he detoured downtown and parked in front of the towering government office building on Seventh Avenue. It being a Sunday, he had to use his key card to get inside the complex. When the key card didn't work, the nervousness that had crept up when his BlackBerry went down now escalated into foreboding. But the meeting with Tibbles in Juneau was still on, as far as he knew. Bitney climbed back into his car and merged onto the highway headed toward Tok. When he woke up there the next morning, he took out his laptop and checked his e-mail. He had messages from two different people telling him their e-mails to his state government address had bounced back. They both wanted to know if everything was okay.

Clearly, everything was not. The administration had apparently cut his service without even telling him he would be fired. It seemed rather unprofessional—vindictive, even. He just wanted to figure out his new job as quickly as possible and put it all behind him. At that point, Bitney decided to call his deputy legislative director and longtime friend, Christopher Clark.

"I better transfer you down the hall to the chief of staff," Clark said.

Tibbles sounded sullen when he got on the line.

"What's going on?" Bitney asked. "I thought I was driving down to Juneau to see you."

"We cut you off on Friday," Tibbles said flatly, according to Bitney.

Bitney found the manner in which the news was delivered particularly hard to swallow, considering that he had recommended Tibbles to Palin for the chief of staff position, essentially hiring his own boss. That the governor to whom he had been so devoted had relayed the news of Bitney's firing through Tibbles a full three days after the fact—only after Bitney asked and without giving him a chance to settle into a new position—was a personal affront that he had not expected. The Palin administration had done nothing to help Bitney transfer into another department, as Tibbles had indicated it would in previous conversations.

"I need to work, and I didn't think it was a death sentence," Bitney recalls. "But I found out I was wrong."

Bitney's unceremonious dismissal raised more than a few eyebrows among his many friends in Juneau. After all, they thought of him as the man who had first given professional heft to the small-town campaign that Palin had run at the beginning of the gubernatorial race. Bitney recognized that Palin's political sixth sense, rather than his guidance, had been her strongest asset. Still, he knew he'd helped raise her standing from newcomer, one whom voters liked and respected but perhaps weren't sure was up to the task of running a state, to full-blown contender.

"What I gave her was a sense of depth on policy," Bitney says. "She had the connection, the connectivity, the charisma, the looks, the story, the appeal, all of that. I mean a great candidate—you can't beat her for a candidate. But she just flat out didn't know issues. She's not stupid—that's not what I'm saying. She just didn't have years in Juneau."

In a moment of candor, Palin's deputy press secretary, Sharon Leighow, told reporters at the time that Bitney had been fired for personal reasons. But more than a year later, as national journalists dug up the dirt around Wasilla, Leighow's story changed. "John Bitney was dismissed because of his poor job performance," she told the Wall Street Journal, declining to elaborate on his failings as the legislative director during one of the most accomplished periods in the history of Alaska government. Not only was Leighow's statement at variance with her original explanation, but it also defied Palin's public praise of her legislative director just a couple of months before he was let go. "Whatever you did, you did right," she had told Bitney at a post-legislative-session press conference.

Despite his concerns about finding work after being fired, Bitney quickly landed a job as House Speaker John Harris's chief of staff. Soon after, Todd Palin called the House Speaker and, according to Harris, expressed his displeasure that the top lawmaker had hired Bitney. It would not be the last time that Todd, a private citizen, would try to influence government hiring decisions to satisfy a personal agenda. Bitney, a man who had broken down into tears on primary day over how much he cared about Sarah Palin and wanted her to succeed, was now the target of an apparent blacklisting campaign. But Harris stood his ground, and Bitney's new job was safe.

Along with Tibbles, Bitney had also recruited his close friend Christopher Clark to join the Palin team as deputy legislative director in December 2006. Like Bitney, Clark had a long history in Juneau, and the two had spent time working as legislative aides together. When the session began, Bitney often found himself so immersed in developing Palin's policies that he relied on Clark to act as the chief liaison with the legislature.

"He had every position statement, every poll response, every survey response, every speech," Clark says of Bitney. "Therefore, he was often consulted for guidance, and so because he was often so busy, people would come through me."

Clark's other main function was to help provide background information to reporters frustrated by unreturned phone calls to the governor's press office when they were under deadline pressure. He had been impressed by Palin's grit and commanding presence during the gubernatorial debates he had moderated as a KTOO radio reporter, and after he joined her administration, Clark grew fond of her "big-picture" leadership style, which gave her more experienced staffers significant freedom. He was also surprised by how tolerant Palin seemed to be when things did not run smoothly, such as the time he had participated in a less than cogent briefing on ethics reform. After most of the participants had left the room, Clark approached Palin.

"Hey, I'm sorry, Governor," he said. "I'm sorry we didn't provide you with a more organized presentation."

"Oh, no, no," Palin replied. "That was very good."

Everything was running smoothly for Clark until July 2007, when his friend and boss John Bitney was fired. Clark knew from observing how Palin dealt with perceived personal slights that because of his close relationship with Bitney, it was just a matter of time before the axe came down on his neck too. Sure enough, Mike Tibbles called him into a meeting in mid-August.

"Hey, Chris, it's been great," Tibbles said, according to Clark. "We know you've been working hard; you've been working like a dog. We've decided to go with a new arrangement. We are going with codirectors instead of a director and a deputy director."

Tibbles gave as the official reason for the dismissal the governor's desire to improve communications with the legislature, an explanation Clark found particularly ironic since he felt the complaints that had started to pile up about poor communications resulted directly from Bitney's termination the month before. Clark's last day in office was September 6. Tibbles offered to try to find him a job elsewhere and did make an earnest attempt to do so, but Clark's heart was not in it. He reunited with his old friend Bitney in Representative John Harris's office.

"Frankly, I felt like both of us had done a good job for the Governor," Clark says. "Her approval ratings went higher and higher and higher during our time with her." After Clark was let go, he had dinner with Palin's future communications director, Bill McAllister, in Juneau. McAllister was still a Channel 2 reporter at the time and, according to Clark, admitted he liked the governor but agreed that Clark had been "collateral damage" because of what happened to Bitney.

Clark wondered how Palin would fare without the brain trust that had stuck with her from the beginning of the campaign. Longtime friend Kris Perry had been with the governor since her Wasilla days, but as good a manager as she was, Perry was no expert on policy or process. Of the other members of Palin's inner circle, only Frank Bailey, who had worked for Alaska Airlines before becoming a campaign volunteer, had been around since the early days.

"I have no doubt that if Bitney and I were still down there in the legislative office, Troopergate would not have happened," Clark says. "Now that seems like an outrageous thing, maybe even an arrogant thing, to say. Why would the legislative office have anything to do with that? Well, see, we were more than just a legislative office. I don't know if the Governor has ever realized this. . . . We were constantly picking up all these little, itty-bitty things that most people may have seen as miniscule, but it is little details that will trip you up."

By July 2008, Palin had begun to generate some national attention in conservative publications and political blogs with her state approval ratings hovering around a remarkable 80 percent. With an impressive record of legislative accomplishment, she could rightfully claim the title as the most popular governor in America. Her name was even being tossed around as a potential dark horse vice presidential pick for John McCain, whose campaign was floundering, unable to stick to a compelling narrative in a political climate that, for Republicans, was dismal at best.

Commissioner of Public Safety Walt Monegan had particular reason to feel good about his role in the governor's administration. Well-known and widely respected in Anchorage for his thirty-three years on its police force, the last five as its chief, the ruddy-faced, barrel-chested cop with a walrus mustache had impressed Palin and her staff so much during the 2006 campaign that they twice asked him to shoot a commercial for her—a request he had denied, citing the nonpartisan role of a police officer. A former marine who was not yet born when his father died heroically in the Korean War, earning the Medal of Honor posthumously, Monegan had seemed the perfect fit for the job of public safety commissioner, which he began the day after Palin took office. In April 2008, he had taken a bow and soaked in the sustained applause when Palin lavished praise on his work to combat Alaska's sky-high domestic- and sexual-violence rates at a conference in Anchorage.

"An indication of our commitment is the participation here of my, of our, Department of Public Safety Commissioner Walt Monegan . . . and I want to publicly thank him," Palin said.

Monegan had recently proposed to create a special task force on sexual abuse using a "vertical prosecution model." His plan was to assign state troopers to investigate cases in rural areas where local authorities were overwhelmed, designate prosecutors to handle the cases in the courts, and offer up social workers to counsel the victims. Though the governor had not yet signed off on the idea, Monegan was particularly pleased that she had noted at the conference her gratitude that he wasn't just paying lip service to the issue of sexual abuse but "finding the solutions and plugging them in."

Monegan had taken a proactive stance on the issue after an Amnesty International study released the previous year drew attention to statistics that found Alaska Native women were more than 2.5 times more likely than average to become victims of sexual assault. On a daily basis, Palin's rural affairs advisor, Rhonda McBride, would take phone calls from Alaskans who told heartbreaking stories about life in the bush. One day she heard from a village teacher who told her that most of the girls in her class had been sexually abused. The teacher's school was so small that one of her female students had to sit with the boy accused of assaulting her while his case made its way through the court system. McBride would often relay concerns to Palin via e-mail, but because she rarely got any feedback, she had no idea if the governor even read anything she sent. She had found a far more receptive audience in Monegan, who seemed equally passionate about addressing the problem.

As the nearly endless hours of sunlight signaled the arrival of the short but glorious Alaska summer, Monegan was filled with optimism about his vertical prosecution plan. He looked forward to his upcoming trip to Washington, D.C., where he was scheduled to meet with Alaska's junior senator, Lisa Murkowski, about acquiring federal funding for it. The governor's acting chief of staff, Mike Nizich, had signed off on the trip, and Palin had not related any concerns to him about vying for an earmark.

Monegan did not know, however, that some members of Palin's administration were exchanging e-mails expressing their confusion and frustration about Monegan's budget priorities. The e-mails would prove critical, once the Troopergate scandal erupted, to the Palin administration's assertion that Monegan was guilty of insubordination—the final reason given to the media in the evolving public explanations for his termination. After first saying that Palin simply wanted to take the department in a new direction, the administration would subsequently argue that Monegan had failed to meet recruitment goals and was not active enough in fighting alcoholism in the bush. The last claim was particularly curious since the demotion Palin offered him was a job that worked more directly on alcohol-related issues.

When Nizich called Monegan into a meeting on July 11 at 3 P.M., the public safety commissioner thought it was to continue a recent conversation about an issue involving security for the governor at her upcoming annual summer picnics. Todd Palin had been expressing concerns that Palin's former brother-in-law, State Trooper Mike Wooten, posed a threat to the safety of the "First Family." To Monegan, this didn't synch up with the governor's decision to drastically cut her own security detail from the half dozen officers assigned to

her at the beginning of her term to one full-time officer in Anchorage and one part-time officer who protected her in Juneau during
the legislative session, but he figured Nizich would update him on
the matter.

Monegan had just returned to Anchorage from a trip to Bristol
Bay to examine how wildlife troopers were handling the commercial fishing season there, so he changed out of his jeans, put on a suit
and tie, and headed downtown to meet with Nizich. When he arrived at the governor's office, Monegan found a spot at the same
conference table where he had sat six months earlier, during the first
week in January, when Todd Palin had called him in to that meeting
to first share his concerns about Wooten, who had gone through a
messy divorce with the governor's sister Molly and had been sanc-
tioned for conduct violations under the previous administration.
Todd had argued to Monegan at that time that Wooten should not,
in the light of those conduct violations, have been allowed to continue to serve, and he had asked the public safety commissioner to
reexamine the investigation that had already been completed. Monegan had agreed to do so. He picked up the paperwork on Wooten
that Todd had assembled, including a report by a private investigator, and said he would make sure the investigation hadn't missed
anything. It had not, which Monegan later explained to the governor's husband.

The meeting with Todd had been the first time Monegan heard
Wooten's name, but it would not be the last. In fact, he would receive dozens of inquiries about him from Palin staffers, along with
three e-mails from the governor herself. One member of Palin's inner circle, longtime aide Frank Bailey, was caught red-handed in his
attempt to get Wooten fired when he reached out to the legislative
liaison for the Department of Public Safety, Lt. Rodney Dial. "Todd
and Sarah are scratching their heads. Why on earth hasn't this, why

is this guy still representing the department?" Bailey said on February 29 in a phone call that was recorded automatically. "I'm telling you honestly, you know, she really likes Walt a lot, but on this issue she feels like it's, she doesn't know why there's absolutely no action for a year on this issue. It's very troubling to her and the family. I could definitely relay that." After initially denying that anyone had pressured Monegan to fire Wooten on her behalf, Palin released the audio of the phone call at a press conference and said that she had not orchestrated it but added that it was "disturbing" and could be seen as a "smoking gun." Bailey was handed a slap on the wrist when he was placed on paid administrative leave for five weeks and rejoined the administration until Palin resigned in July 2009.

Monegan also reported having two conversations on the Wooten matter with Palin, though she later denied that either conversation had taken place. Monegan finally told her, he says, that he needed to keep her at arm's length on the sensitive personnel matter, while he dealt with Todd, a private citizen, regarding any ongoing concerns the family might have. Although Monegan's current meeting with Nizich was held in Governor Palin's office, the governor was again not present. Nizich cut right to the chase.

"The governor really respects and admires your ability and your interest in handling the bush areas," the acting chief of staff said, according to Monegan. "So she wants to offer you the job of being the director of the Alcoholic Beverage Control Board."

Nizich's words felt like an electric shock going through Monegan. The Alcoholic Beverage Control Board worked under the Department of Public Safety. He was being offered a demotion.

"I take it that means I'm no longer the commissioner of public safety?" he asked.

"That's correct."

"When's it effective?"

"Immediately."

Monegan paused for a moment to reflect. "Well, let me tell you, I'm not really interested in that job," he said.

"Well, think about it," Nizich said. "Think about it overnight and then give me a call tomorrow."

"Okay, I can do that, Mike."

Monegan knew that as a commissioner, he served at the governor's pleasure. The final decision had apparently been made, and there was no point in arguing about it. But he could not just leave without at least trying to get a real explanation for why he had been fired so suddenly. "This is out of the blue. I mean, I didn't even know anybody was mad at me," Monegan said. "Nobody ever said anything." He paused before adding, "Was it Wooten?"

"No, she just wants to take the department in a different direction," Nizich said, echoing the first talking point that the governor's office would soon distribute to explain the firing.

Monegan pressed. "What direction?"

"A different one."

Monegan said he'd get back to Nizich the next day. The two men shook hands, and Monegan left the governor's office. On his way out of the building, he took off his government ID and handed it to the receptionist.

That Saturday, he confirmed with Nizich his decision not to accept the demotion. The next day, he returned to clean out his office, still without having heard a word of thanks for his service or an explanation from Sarah Palin, the woman he had been proud to serve for nineteen months.

When John Bitney reflected on the Monegan dismissal, it sounded all too familiar. "Firing people isn't fun," he says. "To have to look at somebody in the face and tell them is not an easy thing for some people to do, and I think that her inability to do that has led to these things being way more dramatic than they ever need to be. Let people go, but give them some dignity."

Less than a week after Monegan's termination, Andrew Halcro, Palin's former gubernatorial campaign opponent turned blogger and radio show host, would become the first to accuse the governor publicly of abusing her power. Two days later, the story suddenly generated its first real burst of steam in the mainstream media when Monegan went public with his assertion that he had felt pressured to fire Wooten. The Troopergate scandal was now the dominant narrative surrounding the Palin administration.

Over a pot of coffee at the Captain Cook Hotel in downtown Anchorage more than six months after his termination and in the midst of his ultimately unsuccessful campaign to become mayor of Anchorage, the half–Alaska Native, half-Irish former cop insisted that the waitress call him "Walt" instead of "Mr. Monegan." Looking a bit uncomfortable in his stuffy suit, he reflected on the events that had led him here. The presidential campaign and the two separate inquiries into whether Palin had misused her position were over, but her decision to fire him would have profound implications for the rest of his life. Asked whether Palin should have taken up herself the unenviable task of notifying him, a prominent member of her administration, that she was letting him go, Monegan paused to consider before answering methodically.

"If I were governor, I would have," he said.

$\star \;\; \star \;\; \star$

5. Plucked

WHEN JOHN MCCAIN met Sarah Palin for the first time at the National Governors Association meeting in February 2008, he had just about wrapped up the Republican nomination for president. She, on the other hand, was a lowly first-term governor lost in a sea of her better-known, more experienced colleagues. But, with one gutsy question, the rookie Alaskan would catch McCain's attention.

As part of the festivities surrounding the event in Washington, D.C., McCain hosted a special meeting at the Willard Hotel with Republican governors who had either endorsed a different candidate during the competitive primary process or, like Palin, stayed out of the race altogether up to that point. After talking about his vision for the rest of the campaign and reminding the governors about the important roles he sought for them, McCain opened the floor to questions.

"What is it that you'd like to talk about?" he asked. "What is it that you think I need to be focusing on? Let's have a conversation because I need your counsel."

Despite the many oversized egos among the ambitious politicians in the room, there was momentary silence. Then Sarah Palin opened her mouth.

"Senator, I'd like to talk to you about drilling in ANWR [the Arctic National Wildlife Refuge]," she said. "I disagree with you on not drilling in Alaska. I think that we have real resources, and we need those resources for our country. And we can do it safely and cleanly and protect the environment."

The ice having been broken, some of the bigger names in the room began to chime in with their own thoughts. Although his opinion on ANWR was not swayed, McCain took note of the courage it took for Palin to challenge him so directly. He admired politicians not afraid to stir the pot, and her name would soon find a place on the list of his potential running mates.

As the convention drew nearer and Barack Obama maintained a solid lead in the polls, the need for a "game-changing" selection became more apparent. The national media began to throw Palin's name around as an intriguing, yet highly unlikely, long shot, and she became a serious topic of discussion within McCain's inner circle. Still, Joe Lieberman had always seemed the more likely choice if McCain decided he needed to heave a long pass into the end zone. The innovative thinking behind the McCain team's consideration of Lieberman was that he and McCain would take a one-term pledge and commit to a nonpartisan style of governing, reinforcing Mc-Cain's independent streak and pigeonholing Obama as a liberal ideologue. Backed enthusiastically by their mutual friend, South Carolina senator Lindsay Graham, McCain had given serious thought to the Lieberman scheme, but it became an unmanageable mess once word leaked to the media that the possibility was real. Conservative leaders were apoplectic about the mere thought of putting a pro-choice Independent-Democrat on the Republican ticket, and the potential benefits did not outweigh the near certain possibility of an insurrection at the convention.

The idea of tapping Mitt Romney for the number two slot would have been laughable just a few months earlier, when McCain looked as if he might actually take a swing at the former Massachusetts governor during some of the testier moments of their primary debates. But Romney had proved himself a highly effective fundraiser for his former opponent and an economics whiz who could very well put his birth state of Michigan into play. Most importantly, McCain had almost uncharacteristically warmed right up to Romney after the two began spending time together and the senator realized that the straight-laced businessman was actually adept at cracking a joke and pragmatic enough not to harbor even a hint of a grudge. But despite Romney's many assets, the drawbacks of running with a man who had not only accused McCain of being a liberal but also owned almost as many houses as the Arizona senator did were considered too great.

Mark Salter had pushed Tim Pawlenty, the young governor of Minnesota, but even he understood that picking a middle-aged white male would be greeted with a collective yawn. "I don't think it's a secret I was a Pawlenty advocate," Salter says. "Put him on the ticket, and he'll get less press than Joe Biden did."

Chief strategist Steve Schmidt had outlined four political goals for McCain to consider in choosing his running mate. This was going to be a difficult race to win, and they needed someone who could do more than just step up to be president at any time, a daunting enough qualification in itself. The vice presidential candidate had to appeal to female voters, win over independents, recapture the maverick label that had made McCain a media darling during the 2000 campaign, and excite conservatives while simultaneously distancing the ticket from the Bush administration. Schmidt knew that if McCain failed to come out of the convention with a lead in the polls, he would have little chance of closing the gap in the final two months. Knowing that only a truly bold and dynamic candidate could offer that possibility, the campaign's top strategists mentioned Sarah Palin's name more and more often as they sweated, literally and figuratively, through the muggy days of August.

Palin was one of several potential running mates asked to fill out general questionnaires about their personal and political lives. Campaign operatives obtained her cell phone number from the Alaska State Troopers, and McCain called her on August 24, just five days before he would unveil her to the world. Yes, she was interested in the job.

★ ★ ★

TWENTY-EIGHT-YEAR-OLD Alabama native Davis White may have technically served as the McCain campaign's director of advance, but on Monday, August 25, 2008, he became something more akin to a secret agent. When he arrived at Ted Stevens International Airport in Anchorage that afternoon, he used his BlackBerry camera to snap a photo of the stuffed polar bear that presided over the terminal. White e-mailed the picture without comment to three top aides at headquarters in Arlington, Virginia. The Secret Service had previously warned the campaign that its e-mail system had been compromised, and White's mission being the most sensitive endeavor of the campaign, the electronic photo served as the only confirmation that it was going as planned.

The next morning, White met Sarah Palin's closest aide, Kris Perry, over breakfast at a hotel on the outskirts of Anchorage. His instructions to Perry must have seemed surreal to the unassuming Wasilla native with a penchant for bear hugs who had gotten into local politics because she wanted to help her friend Sarah. White explained that a Learjet 35A carrying Perry and the governor would leave the following day, Wednesday, at noon for Arizona. On Thursday morning, White would connect Palin with the Republican presidential nominee, John McCain, at his Sedona ranch. If McCain decided not to offer her the vice presidential slot, White would take Palin and Perry back to Alaska safely and quickly. If the senator did offer her the job, the campaign would send for her husband and kids in Alaska, and the Palin family would experience a consequential life change.

Perry assured White that it would be at least a full day before either the media or Palin's other Alaska aides noticed that their governor was missing. She was scheduled to sign the gas-pipeline legislation on Wednesday morning, and a lull would be expected after that public ceremony. Still, White explained that the campaign could not risk someone noticing that all of the Palin kids had been taken out of school, so whatever happened, the children would have to stay home and out of sight on Thursday morning and wait for their marching orders at Perry's house. Another McCain advance staffer, John Berrier, would rent a fifteen-passenger van in Anchorage. As soon as he received the green light on Thursday, Berrier would drive Todd Palin, the kids, and chief of staff Mike Nizich to the airport and get them on a G4 airplane to join Sarah in Middletown, Ohio.

After his meeting with Perry, White phoned Tom Yeilding, his best friend from their hometown of Mountain Brook, a suburb of Birmingham, Alabama. Yeilding had once done advance work for Vice President Dick Cheney, and White trusted him implicitly—the only qualification that campaign manager Rick Davis had said was essential for this job. Yeilding had since left the political world and was now in the construction business. He was on a work site in Tennessee when he got the call.

"I've never asked you to do this, but I need you to take me seriously," White said into the phone. "I need you to walk off the site right now and get on a flight to Cincinnati and call me when you get there."

Yeilding was dumbfounded. "Davis, I'm the foreman on this crew," he said. "I've got a dozen guys working for me. We're about to put up some of these beams."

White understood quite well how odd his request must have seemed, but he had no time for arguments. "Tom, this is important. You're the only person I trust."

"I don't have clothes," Yeilding protested. "I don't have anything."

"Wear whatever you're wearing. You are not going to look like a campaign staffer."

Yeilding could hear the intensity in his old friend's voice. He dropped what he was doing, drove to the airport, and got on a plane to Cincinnati. When he landed, he again spoke to White, who told him to drive about forty minutes to Middletown, find a hotel there, and book twelve rooms under the name CraneWorks, Yeilding's construction company. He found a place called the Manchester Inn. It may not have been up to the standards of the Ritz-Carltons, J. W. Marriotts, and Four Seasons that Palin would stay in over the next two months, but it was just about the last venue anyone would look in to find a vice presidential candidate.

The next morning, Davis White watched as a black Jetta pulled onto the tarmac at the executive airport in Anchorage and came to a stop behind the Learjet. Todd Palin was behind the wheel with his wife sitting shotgun and Kris Perry in the backseat. Wearing a black top and skirt and pink flip-flops and carrying just one small bag, Sarah Palin got on the plane with Perry and White. At the refueling stop in Seattle, the three disembarked to watch former president Bill Clinton speak live at the Democratic National Convention in Denver. There was not much risk that anyone at the private airport would recognize the governor of Alaska, but White was nonetheless relieved when they landed in Flagstaff with the secret still secure.

At the Flagstaff airport, deputy campaign manager Christian Ferry greeted them and drove the group in his rented white Chevy Tahoe to the home of Bob Delgado, a close friend of the McCains and CEO of Anheuser-Busch beer distributor Hensley & Co., Cindy McCain's family company. They arrived there at around 10 P.M., and Palin was introduced to Delgado, Steve Schmidt, and Mark Salter. Over a late pizza dinner, Palin spent the next couple of hours speaking on the telephone with campaign attorney A. B. Culvahouse and answering difficult questions from Schmidt and Salter.

For his part of the vetting, Culvahouse focused on the situation surrounding Palin's firing of Commissioner of Public Safety Walt Monegan a little more than a month earlier. She insisted to the campaign attorney that she had done nothing wrong.

Schmidt and Salter discussed several topics with Palin, including how she would handle her difference of opinion with McCain on drilling in ANWR. The top aides could tell right away how toughminded she was, but Salter wanted to make sure she was left with no doubt that this experience would be unlike any she could ever imagine. "I hope you understand that if the senator were to offer you this and you agree, no matter what you've done in your life professionally, nothing will prepare you for the intrusiveness of it," he told her. "So if you've got anything out there, it's in your interest to make sure we know about it."

The governor revealed that her seventeen-year-old daughter was pregnant. It was far from an ideal situation, but life wasn't perfect. Bristol was mature for her age and in love with the soon-to-be father, Levi Johnston. The young couple's plans to marry would make their current state of affairs more palatable to the public.

Another topic that Salter and Schmidt broached was Palin's view on evolution. There was some unspoken concern among the two top aides that the very religious governor might be branded a fundamentalist on matters of faith. "I'm the daughter of a science teacher. My father showed me fossils. I know about evolution, and I accept evolution," Palin assured them. "That doesn't mean that God didn't set everything in motion." It was another solid answer. She had passed the first test, but the campaign's eleventh-hour vetting would lead to some unpleasant surprises down the road.

At 6 A.M. the next morning, Palin, Perry, Schmidt, Salter, and White packed into the Chevy Tahoe with Ferry behind the wheel. Ferry had thought ahead by equipping the vehicle with "baby-on-board" pull-down window shades so that no one could see inside while they were en route. When they arrived at McCain's Sedona ranch forty-five minutes later, the Secret Service agreed to allow them to enter the complex without stopping the vehicle to be swept, which would risk exposing its occupants to an enterprising reporter or other prying eyes. McCain's traveling press corps had already been told that the senator was having coffee at his ranch and would not be departing until later in the morning.

McCain greeted Palin and the vehicle's other occupants and then walked with the governor to the river that runs through his ranch for a sit-down chat. After about an hour of alone time with Palin, the senator excused himself to speak with Salter and Schmidt for a few minutes. As the three men talked, it became clear that McCain considered Tim Pawlenty the other finalist for the position and that his mind was still not 100 percent made up. He encouraged his two top aides to help him weigh the pros and cons of Palin versus Pawlenty. Had McCain decided at the last moment that he did not want to go through with one of the biggest gambles in presidential-campaign history, Palin would have been thanked for her time and a call put in to Pawlenty within minutes. But the old fighter pilot decided he was up for one last daring maneuver.

After excusing Salter and Schmidt, McCain reconvened with Palin along with his wife, Cindy. The Arizona senator asked the Alaska governor if she would be his running mate, and she accepted the offer immediately. Cindy McCain had a staffer take a photograph of the three of them to memorialize the moment. Palin called Todd in Alaska to break the news and confirmed to Kris Perry that it was on to Dayton. Though grinning from ear to ear, the governor was strikingly poised. It must have seemed like her whole life had been leading her to this moment. Others in her shoes might have hesitated, at least for a moment. But Sarah Palin had no doubt that she was ready.

The group wasted no time in driving back to Flagstaff and boarding the cramped Learjet. Schmidt and Palin sat in the rear bench seat, while Salter and Perry occupied the middle row with White and Ferry in the front. During the flight to Ohio, Schmidt and Salter did their best to instill the confidence that anyone in Palin's situation would need, but they were also frank about the importance of the next day's rollout. They discussed how they would avoid the pitfalls that had plagued the days and weeks following George H. W. Bush's 1988 unveiling of his running mate, Indiana senator Dan Quayle. Quayle had been riddled with accusations that he was too inexperienced and not up to the intellectual challenge of the nation's second-highest office. To try to skirt the distinct potential for similar problems, the campaign would ensure that their vice presidential rollout would center on carefully scripted speeches rather than unpredictable interactions with the media.

After a refueling stop in Amarillo, Texas, the Learjet touched down in Middletown, Ohio, at about 5 P.M. Two fifteen-passenger vans—one equipped with a baby seat for Trig Palin, Sarah's infant son—awaited them on the tarmac. Palin got into one of the vans, which drove fifteen minutes down the road to the Manchester Inn. Upon their arrival, she accepted her key to the appropriately named Presidential Suite, Room 508, where she temporarily became the proud matriarch of the Upton family, the surname of Tom Yeilding's boss at CraneWorks.

Speechwriter Matthew Scully and Nicolle Wallace, the senior advisor tasked to work closely with Palin, landed in Cincinnati at about 8 P.M. They met their driver at the airport and headed down the dark, windy roads to Middletown. Scully assumed that Wallace knew the identity of the candidate they were about to meet, but she was just as clueless as he was. For a campaign that would later earn a well-deserved reputation for rampant leakages, the secret's still-airtight status was a significant accomplishment.

When they arrived at the hotel more than an hour later, Scully was surprised by the lack of activity on the poorly lit street. He thought there would be some kind of noticeable buzz. Instead, it was just Salter sitting on the steps leading up to the lobby, tapping away at his BlackBerry, while Schmidt leaned against a post talking into his cell phone. Few words were exchanged before Salter and Schmidt ushered Scully and Wallace to the front desk, where they each picked up a key in an envelope with CraneWorks written on it. An elevator took the group of four up to the fifth floor, where Scully figured that the two top McCain aides would have to let the secret out at last. Instead, Schmidt turned to his right as he left the elevator without speaking a word, and the other three followed.

Considering the intensity of the mystery, Scully could not imagine that he was about to meet Mitt Romney or Tim Pawlenty. It could have been Lieberman, though even that prospect did not seem so unforeseen as to require this level of secrecy. He even thought half-seriously about the possibility that Colin Powell might be about to greet him on the other side of the door.

The group came to a stop in front of Room 508, and the moment of truth had arrived. Still, Schmidt decided to unveil the vice presidential pick game show style, without first saying who it was. He turned to address Scully and Wallace, relishing the drama of the moment. "I'm about to introduce you to our nominee. You are the seventh and eighth people to know about this," Schmidt said, embellishing the number, but not by much. "There should be no communications: cell phone, BlackBerry, news to loved ones. Nothing."

In a gesture of confidence in the team, Schmidt trusted Scully and Wallace enough not to confiscate their electronic devices. He opened the door and the group walked into the suite. Kris Perry was sitting in the common room, but she was hardly a familiar face. Schmidt led them a few steps down a short hallway and turned to the right. At the threshold of the bedroom, Scully instantly recognized the woman who sat in a chair in the corner, wearing a sweater, casual pants, and heavy socks. He was flabbergasted, but in the best possible way. He had never heard any of the chatter within the McCain circle that Palin was a serious possibility, but he knew a bit about her career in Alaska and was particularly excited about the addition of a woman to the ticket.

After the shock had worn off sufficiently to hold a productive conversation, the McCain aides chatted informally with Palin. On the TV behind Scully's shoulder, Barack Obama's historic convention speech had just gotten underway amid the glittering lights of a jam-packed Invesco Field in Denver, as if anyone in the room needed another reminder of what they were up against. Palin spoke about her family, career path, and major achievements in Alaska, appropriately introducing herself like a stranger from a distant land. When Wallace asked her about energy issues, Palin spoke fluidly about AGIA, ACES, and national policy. The latest seasoned political veterans to meet her could not help but be relieved by the almost mystifying composure of this obscure first-term governor who had been plucked unnoticed out of the frozen North a day before and was about to become the most-talked-about person in America.

The aides retreated to their respective rooms and left Palin with some time to prepare mentally as best she could. Scully had prepared in advance a generic announcement speech for whomever the vice presidential candidate might be, but McCain's unorthodox pick obliged the speechwriter to make many more changes than he had anticipated. Working alone at first, he kept a hard copy of the skeleton speech by his side while he typed out the first draft of Palin's introduction to the nation. In a simple online search he conducted, one particular phrase from a speech she had given in Alaska jumped out at him: "a servant's heart." He added that into the draft.

Meanwhile, Davis White returned to the airport with Tom Yeilding, who was still decked out in his CraneWorks gear. As the two men waited for Palin's family and chief of staff to arrive, Yeilding gave his old friend an extra CraneWorks hat to keep the construction company ruse going. They both chatted amicably with airport workers about their "boss," whom they said was arriving home from a fishing trip in Alaska. The G4 plane touched down shortly before 11 P.M., and White and Yeilding reunited Mike Nizich and Todd, Bristol, Willow, Piper, and Trig Palin with their mother at the Manchester Inn. Next, White drove to the event site in Dayton where the governor would be unveiled the next day. The podium had been set up to accommodate a candidate expected to be over six feet tall, and there were only seats for two family members on stage. He made the appropriate adjustments.

The Palin children had been told they were going to Ohio to celebrate their parents' twenty-fifth wedding anniversary and were still in the dark when they got to the hotel, although they had more than an inkling that this was not just a spontaneous family vacation to the Midwest. After exchanging warm greetings with her family, the governor decided not to deliver the life-changing news herself. Instead, she asked Steve Schmidt to tell her children that their worlds were about to be turned upside down.

"I have an announcement to make," the broad-shouldered senior strategist said as everyone in the now crowded suite looked on. "Senator McCain has asked your mother to join him to be the Republican candidate for vice president. It is going to be a fun and exciting adventure, and anything that you all need, let me know. There's a team of people. There will be more and more people around the next couple of days."

The kids seemed excited about the stunning news, but contrary to their mother's subsequent rendition of events, none of them was given a real opportunity to reflect upon the idea of embarking on a campaign that would change everything, win or lose, and turn Bristol's pregnancy into national news and tabloid fodder for months and years to come.

When asked by *Fox News*'s Sean Hannity a couple of weeks later about how her family had learned the news, Palin was not forthcoming. "It was a time of asking the girls to vote on it, anyway," she said. "And they voted unanimously, yes."

If Palin did, in fact, ask the girls to take a vote, it was only *after* she had already accepted McCain's offer, and Schmidt had already announced to them her decision to accept it. Even the official timeline provided by the McCain campaign established that the children were told, not asked.

"Didn't bother asking my son," Palin quickly added during the Hannity interview. "Because, you know, he's going to be off [in Iraq] doing his thing anyway, so he wouldn't be so impacted by, at least, the campaign period here."

Palin's nineteen-year-old son, Track, would of course be profoundly impacted by his mother's campaign. Less than two weeks after the big news broke, a horde of national journalists would descend upon Fairbanks to report on his army unit's deployment to the Middle East, scribbling notes as a military spokesman provided background about Track's training and character. Over the course of the next two months, Palin would not follow the precedent set by McCain and Joe Biden, both of whom spoke infrequently about their sons' military careers. Instead, she cited Track's service in almost all of her stump speeches and used his name as a convenient rebuttal whenever protestors interrupted her rallies.

"You know what? I got a call from my son today," she said after one such disturbance in St. Louis. "He's been deployed over to Iraq. He's fighting for our freedoms, including their freedom to say what they want to say."

In Estero, Florida, she revamped her now standard crowd-pleasing protester rebuttal, making it a bit more personal than usual. "You know, bless your heart, sir. My son's over in Iraq fighting for your right to protest right now," she said as she pointed an accusatory finger at the offender while bestowing her blessing.

Though he was not consulted about whether he wanted his mother to become the vice presidential nominee, Track was on record as having expressed a desire for her to stay out of the national limelight. After flirting with a run for the U.S. Senate in 2004, Palin told the *Anchorage Daily News* that her son's objection was the deciding factor since she required unanimous consent from her family. "How could I be the team mom if I was a U.S. senator?" she said at the time, as she endorsed Lisa Murkowski's opponent Mike Miller in the Republican primary.

The governor had been out of the state for two full working days now, but no one in Alaska seemed to notice. The *Anchorage Daily News* and Channel 2 had not been following her schedule closely, and the McCain campaign succeeded in encouraging reporters to continue to speculate on the air and in breathless blog posts about how Tim Pawlenty had cancelled scheduled media interviews or how Secret Service agents had swept the Michigan home of Mitt Romney's sister.

Back at the hotel, Scully worked through the night on Palin's speech. Sometime after 3 A.M., he got up to get a cup of coffee, smiling to himself as he passed Room 508, knowing that behind that door was the world's biggest political secret. He took a nap from 5 A.M. to 6 A.M. and awoke refreshed and ready to discuss with the governor the speech he had drafted for her.

Palin and Scully met in the fourth-floor room that the campaign had set up for staff use, which was coincidentally called the Alaska Suite. Over another cup of coffee, the speechwriter opened his laptop and began working collaboratively with the governor on edits. She was highly engaged and asked frequent questions about how various lines in the speech would figure into the overall strategy of the campaign she had just joined. The TV humming in the background was tuned to *Fox News*. By tracking flight paths online, some enterprising reporters noticed that a private jet departing Anchorage had landed in Middletown on the previous night, and the rumors were multiplying that McCain had made the shocking decision to tap the governor of Alaska (pronounced "Pay-lin") to be his running mate. Palin barely glanced at the screen as she reread the speech over and over. Each time she repeated the newest version aloud, she and Scully would find new places to improve it.

Once the speech had been molded into shape, Palin was asked whether she wanted to read it from a written copy or use a teleprompter. She decided on the latter, even though she would not have time to practice on the machine. "It's okay," she assured her new aides. "I'm pretty good with a teleprompter."

As the morning progressed and Pawlenty and Romney were each confirmed not to be the pick, campaign aides realized that they had better get Palin to the rally site before satellite trucks started to arrive at the Manchester Inn. The new candidate was escorted down the staircase at the back corner of the hotel, just on the off chance that a guest on his way to the free continental breakfast might recognize the governor of Alaska. The now rather large group then piled into the two white vans as White and Ferry scanned for any sign of reporters or TV crews. They took a short drive down the road before pulling into a nondescript auto body shop where a black Dodge Charger with tinted windows followed directly behind them. The occupants got out of their respective vehicles.

"This is the vice presidential nominee, Governor Sarah Palin of Alaska, and her husband, Todd," Ferry announced to the burly men who had been in the Dodge Charger. "This is the Secret Service."

Sarah and Todd Palin climbed into the Dodge and entered a new world. The two vans followed the Secret Service vehicle into the basement of the event site, where White received a phone call from another old friend whom he had grown up with in Alabama. It was President George W. Bush's personal aide, Jared Weinstein, who said that his boss wanted to speak with Governor Palin. White handed his cell phone to Palin, who exchanged pleasantries with the president for about two minutes. She then headed to the large gymnasium's locker room and waited with her family for the event to begin.

★ ★ ★

JUST BEFORE THE MCCAIN campaign confirmed that Palin was indeed the pick, Republican political operative Tucker Eskew had fired off an e-mail to his fellow Bush administration alumni, Schmidt and Wallace. Eskew believed in communicating simply, and the personable southerner with the thick drawl had some free advice for his

Yankee friends running the McCain campaign. If, indeed, it was Palin, he said, they should break the message down into the three *e*'s: energy, executive experience, and ethics reform. A veteran of Bush's down-and-dirty 2000 South Carolina primary campaign against McCain, Eskew was a master at message discipline—exactly the kind of operative Palin would need around to keep her on point. Wallace wrote back immediately, asking Eskew if he had a couple of months to spare.

Eskew was tasked with providing the nationally untested candidate with political insights, advice, and, most importantly, criticism. Palin did not ask her new chief political adviser to share his backstory, but Eskew understood that longtime staffers who remembered quite well some of the nastier attacks against McCain back in 2000 might not meet his arrival in the campaign with open arms. He approached Mark Salter and asked the longtime McCain confidante if it would be prudent to let McCain know he'd had nothing to do with the lies told back in South Carolina about his fathering a black child out of wedlock. Salter told him it wasn't necessary—Eskew had the senator's trust.

When John McCain took the stage in Dayton, Ohio, shortly after noon, the campaign had already confirmed that Palin was indeed the pick. But many in the capacity crowd of about ten thousand at the Nutter Center who had been waiting there for hours still did not know the identity of the running mate he was about to unveil. When "the next vice president of the United States" entered with her smiling family in tow, the age difference between McCain and Palin made for a striking contrast. The experience argument had officially been tossed out the window, but, once again, McCain could rightly claim to be running an unconventional campaign.

After introducing herself to the enraptured crowd, Palin sounded a bipartisan note by acknowledging the path that Democratic vice

presidential nominee Geraldine Ferraro had carved in 1984 and prais-
ing Hillary Clinton, "who showed such determination and grace in
her presidential campaign." After the speech, Ferraro called Palin to
tell her how honored she had been to hear her name. The next day,
however, Palin dropped references to Clinton from her stump speech
after the Democrat's name drew boos at a rally in Pennsylvania.

The McCain campaign knew full well that Palin's core support
had always consisted of social conservatives. But in a political environment in which their relative influence seemed to have shrunk as
quickly as President Bush's approval rating, senior aides were more
interested in her capacity to woo the legions of independents she
had been able to win over as a reformer in Alaska. "People thought
we did it for the base," Mark Salter recalls. "But really it wasn't done
for the base—I mean that wasn't the motivation behind it."

Still, McCain aides were elated by Palin's surprisingly magnifi-
cent ability to coalesce the legions of social conservatives who had
been anywhere from leery about the Arizona senator's nomination
to downright hostile. During the vetting process, there had been
particular concern over the first veto Palin had issued as governor
when she nixed the bill that would have banned state benefits to
same-sex couples. But it never became even the slightest of issues,
as conservatives by the millions were swept away with the overriding sense that she was one of them. They were thrilled that she had
given birth to a baby with Down syndrome. They were thrilled
that her husband worked in the oil fields. They were thrilled with
her accent, which, for whatever reason, sounded more like she
hailed from the upper Midwest than Southcentral Alaska. They
were thrilled that she could handle a rifle. They were thrilled with
Sarah Palin.

They also opened their pocketbooks. On the day Palin was
named to the ticket, online donations, which had been averaging
around $250,000 a day during the previous week, shot up to $4.5

million. But in order to provide a sustained boost to the Republican ticket, Palin needed to do more than draw American-flag-waving crowds to high school football fields and minor-league baseball stadiums. With that in mind, her Dayton speech was layered with references to her energy successes and her reputation as an alert government watchdog. "I told Congress, 'Thanks, but no thanks,' on that Bridge to Nowhere," she declared in one of her many memorable pronouncements.

The line had been born out of her private conversation with Matthew Scully. Palin had mentioned to her new speechwriter that she had opposed the infamous Gravina Island Project, which was primarily intended to provide access to Ketchikan's airport before earmark-abuse critics, led by none other than John McCain, had helped turn the bridge proposal into a symbol of government waste. Palin did not point out that she had supported the bridge ardently during her gubernatorial campaign and abruptly turned around and spoke out against it only after it had brought national embarrassment to Alaska's earmark-hungry politicians. She also neglected to get into the details about how she had declined to give back the money the federal government had appropriated for the project and did not stop construction from going forward for what was essentially a "Road to Nowhere," which ended abruptly where the bridge would have been built.

Alaskans familiar with Palin's history on the bridge project immediately sent out alarm bells to the national media. Bob Weinstein, the Democratic mayor of Ketchikan, helped circulate a photograph of Palin holding up a T-shirt reading "Nowhere Alaska—99901" during a 2006 visit to the city.

"We need to come to the defense of Southeast Alaska when proposals are on the table like the bridge, and not allow the spinmeisters to turn this project or any other into something that's so negative," Palin had told the *Ketchikan Daily News* that August.

Weinstein and other Ketchikan residents recalled how Palin had lent her trademarked populist touch in deriding the "Bridge to Nowhere" epithet during her visit to the area. She had indicated that she knew the feeling of being insulted by negative insinuations about out-of-the-way places.

"Okay, you've got valley trash standing here in the middle of nowhere," she said at the time. "I think we're going to make a good team as we progress that bridge project."

As difficult as it was for the McCain campaign to explain her previous comments when Palin used the phrase she had once deemed offensive, they found it harder yet to rationalize a comment she had made in October 2006, saying she would continue to fund the bridge "while our congressional delegation is in a strong position to assist." It was obvious code for her support of a federal earmark for the bridge.

Mayor Weinstein and other Palin critics say that Palin shifted her position on the bridge in 2007, just as she had cast her eyes on growing her national profile. They note that her office sent out a press release about the matter in the wee hours of the morning so that it would be sure to hit the East Coast news cycle but failed to notify relevant public figures in Alaska. "She didn't call me. She didn't call the borough mayor. She didn't call our legislators," Mayor Weinstein recalls.

A former McCain aide among those tasked with defending Palin's claim to have taken a courageous stand against the bridge later said the decision to keep the "Bridge to Nowhere" line in the Dayton speech had been a poor one. Yet, once she had made the "thanks, but no thanks" claim, the campaign felt compelled to defend it rather than revise it. "It was a very difficult argument," the aide now admits. "It lent itself to mockery."

After Palin received another enthusiastic reception on Saturday at an event just southwest of Pittsburgh, the newly formed Republi-

can ticket headed to the St. Louis area for a Sunday evening rally in
O'Fallon. These early campaign stops were not about proving that
Palin was equipped for the task of assuming the presidency if necessary. There would be plenty of opportunities to demonstrate that
later. For the time being, the focus was on image. When the Palin
family had arrived in Ohio, each member carried a simple overnight
bag, having been plucked from Alaska with almost no warning.
They were all tired, unprepared, and underdressed for the monumental events just around the corner. Something had to be done.

Todd Palin's appearance was the most immediate concern.
There was already some muffled snickering among a few of the
Beltway-centric McCain staffers. Some wondered how the spouse
of a sitting governor could possibly have gotten by for so long without a properly tailored suit, perhaps neglecting to consider that
cocktail parties and dinner galas on Alaska's North Slope were
rather infrequent affairs.

McCain advisers Steve Duprey and Greg Wendt took Alaska's
First Gentleman to Saks Fifth Avenue across the street from their
St. Louis hotel. The duo helped fit him with two suits, a sports jacket,
a few good button-down shirts, several pairs of pants, some ties and
belts, and a pair of dress shoes—spending just over $7,500 in all.
Wendt joked with the other two that the shopping spree was not exactly the usual "guy's night out," but Todd was cooperative. "I'm
here to do what you want me to do that helps support Sarah and the
ticket," the governor's husband told the aides.

On Sunday night, the Palin family arrived in St. Paul, Minnesota, where the topic of conversation was all Sarah, all the time,
as the national debate swirled on about whether John McCain had
made a wise choice. While conclusions varied widely, the media
swarm in St. Paul left no doubt about one thing: Sarah Palin had
changed the race. Cable news, gossip blogs, and glossy magazines

could not get enough of the former beauty queen who shot her own dinner, and she quickly overtook Obama on the celebrity scale.

As soon as Palin's candidacy was announced, some of the nation's most experienced investigative reporters smelled blood and descended on Alaska. The Windbreak Café in Wasilla overtook The Palm in Washington, D.C., as the hottest place for a power lunch. Reporters uncovered Palin's per diem charges to the state of Alaska for living in her own home and state-expensed trips for her children to fancy hotels, and they raised other questions that challenged her purportedly impeccable ethics credentials.

But not all of the reporting was entirely fair. One of the most common mistakes journalists from the Lower 48 made was to attach particular significance to criticism from prominent state Republicans like Lyda Green, unaware that despite their shared party affiliation, their relationship with Palin had long been contentious. In a few instances, unsubstantiated claims began to surface as undisputed fact in mainstream accounts, such as unconfirmed reports that Palin had tried to ban books as mayor of Wasilla, including one title that sought to explain homosexuality to children. Though no national news agency ran with the most baseless rumor that began to take hold in liberal blogs, some reporters did make private inquiries about whether Palin had faked her recent pregnancy to cover up for her daughter Bristol. Most involved in the campaign soon shared the conviction that Schmidt and others had already held for months. The amorphous entity known as "the media" was in fact a mortal enemy—and to be treated as such.

The campaign had reaped the benefits of its impressive performance in keeping its startling vice presidential pick a surprise until the last moment, but now that the secret was out, it began to face some of the repercussions of its own good work. Like everyone else outside McCain's inner circle, staffers in the communications shop at campaign headquarters had been left in the dark about the Palin pick until the day it was unveiled. Never having considered her among the most likely selections, the press office suddenly faced the nearly impossible task of assembling every conceivable detail of her life and political career and crafting responses to an unceasing barrage of incoming questions.

Maria Comella, a veteran of Rudy Giuliani's underwhelming run for the Republican nomination, had been brought in as the traveling press secretary for the soon to be announced candidate in mid-August. During the two weeks after she was hired, Comella was tasked with helping plan the vice presidential rollout, but since she did not know the candidate's identity until the morning Palin was announced, it was like working blindfolded. Just hours before the selection, the campaign's top communications staffers had put together background information and talking points on the five most likely vice presidential selections, of which Palin was not one.

After the surprise unveiling, Comella and her colleagues scrambled to learn as much as they could about the obscure governor, but they hesitated to respond to reporters' inquiries or to put out statements since they were so unfamiliar with the candidate themselves. An additional frustration was the length of time it took to get answers to the inquiries they filtered down to Palin and the three Alaska staffers who had joined her at the convention. Reporters had already begun asking questions like whether she had once supported Pat Buchanan's presidential candidacy and if she had actually crossed into Iraq during her visit to the Middle East. Some of the staffers tasked with handling issues like these felt that Palin was not being forthcoming enough in dispensing the information they needed to handle the media inquiries.

Comella was also tasked with drawing up hundreds of flash cards to get Palin up to speed on foreign affairs and major national issues. The candidate was assumed to possess a rather minimal knowledge base. For instance, one card noted that the current prime minister of the United Kingdom was Gordon Brown. After they were filled out, foreign policy adviser Steve Biegun approved the note cards, which were then passed on to Palin. But the governor didn't find them very helpful in achieving her goal of understanding issues more deeply, causing some unspoken friction with Comella, which Palin related to senior advisers.

On Monday, the nation's attention turned to the Louisiana coastline, where Hurricane Gustav threatened to wreak havoc almost three years to the day after Hurricane Katrina made landfall in the region. The purportedly duty-bound cancellation of President Bush's and Vice President Cheney's scheduled appearances on the convention floor that day brought no tears to the eyes of any of the McCain aides, who were trying to distance the new ticket from the administration. And the hurricane, which turned out to be far less devastating than had been feared, provided a perfect opportunity for a good old-fashioned info drop. That morning, the campaign released the following statement, which it attributed to Todd and Sarah Palin:

> *We have been blessed with five wonderful children who we love with all our heart and mean everything to us. Our beautiful daughter Bristol came to us with news that as parents we knew would make her grow up faster than we had ever planned. We're proud of Bristol's decision to have her baby and even prouder to become grandparents. As Bristol faces the responsibilities of adulthood, she knows she has our unconditional love and support. Bristol and the young man she will marry are going to realize very quickly the difficulties of raising a child, which is why they will have the love and support of our entire family. We ask the media to*

respect our daughter and Levi's privacy as has always been the tra-dition of children of candidates.

The statement had been the result of hours of meetings and several drafts. At the last minute, Todd and Sarah Palin and campaign advisers agreed that they should take out the line, "We're proud of Bristol's decision to have her baby and even prouder to become grandparents," having decided it trod too close to sounding as if they were celebrating a teenage pregnancy. But when Comella blasted the statement out to reporters, she accidentally sent an earlier draft, which contained the line meant to be deleted.

Comella did not realize her mistake at first, but Palin recognized it right away. The governor asked her assistant to call Comella in for a meeting. Comella took full responsibility, agreeing that it had been unacceptable, and Palin seemed to appreciate Comella's contrition, telling her flatly, "It happens." But once the two women parted ways, Palin made clear to the senior aides running the campaign that she wanted Comella off the plane. Her wish was granted immediately. Tracey Schmitt, who worked with Steve Schmidt in the Bush administration, agreed to take over the reins as traveling press secretary, having been given just hours to pack her bags. Comella would remain behind at campaign headquarters.

It was widely, yet incorrectly, assumed in media circles that Palin had not disclosed her daughter's pregnancy to the McCain campaign before she was chosen, and the pick began to take on the appearance of a disaster in the making. According to a CBS News poll, the Democrats had ridden a five-point bump out of their convention—including a whopping eighteen-point gain with independent voters—expanding Obama's lead to eight impressive points. Some talking heads began to wonder aloud whether Palin might go the way of Thomas Eagleton and exit the race, citing family concerns. Eagleton had been forced to withdraw from the 1972 Democratic ticket after revelations of mental health problems surfaced.

The logistical operation surrounding Palin was also not going smoothly. The simple act of moving her from place to place had already become a colossal task, and Steve Schmidt realized he had to make some changes. He asked Andrew Smith, his former roommate at the University of Delaware, to take on the job of chief of staff. Smith was a brash New Yorker who wore his cynicism on his sleeve, and his personality and life experiences were far from in synch with Palin's. Furthermore, his background was in finance, not politics. But he already had the chief strategist's trust, which was no small thing, and Schmidt knew that his old friend had the ability to create a sense of order out of chaos, which was exactly what the vice presidential operation needed. Still, many former traveling aides would later lament that Smith did not have the appropriate experience for the job and that his lack of familiarity with national politics contributed to strained relationships with Palin and others on the plane.

With Palin's new team in place, the nascent vice presidential campaign needed more clothes. Now that Todd had been taken care of, the next order of wardrobe business was to make sure the already eye-catching candidate looked and felt her very best. Nicolle Wallace was charged with organizing the spending spree, and she reached out to New York fashion stylist Lisa A. Kline, who specialized in outfitting television news anchors. Wallace originally authorized Kline to spend up to $30,000 to buy three outfits for Palin to wear during the convention and three additional suits for the campaign. But once aides came to the conclusion that the entire Palin family had to be outfitted with a new wardrobe, Kline was provided with a list of everyone in the family's measurements. Though never told to throw the original budget out the window, the stylist felt there was an understanding that excessive cost was not a concern.

"They just said, 'Please get it done,'" Kline recalls, speaking out for the first time since the wardrobe she purchased laid the groundwork for a harmful distraction later in the campaign. "To be honest with you, I didn't look at labels. I looked at the job in front of me."

With just a couple of days in which to work, Kline hired a second stylist and a tailor to assist her, and the trio began a series of boutique raids in New York City that might have made Paris Hilton blush. The quick Manhattan jaunt included stops at Bloomingdales, Saks Fifth Avenue, and other high-end stores, and the crown jewel was a Valentino jacket that cost about $3,000, which Palin would wear on the night of her convention speech.

"As a stylist, I have a lot of avenues to get discounts," Kline says. "I called everyone I knew. It was Labor Day weekend and there wasn't a person around. Had I had a month to do this, it could have been done for such a more reasonable amount of money."

After Kline arrived in the Twin Cities, she convinced the Minneapolis Neiman Marcus to open its doors at 7 A.M. on Tuesday morning so she could make some additional purchases for the Palin family to wear when they greeted John and Cindy McCain on the tarmac later that day. The Neiman Marcus clothes were bought using a personal credit card placed on file by a wealthy donor to the Republican National Committee, Jeff Larson.

"There was no time to really say, 'Well these shoes are six hundred, but these shoes are four hundred, so we are going to buy these and hope that they fit,'" Kline says. After Kline went on her latest spending spree, the hotel delivered to the Palins' suite two long clothing racks to display the new wardrobe. Kline and her assistants set up a makeshift assembly line at a large conference table in the middle of the room next to the racks. Each member of the Palin family would don a new outfit as quickly as possible and then hand it to the tailor for proper fitting. Piper, Willow, and Bristol tried on outfits and shoes made by designer Tory Burch, as well as some lower-end purchases, like a dress for Piper from The Gap. The governor wore designs by Cole Haan, Kate Spade, Jimmy Choo, and Prada. While the stylists worked on outfitting the immediate family, another staffer accompanied Sally and Chuck Heath on a second trip to a department store. An Armani blazer was purchased for Sally and a $90 pair of socks for Chuck, who much preferred mining for gold to wearing it.

Though later ridiculed as a spendthrift, Sarah Palin was one of the few people in the room who expressed concern over the exorbitant expense of some of the clothes. As she tried to decide what to wear for the scheduled photo shoot with *Time* magazine, she was much more interested in preparing for the substance of her formal introduction to the country. She did have to admit that she liked the "Johnny Choo" shoes, which a smiling staffer told her were actually called Jimmy Choos. But when she picked up a necklace and examined its price tag, she declared, "I'm not wearing this. This is way too expensive."

In fact, Palin was so concerned that Kline and the governor's personal assistant, Bexie Nobles, began removing some of the price tags on clothes she had not yet seen. Todd Palin was even more unenthusiastic about the new clothes that were added to the purchases made for him in St. Louis. When Ben Veghte, his newly assigned personal aide, obtained garment bags to pack up the new clothes, Todd told him to leave them behind.

Kline estimates that the Palins ultimately rejected over half of the clothes she offered them. Much of the unused wardrobe was returned over the subsequent days and weeks, and about halfway through the campaign, Kline noticed that the governor had stopped wearing the pricey attire she had originally bought. Most of the purchases ended up packed away in the belly of the plane and never worn by Palin. Still, additional spending on new clothes continued on the road, eventually escalating to the $173,000 that was ultimately filed with the Federal Election Commission.

Meanwhile, Palin remained characteristically composed as she prepared for what promised to be the most highly anticipated speech by a vice presidential candidate in the nation's history. Though there were few signs of panic within the campaign, everyone knew that the old axiom that the bottom of the ticket does not matter in the end no longer applied. A strong argument could be made that Palin's address to the convention delegates had become even more important than McCain's. She had to demonstrate that she could deliver a punch as well as she could take one.

Scully was pleased with his first draft. It was a serviceable speech, but he could not claim it to be anything extraordinary. He was delighted with the level of interest Palin took in improving it, tweaking the syntax to cast it in her own voice. On Thursday, Scully watched her read it through from start to finish over a dozen times. She had memorized every pause and point of emphasis, as if it were a song she had been performing for years.

By the time Wednesday night rolled around, Palin's confidence was palpable. Backstage, staffers looked on in amazement as she joked with her hair dresser and makeup artist just five minutes before she was scheduled to go on and apologized to Lisa Kline that the stylist had to be with her in St. Paul and not home to accompany her children on their first day of school. Once again, Palin had no doubts about her own preparedness.

No one inside the Xcel Energy Center knew quite what to expect, but the anticipation was intense. Sitting in the mezzanine level with the Palin family was Bristol's eighteen-year-old fiancé and father of her unborn child, Levi Johnston. The former hockey standout wore a stylish new suit, which Kline had picked out. Johnston appeared a bit nervous as he gripped Bristol's hand, but just as the scene was designed to show, he seemed to fit in just fine as the newest member of Alaska's First Family.

Everyone who had seen Palin practice the speech knew she had a good chance of exceeding her critics' bargain-basement-level expectations. But no one expected her to deliver the "perfect ten" that would send the convention delegates into a frenzy and impress a national audience of over thirty-seven million people. It was her piercing barbs directed against Obama that Palin had relished most. "I guess a small-town mayor is *sort* of like a 'community organizer,' except that you have actual responsibilities."

Condescending jabs like these might have crossed the line of good taste if delivered by other candidates, but Palin had taken so much heat over the previous week that most deemed them justified counterattacks. In the accolades bestowed upon her in the hours and days after the speech, political pundits could barely seem to find the words to describe just how impeccably poised, resolute, and downright likeable she had been.

In her home state, Palin's backers were overwhelmingly supportive of the Alaska girl who had stepped into the ring to deliver a prime-time knock out, but not everyone in Alaska was so enthralled. Critics scoffed when she asserted, "We began a nearly $40 billion natural gas pipeline." The use of the word "began" seemed to carry the false implication that a construction contract had been signed on a project that everyone in Alaska knew was far from guaranteed to ever see the light of day.

Democrats began to wonder if the bipartisan Sarah Palin they had known and worked with had suddenly disappeared into the ideological coven of the national Republican Party. State Representative Les Gara, who had worked closely with Palin on her landmark AGIA legislation, took personal offense at her depiction of Obama as out of touch. Gara, who was raised in a foster home before going on to attend Harvard Law School, remembered thinking at the time that "she called a guy who grew up in a broken family an elitist. That's what she called Barack Obama at the Republican National Convention."

Similar reactions among state Democrats would have profound implications for Palin's postcampaign return to Alaska. But the personal sensibilities of Alaska's state legislators were not exactly at the forefront of the minds of Palin and her new team. They had managed to turn a vice presidential pick that was widely assumed to be a disaster just hours earlier into what now looked like a stroke of political genius. In just a couple of days, new polls would reveal a surge of national support, especially among independent women, which would help the Republican ticket take its first lead since the campaign began.

Though he gave Palin all the credit she deserved for her impeccable delivery, Matthew Scully couldn't help but feel satisfied by the standing ovation to which he was treated at the Minneapolis Hilton bar that night. He had been immortalized as the author of the already legendary speech, and McCain approached him on two separate occasions to reiterate how much he had enjoyed it.

"I just fired Salter," the senator joked of his own longtime scribe.

$\star$ $\star$ $\star$

6. The Iron Curtain

OTHER THAN THE CURTAINS that divided the passenger compartment in half, there was nothing particularly notable about the one-hundred-seat JetBlue Embraer 190 that shuttled the new Republican vice presidential nominee around the country. The plane was, of course, custom-painted with the McCain/Palin logo splashed across the exterior. And the journalists who covered the candidate's travels were, as they had been since the days of the "boys on the bus," confined to assigned seats toward the back of the plane. The far rear was the Secret Service's realm, where the agents often made for difficult hurdles to be surmounted on excursions to the rear lavatory.

The conspicuous gray curtains were a psychological barrier as well as a physical one. They divided the plane into two zones that sometimes seemed, in the heat of the mentally exhausting campaign, as estranged as West and East Berlin once were. None of the reporters could say for sure what went on in the front of the plane, but they had a pretty good idea that life was a little better up there, especially during meals. Whiffs of hot pizza and freshly prepared dinners would sometimes drift to the back of the plane as the disillusioned reporters munched on their cold sandwiches. Rumors that a secret stash of Diet Dr. Pepper had been shipped in, just for the governor, were surreptitiously confirmed by a brave flight attendant, who agreed to disobey orders and offer cans of the forbidden soft drink to the media.

The curtains were not a bona fide reason why the relationship between the campaign and the media became particularly antagonistic in the first half of Palin's candidacy, but they did not exactly set a positive tone. They were always tightly drawn, except during takeoffs and landings when FAA regulations required that they be opened. It was as if the campaign's handlers were concerned that a deranged *New York Times* reporter might leap from his seat, sprint down the aisle to the front of the plane, and demand of Palin whether she knew both ways to pronounce "Qatar."

Despite the enormous national interest in all things Palin, her traveling press corps was notably smaller than the presidential candidates', with no more than twenty members of the media on most flights and a core group of one embedded reporter/producer from each of the five television networks. No wire service or newspaper reporters traveled regularly, and NBC was the only network that devoted a correspondent and full crew to Palin coverage around the clock. Though Barack Obama, Joe Biden, and John McCain were not exactly having freewheeling conversations with the press at this stage of the campaign, the extent to which Palin's aides made sure to keep her out of range of any interaction whatsoever with the media seemed extreme. Aside from a strictly off-the-record "meet and greet" at the back of the plane during her first solo flight, the least-known vice presidential candidate in modern history did not take a single question from the traveling press for the first three weeks of her campaign. Instead, her strategists had her deliver the same carefully crafted stump speech to the massive crowds that greeted her around the country while preparing her in private for a string of high-profile interviews with television network anchors. Though the staffers who briefed her on policy were impressed by her ability to absorb new information quickly, there was quite a lot of it to learn.

Since the rallies hardly ever produced any genuine news, every minor deviation from Palin's stump speech seemed significant to the journalists, who spent up to seventeen hours each day within shouting distance of her but never any closer. Reporting on the 2008 presidential campaign had been revolutionized by BlackBerries, air cards that allowed Internet access from almost anywhere, and FTP sites that made it possible to distribute video quickly, even when live satellite feeds were not an option. Though both the McCain and Obama campaigns sometimes complained that the nonstop blogging came at the expense of the big picture, both also relentlessly flooded reporters' in-boxes with an incessant barrage of e-mail directing attention to the sometimes trivial moments on the trail that they would have you believe might swing the election.

Palin's staff knew that the embedded reporters were particularly hungry for any kind of real news, but her traveling aides were under orders to keep their mouths shut. During one mid-September flight from Green Bay to Minneapolis, a senior Palin staffer made the exceedingly rare journey across the demilitarized zone to the back of the plane to speak to the information-starved journalists who resided there. But the briefing was far more notable for what it said about the Palin campaign's secrecy than for any insights it provided.

"We go into today with a candidate who's got, on background, enormous clarity and action versus a candidate of contemplation and confusion," the aide said. The insistence that this entirely useless statement be kept on background (meaning that it could not be attributed) would have been laughable had it not been uttered so earnestly.

From the beginning, Palin and many of her staffers disagreed with the strategy of ignoring the traveling press. The candidate knew she could apply the personal touch that had worked so well on reporters in Alaska, but senior aides at campaign headquarters repeatedly denied her requests to venture to the back of the plane. In fact, reporters saw much more of her daughter Piper, who took an interest in goofing around with journalists and the lower-level campaign staffers who sat near them, signing the occasional autograph on one of the "Vote for Piper's Mom" bumper stickers that adorned the plane's interior, and playing a game that involved rolling an orange down the aisle. At the very least, Palin wanted to talk to some of the reporters back home in Alaska with whom she had developed such strong relationships. But that request was also denied.

The fact that the other candidates were not talking to their own traveling press corps either did little to mitigate the growing perception that Palin was a candidate in hiding. After all, Biden was doing local interviews on a daily basis, and McCain and Obama had each been through the media gauntlet over nearly two years of campaigning. In retrospect, the decision to rely exclusively on much-hyped television interviews, rather than lower-stakes interactions with the traveling press and friendly conservative talk radio, was shortsighted.

"Everybody knew deep down that we made a huge mistake in not allowing her to do the media," a former communications staffer said after the election, adding that the campaign suffered from a mentality that stressed shifting tactics to respond to each individual crisis rather than sticking with a consistent strategy.

As Palin's reticence became a frequent topic in newspaper editorials and on cable news shows, the candidate grew increasingly concerned about how she was being handled. Though the press on board the plane appreciated the personal television sets affixed to the back of all the seats, the easy TV access was a constant source of frustration for staffers who looked on hopelessly as Palin spent hours upon hours watching critical commentators tear her to shreds. Aides would have preferred to see her reading books like *The Looming Tower*, a history of terrorism leading up to the September 11 attacks, which Steve Schmidt had given her at the beginning of the campaign. Several staffers who traveled on the plane recall that she carried *The Looming Tower* in her purse, but some were concerned that they never actually saw her reading it.

As the campaign progressed, Palin told one of her personal aides, Jeannie Etchart, about how she used to enjoy the escapism that glossy celebrity magazines like *People* and *Us* provided while she flew around Alaska on state business. Etchart took the hint and relayed the request to a campaign advance team, who picked up a selection of tabloids far removed from political commentary. Palin enjoyed them for a while but lost interest once they started featuring stories about her and her family. After that, she mostly stuck to her briefing papers and the few publications left that were truly safe from political talk, like *Runner's World*.

Palin also devoted an admirable amount of time to reading and responding to the handwritten notes and heartfelt cards that supporters at her rallies often handed her. People who had included their e-mail addresses on the notes they gave her on rope lines must have been surprised when they received responses from the candidate herself just hours later. There is no doubt that Palin enjoyed almost every minute of the boisterous rallies where tens of thousands of people hung on her every word. She often became so absorbed in conversations with people she met before and after events that her campaign schedule suffered. No one seemed to want to pull her away during these moments when she was at her best.

Palin's sway over rank-and-file Republicans was so strong that McCain and his senior aides decided to schedule far more events in which the top and bottom of the ticket would share the stage than they had originally planned. McCain, too, fed off the energy of the crowds, but he was left with no doubt that most of the people who waited in line for hours were there to see his running mate. Palin always spoke first, but she was in no way treated as the opening act. Often, the moment she finished her stump speech and introduced the American hero beside her, dozens of people would start to file out, eager to beat the traffic. One man at an early September rally in the idyllic small town of Lebanon, Ohio, seemed to say it all when he proudly waved two homemade signs. "America Respects John McCain," the sign in his left hand said. "America Loves Sarah Palin," read the one in his right.

After a couple weeks on the trail, Palin was slated to take a three-day detour to Alaska so she could repack, speak at her son's army deployment to Iraq, and finally conduct her first national interview of the campaign with *ABC News*'s Charlie Gibson. In her final rally with McCain before heading home, the Republican ticket was treated to its largest crowd yet. Over twenty thousand people packed a field on a bright and sunny late-summer day in Fairfax, Virginia, a wealthy suburb of Washington, D.C. As the motorcade made its way into a jam-packed Van Dyke Park that morning, rally goers booed and turned their thumbs down at the sight of the van marked "Press." When the program began, former Tennessee senator and one-time presidential candidate Fred Thompson performed his duty as the introductory speaker by riling up the party faithful to an even more fervent pitch and helpfully pointed out the location where the journalists were sitting.

"I hope they brought their brie and Chablis with them," the multimillionaire screen actor sneered before introducing Palin.

As she did throughout her first month on the campaign trail, Palin stuck to her stump speech, describing once again, for example, how she took the previous governor's private jet and "put it on eBay." Though almost everyone in the crowd had surely heard the lines before, they responded with raucous cheers. They were in no way sick of her promise to "shake things up in Washington," as they applauded that familiar refrain too. As happened wherever she went, Palin had to pause at times to let the chants of "Sarah! Sarah!" finally die down.

After taking a few extra minutes to work the rope line, she boarded her plane at Dulles International and strapped in for the nearly ten-hour journey to Fairbanks, which included a refueling stop in Great Falls, Montana. With the plane uncharacteristically full, the takeoff was delayed because it was overweight—or as the captain politely described it over the intercom, "We can definitely take off from Dulles, but I'm not sure we'll be able to take off from Montana."

Few on board were eager to test the pilot's judgment, and the plane finally took off only after staffers removed some baggage. Palin spent much of the flight preparing for her big interview with Gibson with the help of her flash cards and the advice of Steve Schmidt, Nicolle Wallace, and Tucker Eskew. She was also introduced to a new face on the team—John Green, a Washington lobbyist who had been detailed by the campaign's senior aides to help investigate, then mitigate, the Troopergate issue. Green spoke to Palin for almost three hours about the circumstances surrounding her firing of Walt Monegan and the political environment in Juneau. He found her forthcoming, though she seemed to overestimate the extent to which the relationships she had built with state Democrats would save her in the end. Despite everything she had already been through, she could still come across as a bit naïve about the level at which she was now operating.

Though convinced she would be exonerated, Palin was deeply concerned about the political ramifications of the investigation that the bipartisan Alaska Legislative Council had voted unanimously to pursue. Before being tapped for the vice presidential slot, she had issued several statements and reiterated to the Alaska media that she was an open book on the matter and would cooperate fully. All of that changed on August 29 when she was named to the Republican ticket. The Senate Judiciary Committee chairman, Democrat Hollis French, put his foot squarely in his mouth by speculating about a potential "October surprise" when the investigation's report was released. The McCain campaign pointed to statements like this to make its case that the investigation was irrevocably tainted.

In part due to the Republicans' success in raising questions about the relevance and legitimacy of Troopergate, the story was low on the list of issues that permeated the campaign. With so much else going on, most voters (and many national journalists, for that matter) simply did not have the time or the desire to immerse themselves in the details of a complicated scenario that they gathered had something to do with a fired cabinet official and a cop. But that, of course, could change. In the meantime, the campaign was fully engaged in working to discredit independent investigator Stephen Branchflower's inquiry, just as the Obama team was doing all it could to keep it in the news.

Palin juggled her concern about the gathering storm in Juneau with preparation for her series of on-camera conversations with Gibson, the first of which took place in Fairbanks. When they aired on ABC later that week, the campaign breathed a collective sigh of relief, her performance having been deemed serviceable. Some observers harped on her apparent lack of familiarity with the Bush Doctrine.

Others noted how mightily she had struggled to explain how Alaska's physical proximity to Russia had lent her a special understanding of that country. But none of the criticisms were particularly damning. In fact, Gibson was just as frequently disparaged as Palin for affecting an accusatory, professorial tone during the interview.

After a final send-off rally in Anchorage, Palin returned to the Lower 48 on Saturday morning. Her first stop back on the campaign trail was a particularly boisterous rally in Carson City, Nevada. It was her first solo event outside her home state, but the rally was also notable for her reinsertion of the problematic claim that she had "told Congress, 'Thanks, but no thanks,' on that Bridge to Nowhere," a line that had been conveniently deleted from her remarks to the Alaska crowds who knew better.

After the event, Palin and her traveling entourage boarded the campaign plane, eager to get to the next stop in Denver after an exhausting day that had begun in Wasilla. The passengers settled in for the hour-and-a-half flight with plastic cups of wine. Someone had remembered that the new season of *Saturday Night Live* was set to begin that night, and there were rumors that former cast member Tina Fey would make a cameo appearance as Sarah Palin. Everyone turned their television sets to NBC.

Sure enough, as the plane began its descent into Denver, cast member Amy Poehler appeared on screen with Fey, who was dressed in a Palinesque red outfit with her hair pulled up in that familiar way. The physical resemblance was striking enough to cause some reporters on the plane to consider momentarily the possibility that the real Sarah Palin had slipped off the plane before takeoff and somehow made her way to New York for the show. But the traveling press were not the only ones cracking up at Fey's mannerisms and accent, which were only barely exaggerated. Staffers could be heard howling in the front section of the plane as well.

"I believe that diplomacy should be the cornerstone of any foreign policy," Poehler, playing the role of an embittered Hillary Clinton, said.

"And I can see Russia from my house," Fey replied in a prideful, singsong voice.

When it was uttered, it was impossible to tell just how defining the line would become to the campaign and Palin's image. It would soon take on such cultural resonance that millions of Americans would come to think the real Sarah Palin had said it.

The candidate watched the skit from her seat at the front of the plane, but her aides explained later that she was getting ready to disembark and was not wearing her headphones. Even if she did not hear herself being parodied before an audience of millions, she knew from just the visuals that it was an impressive characterization. Her keen political instincts were right on the mark. She wasted no time in asking her aides about when she might make an appearance on the show. It would be far better to laugh along with the joke than to shrink from it, she knew quite well. For the time being, the answer was no, but she would keep pushing for it in the coming weeks.

The next day, Tracey Schmitt sent out a short statement confirming that the governor had watched the skit. "She thought it was quite funny, particularly because she once dressed up as Tina Fey for Halloween," Schmitt wrote.

The statement seemed to strike the appropriate tone. But former Hewlett-Packard CEO and McCain economic adviser Carly Fiorina was not amused, and she wanted the world to know it. Fiorina declared on MSNBC on Monday that Fey's portrayal of a ditzy Palin had been sexist. Apparently cognizant of Fiorina's concern, Palin stressed in an interview with Sean Hannity, two days later, that she had indeed watched the skit, but "with the volume all the way down." Palin insisted that, despite missing out on Fey's biting satire, she found her physical characterization hilarious. "Again, I didn't hear a word she said, but the visual was spot on," she stressed. It was a needlessly cautious case of backtracking and emblematic of how the McCain campaign often reacted with a series of discordant responses to every perceived concern, rather than taking a steady approach.

Meanwhile, Palin's relationship with the traveling press remained nonexistent. She still had not taken a single question from the members of the media who crisscrossed the country with her. But that changed when she made an unscheduled stop at Karl's Restaurant and Bar in Cleveland. The designated journalists called "the pool"—typically wire reporters, a national newspaper reporter, a still cameraman, a TV producer, and a TV crew—were ushered into the small diner to take notes to share with the rest of the media. Palin came in with her husband and began shaking hands with the ten startled patrons. Most had come in for a morning coffee but ended up under the glare of television cameras capturing their interactions with the candidate who introduced herself as "Sarah."

Finding himself within earshot of Palin for the first time in the three weeks he had been covering her, a reporter asked for her reaction to the big news of the day: the government's decision to bail out AIG. Palin said she was disappointed that another bailout was in order but understood that it had been necessary. Before her aides ushered him out of the diner, the reporter noted that the press in the back of the plane felt neglected.

"Are you getting lonely?" Palin asked. "Gee, yeah, come on up then!"

The candidate's offer was not seconded by the staffers in charge of press access. In fact, one nervous aide asked for the reporter's audio recording—a request he politely declined. Another staffer approached the journalist on the sidewalk outside the diner and noted that questions had not been "allowed" in the public restaurant. Despite their overzealousness, these aides were merely doing their jobs in the manner expected of them. They knew that even the slightest deviation from Palin's daily script would be met with an eruption back at headquarters from top aides who worried that she could not be trusted to freelance.

As part of an effort to mitigate the escalating questions about her lack of foreign policy experience, the campaign next announced that Palin would meet with an ensemble of foreign leaders in New York City for two days during the United Nations General Assembly. The first day's discussions with Afghan president Hamid Karzai, Columbian president Alvaro Uribe, and former secretary of state Henry Kissinger on September 23 were to take place in various locations around Manhattan. They would be closed to the press, but as was customary, the campaign said it would allow the full media pool in for a photo op at the beginning of each meeting.

After hours of internal debate, however, the communications team at headquarters decided only to allow television cameras. The campaign informed the writers and TV producers while they were on the way to Palin's first meeting that they would be barred from the photo ops. Upholding this decision would eliminate any risk of an unexpected question from a reporter or the potential for awkward small talk between Palin and a world leader being picked up by an audio device and hitting the cable news cycle. Most of the traveling staffers knew that the move would spark a rebellion at the television networks, which required an editorial presence at all photo ops for the exact reasons the campaign staff did not want one.

"That was a slow ball that rolled and rolled and got bigger and bigger," recalls traveling deputy chief of staff Chris Edwards, a veteran of the Bush White House. "I said, 'How is this happening? Why is there this lack of communication between headquarters and the road?' I knew what the coverage should be. . . . I've done this for eight years."

After the networks banded together and threatened to pull their cameras, the campaign backed down and allowed the pool producer and print reporter in. But the damage had been done as reports quickly surfaced about the unprecedented attempt to change the well-established rules at the last minute.

"It was that moment that I realized we have a problem," Edwards recalls. "I'd never been in an environment where the press had become this hostile toward the campaign, and I felt like we'd lost control."

The still-deteriorating relationship with the national media notwithstanding, the interest in all things Palin remained at an astonishingly high level. Even in Manhattan, where celebrity sightings were as common as discarded pizza boxes, the Alaska governor was a show stealer. On the way to her meeting with Henry Kissinger, her Secret Service escort and the New York Police Department had to struggle to push back a mass of humanity that had gathered around her vehicle, which was stalled in midtown traffic. Even campaign trail veterans who had seen enraptured crowds before were stunned as hundreds of people in the liberal bastion of midtown Manhattan stopped what they were doing to fight for a glimpse of Palin and snap pictures on their camera phones.

That night, Palin retired to her suite in the Omni Hotel, where she received another briefing from foreign policy adviser Steve Biegun on her scheduled meetings the following day with the leaders of Iraq, Pakistan, and India. In her first conversations with senior aides in Arizona, Palin had promised that no matter what happened over the next two months, she would always be prepared. And despite the serious multitasking that she was suddenly faced with mastering, she had not let them down during the first month of the campaign. Though her knowledge base certainly left something to be desired, she seemed to ask all the right questions. Biegun and McCain's foreign policy adviser, Randy Scheunemann, were particularly impressed by her ability to absorb new information and her diligent habit of studying up on policy well into the night.

And she did not just want to regurgitate spoon-fed facts. An instinctive challenger, she thought for herself and would sometimes push back against McCain's positions when she could not pretend to agree with them.

"She's a tremendous messenger," says Douglas Holtz-Eakin, McCain's chief economic adviser who traveled with Palin during the week after the convention. "Look, if you're a policy person, you're largely some failed geek. If you can get someone who can take that to the crowds, it's amazing. And she cared. She actually wanted to know why things were the way they were."

In addition to getting ready for her second round of meetings with world leaders, Palin was also tasked with preparing for her morning with *CBS News*'s Katie Couric. Nicolle Wallace, a former *CBS News* analyst, arrived at the Omni Hotel after 9 P.M. to brief her on the kinds of questions Couric might ask. But with so much going on, Palin did not treat the Couric interview as a priority. She had gotten by with Charlie Gibson just fine. Couric, it seemed, would not be any more difficult.

The next morning, Palin convened with her staff for a last-minute briefing before she sat down with the *CBS News* anchor. Much to her aides' surprise, Palin did not want to talk much about the Couric interviews. Instead, she focused the meeting on a questionnaire that her hometown paper, the *Mat-Su Valley Frontiersman*, had sent her to fill out. Her aides had provided their own answers to the fourteen questions that the Wasilla newspaper had asked, but Palin was displeased that they had not given her time to look them over until now. "This is not how I do things," she said. "I told you guys this week that this was a priority and it took you four days to turn it around. This is my priority."

It was, to say the least, an odd priority for the vice presidential candidate to have settled on as she was about to begin her second round of interviews with a national news outlet. The CBS interviews were divided into two parts and were slated to take up an hour and fifteen minutes of Palin's day. The news anchor and the candidate first sat down in the hotel that morning before going on a "walk and talk" outside the United Nations. It was clear to everyone who watched the beginning of the seated portion of the interview that Palin was dangerously out of synch.

Couric wasted little time before getting into the most topical question. "Why isn't it better, Governor Palin, to spend $700 billion helping middle-class families who are struggling with health care, housing, gas, and groceries—allow them to spend more and put more money into the economy instead of helping these big financial institutions that played a role in creating this mess?"

Palin latched onto Couric's phrasing of the question in the context of everyday life, and her answer turned into an early Christmas present for Tina Fey, who needed only the verbatim transcript to satirize the candidate on the following Saturday. "That's why I say, I, like every American I'm speaking with, we're ill about this position that we have been put in where it is the taxpayers looking to bail out. But, ultimately, what the bailout does is help those who are concerned about the health care reform that is needed to help shore up our economy. Um, helping the, oh, it's got to be all about job creation, too, shoring up our economy and putting it back on the right track."

It did not get any better from there. Palin tried in vain to find the right talking point but continued instead to fill the gaps with a nearly indecipherable avalanche of disconnected words. She glanced down repeatedly, perhaps in the hopes that the floor might open up. Her painfully convoluted answer to a question about her foreign policy experience concerning Russia was one of the most perplexing moments, considering that in her role as the commander in chief of Alaska's National Guard, she had, in fact, been briefed on Russian jet incursions near American air space. For whatever reason, she did not think to mention that to Couric, even though she must have known the question would be asked following the attention the issue had generated after the Gibson interviews.

After the slaughter ended, Nicolle Wallace made an attempt to reinstall some much-needed confidence and reassure Palin that she had done a fine job. But the candidate knew it had been a disaster. She was particularly distraught over her inability to come up with a single Supreme Court case, besides *Roe v. Wade*, with which she disagreed. "Well, let's see," Palin had said when Couric had asked her to do so. The candidate intermittently hummed, gulped, and inhaled deeply. "There's, of course, in the great history of America there have been rulings that there's never gonna be absolute consensus by every American, and there are those issues, again, like *Roe v. Wade*, where I believe are best held at a state level and addressed there."

She kept talking, but the answer never came.

As governor, she had spoken out against the ruling in the Exxon-Valdez case, which was particularly pertinent to Alaska, and there were other recent Supreme Court cases with which she disagreed. "I wish I had just used one of those," Palin lamented privately after the interview. The unexpressed thought swirling through more than one aide's mind was, "Well, why didn't you?" Her aides later discussed with her a couple of court cases that she could bring up with Couric in one of the next week's interview installments, but Palin failed to do so.

She next headed to Philadelphia, where she began to prepare for her upcoming debate with Joe Biden. There, aides told Palin that her grueling interviews with Couric had only been the opening act. There would be another full session with the *CBS News* journalist in just a few days. Palin protested the decision to go back for what could be another massacre, but to no avail. Steve Schmidt and Rick Davis pulled her aside and told her in no uncertain terms that the first round of Couric interviews had been a disaster, and the repercussions had been severe. Still, she was not the first politician to have bombed an interview, and the solution was to buckle down and make sure she was prepared the next time.

But Palin's attention was still floating back to Alaska. She had become increasingly concerned with her slipping popularity in her home state; it would never again approach its former heights. She had related her anxiety about the matter so frequently that senior McCain aides worried that she had lost focus. Steve Schmidt agreed to commission an internal poll, which showed that her approval rating was at a still impressive 79 percent in Alaska, but Palin was suspicious that he had skewed the results to placate her. The level of trust between the candidate and the McCain campaign's senior advisers would continue to nose-dive.

★ ★ ★

THE FOLLOWING MONDAY, Katie Couric sat in the second row of a white twelve-passenger van in Columbus, Ohio. On the flight from Philadelphia, she had conducted her second interview of the day with Palin and was now getting ready for her third, which would be a sit-down discussion with both members of the Republican ticket. Then the *CBS News* anchor would have two more chances to tie up any loose ends in a post-rally backstage interview and a final twenty-minute chat aboard the Straight Talk Express bus. When all was said and done, Couric would have interviewed Palin seven times over the course of her two days spent with the candidate.

There was not much time to make last-minute preparations as the *CBS News* van rolled toward the Capital Center, where a crowd of several thousand had been accumulating for hours. Couric looked over the stack of notes she had compiled with her researcher, Brian Goldsmith. "And then I'll ask her the one about what books and magazines she reads," she said.

Couric had come up with that question herself. Having already covered so much policy ground, it seemed appropriate to ask a question that might shine a light on how Palin formulated her general worldview.

"That's a really great question," said *CBS Evening News* executive producer Rick Kaplan from the back row of the van. Kaplan, whose commanding presence always loomed nearby wherever Couric went on the road, was keenly aware that his anchor had been on a serious roll. Her first pair of interviews with Palin the week before had struck just the right tone: assertive and persistent but not disrespectful or condescending.

The *CBS News* embedded reporter (and coauthor of this book) suggested a foreign policy question about how the United States should respond in the event of a Chinese attack on Taiwan. With doubts continuing to swirl about Palin's knowledge of international affairs, it seemed like a good opportunity to test how deeply she had thought about a critical, yet less talked-about, region of the world. But Kaplan shot the idea down, knowing it could open Couric up to accusations of being unfair to Palin. "I don't want any 'gotcha questions,'" he said.

The joint interview with McCain went relatively well, and the indoor rally in Columbus was animated as usual. Despite her interview performances, Palin could always be counted on to deliver on stage. But miscommunications between her traveling staff and headquarters had given her the impression that once the rally ended, she would have a moment to herself before meeting with Couric on the Straight Talk Express. Instead, Couric and her crew were waiting backstage, behind the blue drapes, to get in a few more questions before the final interview aboard the bus.

"When it comes to establishing your worldview," Couric said. "I was curious, what newspapers and magazines did you regularly read, before you were tapped for this, to stay informed and to understand the world?"

It wasn't the exact question Palin's aides had anticipated, but it was close. They had guessed that Couric, or a future interviewer, might ask the governor what nonfiction books she had read recently. Despite the straightforward query, Palin tensed up visibly.

"I've read most of them, again with a great appreciation for the press, for the media," she said.

"Like what ones specifically?" Couric pressed.

"All of them," Palin said, throwing her hands in the air. "Any of them that have been in front of me over all these years. I have a vast—"

"Can you name a few?"

"I have a vast variety of sources where we get our news, too."

Later, campaign aides would agree that it had been a simple question that deserved a simple answer. Whether it happened to be the *Anchorage Daily News*, *Newsweek*, or the *Wall Street Journal*, Palin could have just told Couric what she liked to read. Instead, the candidate had taken the question as a personal affront, as if Couric were somehow suggesting it was impossible to keep up on current affairs from the far-off reaches of the American frontier.

From his vantage point behind the cameras, Chris Edwards looked on in horror at Palin's refusal to answer the question. He was the one who brought press clippings to her room each morning, and he knew that she got her news from a variety of sources. Why didn't she just answer the question? In a near panic, he caught up with Tucker Eskew. He pulled Eskew aside and told him that tonight's version of *The CBS Evening News* was not going to be prettier than the ones that had aired the week before.

From the first segment that aired on September 24 through Palin's final, cringe-worthy nonanswer about the Supreme Court that was broadcast on October 1, the cumulative effect of the Couric interviews was ruinous. Why had this accomplished politician who had proven herself to be a highly skilled communicator barely been able to communicate anything at all? There was no simple answer, but her fixation on her popularity back home had certainly been a contributing factor.

Palin's public explanations for the collective disaster amounted to blaming the referee. In a counterproductive attempt to redeem herself, she began to reference the Couric interviews frequently at rallies. At a packed tennis stadium in Carson, California, on October 4, she lamented that Couric asked her questions that made her think, "C'mon, let's start talking to the American people about the issues you guys want to know about."

Palin did not expound upon the matter of which issues the public did not want to know about. The financial crisis? Global warming? Cross-border raids into Pakistan? Though some of her staffers took issue with the way in which the interviews had been edited, none of them complained about the questions.

Several former aides now agree that Palin's biggest handicap during the interviews was that she was flat out unprepared and unfocused. The perfect storm of the interviews, meetings with world leaders, an ethics investigation that threatened her reputation, her declining approval rating in Alaska, and an impending debate against a veteran national political figure seemed too much for her to handle all at once. Understandable enough. But this was the big arena, and big time plays were needed.

Perhaps the most harmful factor leading to the Couric debacle was Palin's misplaced confidence in her own ability to improvise her way through the interviews. There had been too much new information for her to learn about national and international affairs for adequate freelancing to be a real possibility for anyone in her position. The advent of YouTube and the twenty-four-hour cable news cycle made Palin's crash even more devastating, as the embarrassing clips were played again and again. As she headed into her debate with Joe Biden, gone were the memories of her poised, eloquent, magnetic convention speech in St. Paul. Expectations had never been lower.

☆ ☆ ☆

7. Taking the Reins

THE OVERPOWERING SMELL OF cheeseburgers and French fries saturated the candidate's suite at the Philadelphia Westin Hotel. About a dozen staffers shuffled around the table set up in the middle of the room where hundreds upon hundreds of five-by-seven-inch note cards were spread out in two-foot-high stacks. Palin had been locked in there for hours, cramming for her debate against Joe Biden. The biggest test of the campaign was less than a week away.

On the heels of the first round of Katie Couric interviews, her margin for error was nonexistent. Joe Lieberman, a veteran of a previous vice presidential debate, had been brought in to give Palin an idea of what to expect. The stifling air shortened everyone's patience, and tensions were running especially high between debate prep coordinator Mark Wallace and foreign policy adviser Randy Scheunemann. It was the note cards that had first led to the long-standing feud between Wallace and Scheunemann a couple of weeks earlier. One of the aides wanted Palin to memorize them, while the other thought it better for her to learn conceptually. The spat made it all the way up the chain to Steve Schmidt, who told Scheunemann in no uncertain terms that he did not have the time for bickering between staffers and that they needed to sort it out. But the two men were still fuming at one another, and negative vibes permeated the room along with the smell of greasy food.

At the end of one cram session, Palin asked her advisers to run through the various trade agreements, including "who's in NAFTA, who's in CAFTA," and so forth. It seemed an unremarkable request at the time. The advisers knew that the governor was, in fact, aware that the NAFTA treaty included the United States, Canada, and Mexico. But someone in the room with a penchant for whispering to reporters was taking mental notes. Come November, the anonymous source would pass Palin's words along as part of a concerted effort to advance the exaggerated narrative that her handlers had been stymied in their heroic, yet futile, efforts to educate an ignoramus.

Steve Schmidt, Rick Davis, and domestic policy adviser Becky Tallent arrived in Philadelphia by train on Sunday, September 28. It was clear by the time they set foot in the suffocating hotel suite on the third full day of debate prep that a dramatic change was needed. Schmidt and Davis had already spoken to John McCain, who agreed to offer up his sprawling Sedona ranch. It did not take much persuasion to convince Palin of the benefits of moving the operation to the desert compound, where she could work in her shorts and T-shirt with her family by her side. Schmidt realized that the candidate would benefit from having a more condensed circle of aides to brief her, so he sent some of the staffers who had been with her in Philadelphia ahead to the debate site at St. Louis. Others who did travel to Sedona were barred from McCain's compound and had to remain at the hotel.

Palin and her downsized contingent of advisers arrived in Arizona the next afternoon. On the first evening of their stay, one of her aides spoke privately to the governor about the importance of speaking in her own voice, rather than regurgitating talking points handed down from the Washington insiders who ran the campaign, all of whom were white males. It was one piece of advice that Palin took to heart.

The preparations were kept informal except for two timed reenactments in which debate conditions were replicated, including the exact distance between the podiums. Randy Scheunemann had flown in to play Joe Biden, an acting role that the archconservative seemed born to play. Scheunemann had sat through years of Biden's speeches during his time working for two Republicans on the Senate Foreign Relations Committee, and he knew the Delaware senator's mannerisms well. Palin struggled to keep a straight face as Scheunemann peppered his performance with "God love ya"s and "literally"s and shifted between long-winded discourses on everything from the war in Iraq to his own mother. A former National Rifle Association lobbyist, Scheunemann as Biden delivered a passionate screed on banning assault rifles. When he waxed poetic on the issue of gay marriage, some of the aides looking on from the sidelines gave up on trying to maintain decorum and burst out laughing. At the end of the ninety-minute session, they broke out into spontaneous applause. Palin's keen memory for detail had manifested itself in her very first formal rehearsal, and she had done even better than they had hoped she would.

The next day, the group decided to move the debate operation outdoors so that they could take full advantage of the beautiful Sedona weather. The new environment continued to have a calming effect on Palin and everyone around her. Gone were the endless stacks of note cards and claustrophobic atmosphere that plagued

the operation in Philadelphia. Palin looked refreshed as she stood
behind her podium in a baseball cap and T-shirt. As evening shad-
ows crept across the well-manicured grass, Cindy McCain came out
from the house to address the group. She insisted that all toil must
end at an appointed hour of 5 P.M., when everyone was to convene
for wine and cheese. There were no arguments.

When Palin nailed a second ninety-minute mock debate, everyone was optimistic about the real thing, which was coming up the
next day. By the time she and her aides left the ranch for St. Louis,
their confidence was high enough that the hottest topic under discussion was whether the governor should wear blue or black. In the
end, she went with black. The background, after all, would be blue.

Just minutes before the candidates shook hands on stage in
St. Louis, Palin collected her thoughts in a room as she was joined
by three top McCain advisers and her longtime Alaska aide Kris
Perry. "Be still in the presence of the Lord!" Perry called out, as
Palin bowed her head and prayed.

Palin would give her own version of this event several months
later in a speech at a Republican Party dinner in Alaska. "So, I'm
looking around for somebody to pray with. I just need maybe a little help, maybe a little extra," she said. "And the McCain campaign,
love 'em, you know—there are a lot of people around me, but nobody I could find that I wanted to hold hands with and pray."

The remark drew laughter at the dinner but consternation
among some former campaign aides, especially the ones who recalled that she had, in fact, deemed them worthy enough compan-
ions with whom to pray. On the surface, Palin's remark seemed like
a harmless, humorous aside. But to some of the staffers who had
spent two months of their lives working around the clock to try to
get her elected, it was hurtful. The comment marked a turning
point for several campaign operatives who had defended her up to

that point but began to wonder about her willingness to exploit their relationship for political gain. "I was initially upset. I think a lot of people were," said one former senior aide who still speaks frequently to other staffers who continued to support Palin through difficult times. "I think that somebody in the group spoke up and said, 'It's not directed at us.'" Still, the aide wondered how the comment could have been allowed to run wild in the news cycle without any clarification from Palin. "Why are people letting her go out and give speeches like this? And why are people not getting ahead of this when she says something like this?"

But all of that was much further down the road. In St. Louis on the night of October 2, the governor's aides looked on approvingly as Palin took the stage and made it immediately clear that she intended to showcase her confidence and personality instead of sparring with Biden over specific details of policy—a fight she could not possibly be expected to win. "I may not answer the questions that either the moderator or you want to hear," she declared with a bright smile. "But I'm going to talk straight to the American people and let them know my track record, also."

There were a few moments that came perilously close to flashbacks of the Katie Couric interviews, such as Palin's response to moderator Gwen Ifill's question about whether any trigger would justify the use of nuclear weapons. "Nuclear weaponry, of course, would be the be-all, end-all of just too many people in too many parts of our planet," she said (mostly the end-all, as Palin-bashing columnist Maureen Dowd gleefully pointed out in a postdebate column).

All in all, however, Palin performed competently and avoided major gaffes. The Republican candidate winked and "darn righted" her way through the debate, delighting her admirers and infuriating her detractors in a predictable way. She was particularly effective in using her methodically unaffected speaking style to break down into simple terms the lessons the country could learn from the economic crisis. "Let's commit ourselves, just everyday American people, Joe Six Pack, hockey moms across the nation, I think we need to band together and say, 'Never again,'" she said. "Never will we be exploited and taken advantage of again by those who are managing our money and loaning us these dollars. We need to make sure that we demand from the federal government strict oversight of those entities in charge of our investments and our savings and we need also to not get ourselves in debt."

Though Biden restrained himself from delivering any of the over-the-top diatribes for which Randy Scheunemann had prepared her, Palin told a confidante after the debate that she'd had a hard time reigning in her smile because the real candidate sounded so much like Scheunemann. Surprisingly, it was the Democrat who struck the most poignant note of the evening when he choked up recalling the death of his first wife and daughter in a car accident that also nearly took the lives of his two sons.

Still, the aides who prepared Palin for the debate were uniformly pleased with her performance. Before a local late-night rally scheduled to keep the momentum going, Palin's inner circle opened a bottle of champagne and toasted the candidate. Feeding off the adrenaline, Palin approached a small group of aides and made a pitch to start bringing up on the campaign trail Barack Obama's ties to his controversial former preacher, Jeremiah Wright. John McCain wanted desperately to become the nation's next president, but not at the expense of facing the inevitable accusations of racial exploitation if he made Wright an issue. She knew quite well about the decree that he had months earlier laid out to everyone involved in the campaign: no one was to touch the controversy. Still, Palin could not understand why she should be held to the rule.

"I just don't want to go back to Alaska," she said in an offhanded comment that would later seem prescient.

Several polls showed that both the general electorate and unde-cided voters thought Biden had won the debate, although most pundits declared that Palin had exceeded expectations. But with McCain unable to gain any traction against Obama in the presiden-tial debates, the campaign had needed Palin to do more than that. Her performance did nothing to change the complexion of the race, the way her stirring convention speech had done a month earlier.

The day after the debate, Palin caused more headaches when she told *Fox News*'s Carl Cameron that she disagreed with the cam-paign's decision to pull resources out of Michigan, effectively ceding the state to Obama. She had not been consulted on that critical move in the chess game, which leaked out in a report penned by the *Politico*'s Jonathan Martin the previous afternoon. "I fired off a quick e-mail and said, 'Oh, come on. You know, do we have to? Do we have to call it there?'" she told Cameron. "I want to get back to Michigan, and I want to try."

The e-mail that Palin sent was, in fact, essentially how she de-scribed it to Cameron. She wrote to her traveling staff and top McCain advisers, "If there's any time, Todd and I would love a quick return to Michigan—we'd tour the plants, etc. . . . If it does McC any good. I know you have a plan, but I hate to see us leave Michigan. We'll do whatever we had [*sic*] to do there to give it a 2nd effort."

A senior aide replied, "Michigan is out of reach unless some-thing drastic happens. We must win oh and hopefully pa."

Palin replied that she "got it," but her subsequent interview with Cameron had shown that she hadn't. She acknowledged as much in a postinterview e-mail to senior staff, writing, "Oops—I mentioned something about that to Carl Cameron and it's now recorded that I'd love to give Michigan the ol' college try." Later in the day, she tried once more. "It's a cheap 4hr drive from WI. I'll pay for the gas," she wrote.

Though senior aides had firmly rejected her request, Palin continued to press them on it in the coming days and weeks. A natural optimist but a novice when it came to national campaign strategy, she was inclined not to give up anywhere, much less on a state that had been a prime target for months. She remembered the massive crowds that had greeted her and McCain in Macomb County the day after the convention ended and in Grand Rapids a couple of weeks later. They were good, God-fearing, salt-of-the-earth people. She figured that she could introduce them to her husband, who liked to ride snowmobiles and hunt, just like Michiganders did. Her instincts told her that if she just had a chance to talk to some laid-off automobile workers face-to-face, she could convince them to vote Republican.

"I know what I know what I know." She repeated that mantra to the people around her throughout the campaign. Sometimes she was right, but her growing determination to do things her own way became a continuing headache for the campaign's strategists, who were more interested in polling data and documented fact than they were in the vice presidential candidate's instincts.

Palin sat in her hotel suite in Costa Mesa, California, on the night after the Cameron interview and began to muse with traveling staffers about what she could do to win back Michigan, despite top aides' firm decree that it was out of reach. She was the candidate after all, and it was time for her to take more control over her own destiny. What if they descended upon the state unannounced in the middle of the night and brought Jay Leno or David Letterman along to cover the triumphant surprise visit? Several of her traveling aides loved the idea, as unorthodox as it sounded. There was a growing consensus on the plane that the powers that be at headquarters were holding her back unwisely. The late-night comedian idea was probably pushing it, but maybe they could wait until the next time they were in Ohio and commandeer the campaign bus at the end of the day's events. They could drive it across the border into Michigan, hold a dramatic public appearance to draw in local media, then drive back to Ohio overnight in time for the next day's rallies.

Though many of her aides were on board with her sentiment, other campaign staffers were becoming irritated by how often she brought up her ideas for campaigning in Michigan. There was a growing sense that the vice presidential plane was becoming a renegade operation, increasingly comfortable with acting on its own. Rick Davis was so concerned about the possibility that the governor would ignore orders and travel to Michigan on her own that he attempted to order Secret Service agents to prevent it. Of course, agents would have been obliged to follow the candidate wherever she decided to go.

In an attempt to appease Palin's desire to campaign in parts of the country that were no longer being contested, McCain aides honored her request to travel to Omaha for a rally to try to shore up Nebraska's Second District. Nebraska was one of two states that split its electoral vote by congressional districts, and the Obama campaign had been making a serious play in Omaha to take advantage of it. At the Omaha rally, Palin was explicit about her still-growing frustration with the cable news coverage of her candidacy, which she refused to ignore.

"The pundits today on TV—one of them was saying, 'Check out the vice president's schedule, check out where she's going—she's going to Nebraska,'" she said at the packed Civic Auditorium Music Hall. "But the pundit was saying the only reason she'd be going there is 'cause they're scared, so they gotta go there and shore up votes.' And I so wanted to reach into that TV and say, 'No, I'm going to Nebraska because I want to go to Nebraska!'"

At the time, it seemed like a harmless, if dubious, statement. But in retrospect, her insistence that she was there because she wanted to be there, despite what the powers that be had wanted her to do, amounted to a public declaration that she was now in charge. It bespoke an attitude that would backfire on her later in the week.

Palin also took the Omaha rally as an opportunity to hammer home her newest attack against Barack Obama—that he had a history of associating with dangerous, anti-American radicals. "This is not a man who sees America as you and I do," she warned.

On the previous day, she had first taken Obama to task for his relationship with 1960's radical Bill Ayers, whose Weather Underground movement had engaged in a bombing campaign targeting the Pentagon and the U.S. Capitol. "Our opponent though is someone who sees America, it seems, as being so imperfect, imperfect enough that he's palling around with terrorists who would target their own country," she said at a Colorado fund-raiser.

Palin was seizing on a story in that morning's *New York Times*, which concluded that Obama's and Ayers's paths had crossed "sporadically," including a coffee gathering in support of Obama's first campaign for political office. "The two men do not appear to have been close. Nor has Mr. Obama ever expressed sympathy for the radical views and actions of Mr. Ayers, whom he has called 'somebody who engaged in detestable acts 40 years ago, when I was 8,'" the *Times* reported.

But the report's downplaying of the relationship between Obama and Ayers did not stop the McCain campaign from dispatching Palin to suggest the two men had been "pals." Furthermore, her use of the plural form in making her claim that Obama palled around with *"terrorists* who would target *their* country" went unexplained. Contrary to subsequent media reports suggesting that Palin had jumped the gun on unleashing the new charge that the campaign had

scripted for her, she was merely following orders, and doing so enthusiastically. Palin had long advocated a tougher line on what she
saw as Obama's questionable personal relationships and was clearly
relieved that the campaign had finally given her the green light to
take up the charge. In fact, she liked the "pals around" line so much
that she asked for, and was granted, permission to use it at the Colorado fund-raiser that was set to begin less than a half hour after
she received it, even though the senior aides who approved the attack had originally planned to have her unveil it in Southern California later that day. The crowd of about one thousand well-heeled
donors in Colorado exploded with raw emotion when they heard it.
At long last, the gloves were coming off.

Despite her running mate's firm decree about Jeremiah Wright,
Palin found herself continuing to express agreement with observers
inside and outside the campaign who thought Obama's relationship
with his longtime pastor was even more relevant than the Ayers
connection. In private conversations with staffers, Palin wondered
aloud whether most Americans fully understood just how close the
Democratic nominee had been to the man who had famously
shouted the words, "God damn America!"

After a few days of hitting Obama with the "pals around" line,
she thought she had done enough on Ayers. Now it was time to
push hard on Jeremiah Wright. McCain was well aware that Palin
was itching to kick the door open, but he stood firm on the matter.
She did not pretend to agree with McCain's decision, though she
said she would honor it. That promise changed rather abruptly
when *New York Times* op-ed columnist and frequent Palin defender
Bill Kristol asked her in a phone interview set up by the McCain
campaign why Wright was not a relevant issue. Palin could have
easily dodged the question, but she decided to answer it head-on.
"To tell you the truth, Bill, I don't know why that association isn't

discussed more, because those were appalling things that that pastor had said about our great country, and to have sat in the pews for twenty years and listened to that—with, I don't know, a sense of condoning it, I guess, because he didn't get up and leave—to me, that does say something about character." Palin concluded by observing rather ironically that the forbidden issue, which she had just addressed at length, "would be a John McCain call on whether he wants to bring that up."

Her refusal to abide by McCain's demand that everyone involved in the campaign ignore the Wright issue seemed to confirm the growing perception among many of the senator's aides that the vice presidential candidate was now acting according to her own interest, rather than the campaign's. They began to view everything she did and said through a filter of suspicion.

Still, even the most skeptical aides could not deny that she was a major draw on the stump. Before Palin had been tapped for the job, the McCain campaign had planned for the vice presidential pick to hit the fund-raising circuit hard. Raising cash had long been one of the vice presidential candidate's main functions, and the vice presidential operations group at headquarters had spent much of the summer drawing up a plan for the future candidate to appear at fund-raising events around the nation. But the Alaska governor was such a strong draw at rallies that senior campaign aides dramatically altered their scheduling plans. Palin only attended one fund-raiser in her first month on the trail.

By the time October rolled around, however, the financially strapped campaign needed her to start hitting the hotel ballroom circuit in earnest. In a one-week span, Palin appeared at ten fund-raisers from Dallas to Pittsburgh. She was less than enthused about spending so much precious time behind closed doors with wealthy donors. She much preferred interacting with the everyday folks who greeted her with passionate cheers at rallies, rather than the tepid applause she usually received at fund-raisers from people who seemed much different from her.

On October 6, Palin's day on Florida's west coast was a study in contrasts. That morning, before a backdrop of hundreds of supporters forming a human flag in red, white, and blue T-shirts, she appeared at a rally in Clearwater. She worked the crowd into a tizzy with patriotic language and drove them to raucous boos when she lamented that Obama's candidacy made her fear for America's future. But she also diverted from her scathing attacks for a moment of sincere appreciation for the thousands who had come out to cheer her on. "Man, some of your signs just make me want to cry," she said.

After the emotionally charged rally, it was off to Naples for a pair of hoity-toity fund-raisers. At the Naples Beach Hotel, about 150 donors from the yacht-club set sipped lunchtime mimosas and Bloody Marys as they listened politely to what Palin had to say. No tear-jerking signage here. Next on the docket was a short trip down the road to the waterfront compound belonging to Jack Donahue, founder of Federated Investors. The first applause line did not come until ten minutes into Palin's speech. The absence of the boisterous adoration she had grown used to at her red-meat rallies clearly took her off her game as she stumbled through her prepared remarks.

Palin had, of course, held her fair share of fund-raisers while running for governor, but the national circuit was foreign territory. At the beginning of the fund-raising blitz, she told one baffled aide that she assumed all the money she raised would go into a vice presidential account to pay for her own half of the campaign's expenses. Even after the process of the "McCain Victory 08" fund was explained to her, she repeatedly complained to aides about how mundane the fund-raisers were and still did not seem to grasp their importance. "These people are already voting for us, so why do they need a picture with me?" she would ask. "My time is much better spent on the rope lines."

The fund-raisers also made Palin increasingly conscious of her own image. She was not used to wealthy women complimenting her on her outfits and asking where she got her shoes, but these were the kinds of things they always seemed to notice. Palin had truly been appalled by the price tags on some of the clothes Lisa Kline and her assistant had bought for her at the convention, but as the pressure to look perfect at all times escalated, she continued to make requests to her traveling aides for additional wardrobe purchases, though never for the most expensive brands.

But the subject of clothes was far from Palin's mind on the night of October 10 when the Alaska Legislative Council voted unanimously to release investigator Stephen Branchflower's newly completed 263-page report on the Troopergate investigation. Branchflower concluded that Palin had abused her power by purposefully allowing Walt Monegan to be pressured to fire her former brother-in-law, Mike Wooten. The report also suggested, however, that the situation with Wooten was not the only reason why Monegan had been terminated and reaffirmed that the governor's decision to fire Monegan had been lawful.

The report was major news in Alaska, and left-leaning blogs rejoiced. Still, though it certainly did not polish Palin's image nationally, the country at large did not greet the report's release as an earth-shattering moment. The McCain campaign was fortunate that the news came out on a Friday night—the most somnolent time of the week for revealing negative information, as Americans turn their attention to weekend activities, and news audiences decrease dramatically. The campaign's communications team released a brief statement that night, highlighting Branchflower's finding that Palin had been within her rights to fire Monegan and suggesting that political calculations had tarnished the inquiry's legitimacy. In the broader context of the campaign, the Troopergate story seemed poised to become only a minor setback.

The next morning, a reporter stood outside the Straight Talk Express and managed to get within shouting range of Palin as she boarded the bus. He asked if she had indeed abused her power, as Branchflower's report claimed. "No," Palin said. "And if you read the report, you'll see that there was nothing unlawful or unethical about replacing a cabinet member. You've got to read the report, sir."

Just as campaign aides had instructed her to do, Palin had chosen her words carefully to focus on the report's finding that she had not acted illegally in firing Monegan and to ignore the section saying that she "knowingly permitted a situation to continue where impermissible pressure was placed on several subordinates in order to advance a personal agenda."

But Palin's careful parsing morphed into blatant mischaracterization later in the day on a conference call with Alaska reporters that lasted all of five minutes. "Well, I'm very, very pleased to be cleared of any legal wrongdoing—any hint of any kind of unethical activity there," she declared.

In one sweeping sentence, the governor flatly asserted that Branchflower's report, which said "that Sarah Palin abused her power by violating Alaska Statute 39.52.110(a) of the Alaska Executive Branch Ethics Act," had actually found just the opposite. The reporters and politicians who had been following the case closely in Alaska reacted quickly. The *Anchorage Daily News* held nothing back. "Palin's response is the kind of political 'big lie' that George Orwell warned against," the hometown paper once generally supportive of Palin now wrote in an editorial. "War is peace. Black is white. Up is down."

As the McCain campaign struggled to find a way to defend Palin's indefensible misinterpretation of the report, a story that might otherwise have died instead caught fire in the news. An autumn chill began to penetrate the late summer warmth, and top aides were reminded that they were running out of time. Nothing the campaign was throwing Obama's way seemed to stick, and so it was necessary to change tactics once again.

Palin wanted to talk about abortion. She had been making that clear in private conversations for weeks. But with the near collapse of the American financial system creating the biggest economic crisis since the Great Depression, senior McCain aides knew they would not win this election by focusing on traditional "wedge" social issues. Still, they were well aware of how eloquent Palin could be in espousing the pro-life principles by which she lived. Abortion was still issue number one for wide swaths of the socially conservative base, and the campaign could not afford to alienate those voters. The campaign decided to grant the candidate her wish.

A prime opportunity to address the issue came on a sparkling fall morning in a jam-packed hockey rink in Johnstown, Pennsylvania, on Saturday, October 11. It happened to be the day after the Branchflower report's release, and in light of Palin's demonstrably false pronouncements about what the report had concluded, the campaign's brain trust was eager to change the subject. Despite a 2–1 edge for Democrats in the voting registration rolls, central Pennsylvania's socially conservative Cambria County had narrowly voted for President Bush in 2004. Although most polls showed the Republican ticket trailing in the state by double digits, the McCain/Palin campaign had decided to make its stand there. There was almost nowhere else to go to get the votes they needed for an electoral majority, and there were no Pennsylvania voters more important than Johnstown's "Reagan Democrats."

Inside the hockey rink, Palin read from a new abortion-centric stump speech penned for her by Matthew Scully. She first went into intimate detail about how she dealt with her baby son Trig's Down syndrome diagnosis and the joys he had brought into her life. The uplifting tone then shifted abruptly to an accusatory screed, as she proceeded to shred Barack Obama for what she described as a "radical" position on abortion. "I listened when our opponent defended his unconditional support for unlimited abortions, and he said that a woman shouldn't have to be quote 'punished' with a baby," Palin said. "Ladies and Gentlemen, he said that right here in Johnstown—punished with a baby."

It did not matter to the outraged audience that when Obama had made the remark, he had been talking not about abortion but rather about the importance of sex education. The crowd's voracious response to the hot-button line had an invigorating effect on Palin. In the days that followed, she often inserted portions of the Johnstown abortion speech into the standard stump speech to which headquarters had instructed her to revert. Later that week, when Palin made her first trip as a candidate to New Hampshire, the abortion issue would come up again, although not in the way the campaign had planned. Her October 15 foray into the Granite State turned into, perhaps, her most tumultuous day of the campaign. Two internal spats with top aides provoked by Palin would demonstrate that the vice presidential candidate had turned a corner. No longer would she play the good soldier when she felt that doing so threatened her own image. Her own political survival was now a primary concern, one as important to her as the viability of the campaign that her running mate had launched nearly two years earlier.

Everyone knew New Hampshire's almost mythical status in John McCain's political life, the state having awarded him resounding victories in its first-in-the-nation primaries in 2000 and 2008. The voters there were McCain's kind of people: pragmatic, blunt, and pleasantly cynical. New Hampshire's four electoral votes could now prove decisive in several scenarios, and the swing state was deemed important enough to take up a full day of Palin's schedule. Her independent, antiestablishment streak might also resonate in the state, although its small population and socially moderate base meant she would not get the kinds of enormous, hyper-passionate crowds to which she had grown accustomed.

Palin's arrival in the coastal town of Portsmouth got off to an inauspicious start, as she was already well behind schedule when her plane touched down. It did not get any better from there. Once she boarded the Straight Talk Express and was on the road to the first rally in Dover, her aides gave her a short briefing on the two New Hampshire politicians who would meet her at the high school gymnasium rally. Senator John Sununu, she was told, was in a tough reelection fight, and former congressman Jeb Bradley was trying to retake the House seat he had lost in 2006.

Palin was less than thrilled with the casual manner in which this information was delivered to her. In fact, she had been increasingly frustrated by how often she felt like she was being pushed in front of local politicians she knew little to nothing about, often just minutes before they were to introduce her at rallies around the country. On October 9, she had sent an e-mail to senior aides and traveling staffers with the subject line "GOOGLE," writing, "Pls let me know who the invited travellers [sic] are before they're confirmed to travel with me. I want to google them myself so I can know my comfort level with an association with politicians whom I've never met before they jump on the bus or plane with the VP campaign." Her reference to the "VP campaign" had seemed at odds with the unified team that theoretically made up the McCain/Palin ticket. Furthermore, it should have been well beneath her pay grade to personally Google the names of politicians who would already have been thor-

oughly vetted by a team of experienced staffers at campaign headquarters who were paid to do just that.

When she was handed Jeb Bradley's bio, which noted his pro-
choice stance and his opposition to drilling in ANWR, Palin put her
foot down.

"Why is he going to be on stage with me?" she asked. "He and I
don't agree on anything."

It was a startling comment when examined in the context of the
political persona that Palin had cultivated in Alaska. The woman
who had chided Andrew Halcro in a debate just two years earlier for
using the abortion issue to divide people was now declaring her unwillingness to be seen in public with a Republican politician who
agreed with her on the vast majority of issues but differed on abortion and drilling. Bradley's record on social issues was not exactly a
liberal one. He had voted to ban late-term abortions, and he was
the only member of Congress from New England to support a proposed constitutional amendment banning gay marriage. But as an
election day defeat seemed increasingly likely, Palin had become
sensitive to maintaining her new image as an ideologically pure social conservative, a credential she saw as largely responsible for at-
tracting the legions of devoted adherents who greeted her each day.
She did not want to lose those people after November, no matter
what the electoral result.

While Palin's traveling aides tried to figure out how to handle
what was clearly shaping up to be an awkward situation, one staffer
suggested that since the governor was already running late to the
first event, Sununu and Bradley could give their introductory remarks before the vice presidential campaign entourage arrived. The
New Hampshire politicians, who had no idea that anything was
amiss, ended up doing just that. When Palin finally arrived in Dover,
she bolted past Sununu and Bradley and quickly took the stage. There
were only about one thousand people there—a small gathering by

Palin's standards—but the gym could not hold any more, and there was a small overflow crowd outside.

After the rally, Palin was finally introduced to Sununu and Bradley. She was gracious to both New Hampshire Republicans as she posed for photographs with them backstage. Bradley was particularly impressed by Palin's common touch as he watched her take off her own earrings and replace them with a pair just given to her by a woman who made jewelry to benefit U.S. troops overseas. He had no idea that Palin's aides had worked out the timing of his remarks so that their candidate would not have to face the career risk of presenting a united front with a pro-choice politician.

Palin's next stop was an outdoor rally on a nostalgic New England boardwalk at Weir's Beach at the southern tip of Lake Winnipesaukee. She had been promised that she could use the hour-and-fifteen-minute drive to the event for state business and personal time in the back of the bus, and she had become increasingly protective of every second of downtime since it was so often excised from her schedule. It seemed like whenever she was slated to spend time with her family or go for a run, she ended up on a bus or an airplane. She would sometimes joke to sympathetic traveling aides from her seat in the third row of the campaign plane, "So, should I run now?" Remarks like these added to the growing "us-versus-them" mentality that Palin now seemed to be deliberately fostering among her own staffers against aides who were either traveling on the McCain plane or left back at headquarters.

Despite the downtime promised to her, Sununu and Bradley had previously been told that they would be able to chat with Palin on the bus between events. When a vice presidential staffer tried to direct the New Hampshire Republicans into a van that would travel separately in the motorcade, McCain's longtime New Hampshire guru Steve Duprey, who was helping out in his home state for the Palin visit, stepped in. He called headquarters to report that Sununu and Bradley were being denied a ride on the Straight Talk Express and that Palin was refusing to go on stage with Bradley. The response from headquarters came quickly: the New Hampshire Republicans were to be welcomed onto the bus and would appear on stage with Palin whether she liked it or not.

Bradley and Sununu were redirected onto the bus, but for most of the drive to Weirs Beach, Palin sat alone at the back and tended to her infant son, Trig. She did come up to chat with the New Hampshire Republicans for a few minutes as the vehicle approached Weirs Beach and, left with no other option than outright mutiny, conceded to the demand from headquarters that she appear with Bradley on stage.

Bradley, who subsequently lost his congressional bid, was still entirely unaware of Palin's reservations about being seen in public with him months after the fact. When provided with a detailed account of what had happened, he seemed taken aback. "I think it's important that Republicans on these conscience votes realize that there are going to be differences of opinion and we not exclude good Republicans just based on one set of ideas," he said. "And I have a pretty conservative voting record on the social issues."

The drama surrounding Palin's reluctance to appear publicly with Bradley particularly aggravated senior McCain aides since the final of three presidential debates was just hours away. The campaign's focus should have centered entirely on John McCain and the soon-to-be canonized Joe the Plumber. Instead, top advisers once again found themselves immersed in a manufactured crisis on the vice presidential side. Worse than that, the Jeb Bradley saga was only the first of two instances that day in which Palin would attempt to push back against her marching orders.

On the previous day, CNN's Rick Sanchez had conducted a live interview with Salon.com reporter David Neiwert, who had coauthored an investigative story highlighting Palin's relationship with members of the Alaskan Independence Party (AIP) when she was mayor of Wasilla. CNN ran a graphic at the bottom of the screen reading, "The Palins and the Fringe," an allusion to the AIP's platform, which calls for a vote giving Alaskans the rather startling option to secede from the union.

Sanchez asked Neiwert if the AIP's ideology was similar to the goals of the group that blew up the Alfred P. Murrah Federal Building in Oklahoma City. Neiwert responded that while Timothy McVeigh had been a lone wolf, the bomber had ideological ties to a "patriots' movement," whose ideals were indeed similar to the AIP's. The report was not entirely evenhanded. Despite a platform befitting the antebellum South, the AIP has played a serious role in Alaska politics. Wally Hickel ran as an AIP candidate, though he did not endorse secession, when he won the governorship in 1990.

It had already been reported that Todd Palin was a registered member of the party from 1995 to 2002 and that Sarah Palin had taped a recorded greeting at the party's 2008 convention. But the governor was incensed by the implications of the narrative that CNN had discussed, which at least one protestor in Dover echoed. She sent the following e-mail with the subject line "Todd" to senior advisers Steve Schmidt, Rick Davis, and Nicolle Wallace, copying her husband on the message: "Pls get in front of that ridiculous issue that's cropped up all day today—two reporters, a protestor's sign, and many shout-outs all claiming Todd's involvement in an anti-American political party. It's bull, and I don't want to have to keep reacting to it. . . . Pls have statement given on this so it's put to bed."

Her suggestion that Todd had nothing to do with the AIP was an embellishment at best and an attempt to mislead her own campaign's advisers at worst. The reference to a single protestor's sign and "many shout-outs" reflected her tendency to extrapolate from minor, anecdotal evidence something far more meaningful.

Schmidt replied to all less than five minutes after Palin sent her e-mail. "Ignore it," he wrote. "He was a member of the aip? My understanding is yes. That is part of their platform. Do not engage the protestors. If a reporter asks say it is ridiculous. Todd loves america."

This clear-cut response from the campaign's chief strategist once again did not satisfy Palin. She responded with another e-mail, adding five more aides to the list, including senior advisers Tucker Eskew and Jason Recher, Alaska aide Kris Perry, traveling press secretary Tracey Schmitt, and personal aide Bexie Nobles. The inclusion of the five additional aides in the e-mail chain seemed intended to rally Palin's own loyal troops in the face of a decision from the very top of the campaign apparatus with which she disagreed. The inclusion of her personal assistant was particularly telling since Nobles was not in a position to have any input on campaign strategy whatsoever.

"That's not part of their platform and he was only a 'member' bc independent alaskans too often check that 'Alaska Independent' box on voter registrations thinking it just means non partisan," Palin wrote. "He caught his error when changing our address and checked the right box. I still want it fixed."

Here again, Palin was exaggerating the truth to bolster her argument, rather than grounding her concerns in the acknowledgment of a demonstrable, if unpleasant, fact. The box that Alaskans have the option of checking when registering to vote states the full name of the party, "Alaskan Independence Party," not "Alaska Independent," as Palin asserted in trying to make it seem more plausible that Todd's AIP membership was merely a clerical error.

Schmidt put the matter to rest once and for all with a longer response. Unable to conceal his frustration with the distraction and with Palin's lack of cooperation and straightforwardness, he wrote,

Secession. It is their entire reason for existence. A cursory examination of the website shows that the party exists for the purpose

of seceding from the union. That is the stated goal on the front page of the website. Our records indicate that todd was a member for seven years. If this is incorrect then we need to understand the discrepancy. The statement you are suggesting be released would be innacurate [sic]. The innacuracy [sic] would bring greater media attention to this matter and be a distraction. According to your staff there have been no media inquiries into this and you received no questions about it during your interviews. If you are asked about it you should smile and say many alaskans who love their country join the party because it speeks [sic] to a tradition of political independence. Todd loves his country

We will not put out a statement and inflame this and create a situation where john has to address this.

Schmidt's challenge to Palin over her suggestion that reporters had been asking her about the issue was particularly blunt since it implicitly questioned her truthfulness. Furthermore, his unwillingness to budge an inch on the matter was a remarkable assertion of his rank over the vice presidential candidate. Palin did not respond, but she was gearing up for future battles in the civil war now in full swing within the McCain campaign.

$$\star \ \star \ \star$$

8. The Final Limp

THOUGH SHE HAD OBJECTED to appearing side by side with a New Hampshire Republican running for Congress, Palin could not wait to share a stage with Tina Fey. Her repeated requests to appear on *Saturday Night Live* finally paid off when senior campaign aides agreed to let her go on the show on the weekend following the drama-filled day in New Hampshire. By midweek, a script still had not been approved, and Palin's traveling staffers offered some input of their own. Senior adviser Jason Recher thought that the governor could play the part of a journalist interviewing Sarah Palin (as played by Tina Fey, of course). The real Palin would ask Fey ridiculous questions about Alaska. "What is it like to live in a state without television?" or "How do you eat if you can't find a moose to shoot?"

Palin liked the implicit jab at the media, but the show's producers had their own ideas. When *SNL* sent the campaign a draft of the script they had written for her, several aides balked at her planned interaction with actor Alec Baldwin, which ran the risk of making Palin look weak. But in the end, the producers won out.

"Forgive me, but I feel I must say this," Baldwin said to Palin at the beginning of the show. "You are way hotter in person."

Recher had suggested that she reply to this line with the funny yet assertive retort, "Hey, weren't you supposed to move to France after the election?" The proposed line almost certainly would have gotten a bigger laugh than the far weaker response that Baldwin and the show's producers settled on: "Oh, thank you. And I must say your brother Stephen is my favorite Baldwin brother."

Campaign aides were stunned when the producers balked at the idea of having Palin and Fey on camera at the same time for reasons that were not fully explained. The whole point of Palin's appearance, from a political perspective, was to prove she could hold her ground face-to-face with her comedic tormenter. In the end, the show allowed the identically dressed women to appear on camera together, but just for a fleeting second.

The episode's reviews were mixed. Palin showed that she did not take herself too seriously, but that had never really been in doubt. The governor was provided with no opportunity to serve up anything close to the biting ridicule that Fey had been heaping on her for weeks. The most memorable segment of the episode was Amy Poehler's Palin-themed rap, which aired during the "Weekend Update" segment. Poehler stole the show as Palin merely sat in her seat, bopping her head to the beat while the comedian reopened some old wounds. "My country 'tis of thee," Poehler sang with her hand over her heart. "From my porch I can see . . . Russia from my house, and such."

The *SNL* episode had poked fun at Palin's allergic reaction to the media, but ironically, by then, she had already made the transition from the most distant to the most accessible of the four candidates. As she became increasingly comfortable with communicating the campaign's message, Palin had begun sitting down for several local media interviews every day. She had also opened up to the national reporters who traveled with her. By contrast, not Obama nor Biden nor McCain had held a press conference in almost a month.

Strangely enough though, Palin balked at doing some interviews that should have been effortless. For instance, she told senior aides that she did not have enough time to prepare for another sit-down with *Fox News*'s Sean Hannity, a conservative commentator who was one of Palin's most prominent backers on television. When her chief of staff, Andrew Smith, sent her an e-mail about her scheduled interview with the *Chicago Tribune*'s Jill Zuckman on providing resources to special-needs children, Palin replied that she would not have time to read over the three talking points he would send her because she was preparing for her deposition in the "Tasergate" case. (The McCain campaign preferred to use the name "Tasergate" instead of Troopergate as a way to highlight that Trooper Mike Wooten had once used a taser on his willing eleven-year-old stepson.) Palin argued that she could spend her time more wisely by preparing for new policy initiatives rather than friendly interviews.

But when her plane landed in Colorado Springs the night after her *SNL* performance, Palin walked right up to a local television crew and began answering the reporter's questions. Sensing an opportunity, the traveling press corps followed in close pursuit. Suddenly, an impromptu media availability was in progress. Palin's press secretary, Tracey Schmitt, did not notice what was going on at first as she waited for the motorcade to start rolling. When she saw that the candidate was surrounded by a swarm of buzzing reporters, she rushed over to the hive, determined to issue every press secretary's favorite two words: "Last question!" But it was only after

Schmitt's third attempt to bring the media availability to a close that the governor finally stopped answering questions.

Most of her traveling staffers found Palin's increasing propensity to make her own decisions to be a heartening development. But the unscheduled press conference angered top aides at headquarters in Virginia, who saw it as yet another example of the Palin plane's inability to rein in a candidate who was supposed to be playing second fiddle to McCain but instead wanted to conduct the entire orchestra. When they found out that she had lamented to reporters about her own campaign's use of robocalls in battleground states, some of them began to wonder whether Palin was intentionally undermining them.

Though her media strategy was disjointed at best, Palin's victim mentality remained as entrenched as ever. On October 22, Nicolle Wallace sent the candidate an e-mail outlining that day's interview with *NBC News*'s Brian Williams, the last of the "big three" anchors to sit down with Palin. After she had completed the interview, Palin replied to Wallace and other senior aides and prepared them for the worst, writing, "Was not a good interview . . . so hang on to your hat with the criticism and mocking that will ensue. Just a head's up—doubt anything can be done about it—the gotcha questions started right out of the shoot and as usual I was perplexed at the whole line of questioning and I'm sure that shown through." Though Palin's day with Brian Williams was not considered anywhere near the disaster that her interviews with Couric had been, her e-mail again showed a candidate stuck in a defensive posture, eager to preempt any discussion of her own performance by criticizing the journalists with whom she spoke.

Veterans of other campaigns knew that some level of antagonism between the presidential and vice presidential operations was to be expected as aides in each group identified with others in their own sphere, but this was now on another level. The natural divide between the Palin plane and the rest of the campaign was threatening to become an uncrossable gorge. McCain loyalists privately grumbled that Palin's increasingly frequent refusal to follow orders proved she cared more about her own future than the success of the current campaign. On the other side of the fence, Palin loyalists found it ironic that her detractors blamed her for going off message when McCain had done the most irreparable harm to his own campaign by insisting that the fundamentals of the economy were strong.

As tensions boiled, the communication link between headquarters and the plane remained unreliable at best. With each new day came more confusion over the governor's schedule, stump speech, and evolving message. Though Steve Schmidt was clearly running the show, the role played by each member of the team beneath him was often undefined. The staffers on the Palin plane found adjusting to the disorganized structure, a reflection of McCain's own free-wheeling tendencies, difficult. Most of them were Bush administration veterans used to a painstakingly organized structure in which everything ran on time and as planned. Though the "Bush people" were now McCain people, there was an unmistakable divide between the new kids on the block and the aides who had been with McCain for years.

"This is how we do things at the White House," the newcomers often remarked in communicating from the Palin plane back to headquarters.

"Well, this isn't the White House, and we are doing things differently," was the most common response.

After its near collapse in the summer of 2007, which led to a massive reorganization, the McCain campaign had spent the last few months of the primaries operating as a cohesive, bare-bones band of true believers, many of whom worked without receiving paychecks. When it was forced to build a much bigger apparatus befitting a general election campaign, the split between the old McCain loyalists and the newcomers, many of whom might have worked for whomever the party's nominee happened to be, became all the more noticeable and problematic. Several of the Bush/Cheney veterans on the Palin plane formed close bonds with the governor during their short two months together on the campaign trail. Most of them were brought into the campaign very late in the game and had little or no contact with McCain whatsoever.

Jordan Hostetter, deputy director of advance for vice presidential operations at campaign headquarters, sums up the sentiment shared on both sides. "I would say there was a very clear distinction between the staff traveling with McCain and with what McCain wanted and the staff traveling with Palin and what they wanted," he recalls.

As difficult a time as the Palin operation had in relaying information internally, it was just as ineffective in dealing with the press. Requests for official responses or clarifications often went unanswered, and there was very little guidance in advance of major events. Reporters were taken completely off guard, for instance, when Palin discarded her stump speech one afternoon in Las Vegas and gave a rousing address on women's issues as she was flanked by five prominent female leaders. The speech should have made major news. Palin had spoken eloquently about equal pay, international justice for women, and other topics that she had barely alluded to since the first week of the campaign. But with no advance notice alerting the networks and national newspapers, reporters barely had time to type up hurried blog posts on the short van ride back to the airport, where they were ushered onto the plane for a three-and-a-half hour flight to Dayton.

As was her custom, Palin surfed through the cable news channels on board the plane, eager to hear the latest things pundits were saying about her. About halfway through the flight, she watched as MSNBC reported a breaking story just published on the *Politico*'s website. According to financial-disclosure statements, the Republican National Committee had spent over $150,000 to outfit the Alaska governor and her family.

Palin ripped off her high-end $350 Bose noise-canceling headphones. They were the very ones recently bought for her by a traveling aide who also made many of the top-dollar wardrobe purchases after the governor was outfitted at the convention. Still, Palin had never specifically asked for top-of-the-line goods, and she seemed genuinely shocked by the total bill being reported. "Who did that?" she demanded. "Who made the decision?"

Nobody responded because there was no simple answer. Despite Palin's refusal to wear some of the more expensive outfits bought for her at the convention, many of the items originally purchased were not returnable since they had already been altered. During her stop home in Alaska, she had picked up some of her own winter coats and other accessories, but staffers deemed many of these items insufficiently attractive for television. Back on the campaign trail, Palin would sometimes ask for a warm coat, more comfortable shoes, or a new skirt, and staffers would respond by purchasing high-end items in whichever city they happened to be at the time. They could hardly be blamed for doing so, since vice presidential operations director Mike Glassner had told five of Palin's traveling aides that they could spend up to $28,000 each, upon being advised by a campaign lawyer of the maximum an individual could contribute to the Republican National Committee. The sizable allowance was in addition to what had already been spent on the governor at the convention. The aides were told to put the items on their personal credit cards and they would be reimbursed.

The governor was not the only one in the campaign who was livid about the report. A heated debate ensued over whether the permission her traveling aides had been given to become personal shoppers to the tune of $28,000 each had been communicated through the proper channels. But one thing was clear: The nonstop shopping sprees added up to a colossal sum that threatened Palin's reputation as a middle-class everywoman.

Tracey Schmitt released a terse statement drawn up at headquarters to try to downplay the purchases rather than justify them: "With all of the important issues facing the country right now, it's remarkable that we're spending time talking about pantsuits and blouses. It was always the intent that the clothing go to a charitable purpose after the campaign."

Though this was one case in which others deserved far more blame than the candidate, the rather toothless official response from the campaign did nothing to diminish the questions that swirled about the clothing debacle and the role Palin herself had played in it.

The emergence of the scandal was nothing but a distraction as Palin prepared for her deposition to be conducted by independent investigator Tim Petumenos—the latest step in the seemingly never-ending Troopergate probe. Although the already-released Branchflower report had condemned her for abusing her power, the deposition was part of a separate Alaska Personnel Board inquiry, which could vindicate her. The personnel board investigation was launched after Palin effectively filed a complaint against herself on September 1, declaring the theoretically neutral three-person panel to be the proper forum for the probe rather than the politically charged state legislature. Petumenos would depose both Sarah and Todd Palin at their hotel in St. Louis on October 24, but the results of his investigation would not be made public until the very night before the election. While it was difficult to resist defending herself over the wardrobe story, Palin's traveling aides concurred that it was in her best interest to bite her tongue while she prepared for a deposition that could have profound implications for her career, no matter what the election result was. But Sarah Palin has never been comfortable with strategic passivity, and she was dying to get her side of the story out.

She guaranteed the reemergence of the dreaded wardrobe narrative a week later when she went off script to address the issue at a rally in Tampa, Florida. Before the event began, speechwriter Lindsay Hayes had been assigned to work with *The View* cohost Elisabeth Hasselbeck, who was traveling with Palin as she stumped across Florida that day. The conservative television personality's presence on the campaign trail was bound to generate significant coverage, and Hayes's task was to help Hasselbeck with her prepared remarks. Hayes mentioned to Hasselbeck the major address on women's issues that Palin had delivered in Las Vegas the previous week and how it had garnered very little media attention. Both women agreed that the clothing scandal, which had died down significantly by that point, was a prime example of the unfair press treatment to which Palin had fallen victim.

Hasselbeck scored a major hit with the crowd when she took the stage and accused the media of being "deliberately sexist" in its Palin coverage. "Instead of the issues," Hasselbeck said in a mad-as-hell tone that drew approving boos, "they are focused, fixated, on her wardrobe."

Hasselbeck's self-described "sassy" diatribe opened the door for Palin to elaborate on the point when it was her turn to address the rally. She began by noting that she had put on her "own" jacket that morning, not realizing how warm the Florida air would be. "This whole thing with the wardrobe, you know, I have tried to just ignore it because it is so ridiculous, but I am glad now that Elisabeth brought it up 'cause it gives me an opportunity without the filter of the media to get to tell you the whole clothes thing," she began. "Those clothes, they are not my property, just like the lighting and the staging and everything else that the RNC purchased."

As evidence that she was not an extravagant spender, Palin went on to cite her favorite consignment shop in Anchorage, her $35 wedding ring, and the pin she wore to honor her son's military service. She neglected to consider that the tirade against the clothes story that she was issuing in front of the television cameras would merely ensure its revival in news reports. As good as her political instincts were, she seemed to have an incurable blind spot when it came to recognizing the benefits she could reap through silence.

Senior aides at campaign headquarters were livid that Palin had gone off script to reinsert this no-win story back into the media narrative with little more than a week before election day. They were especially peeved since they had specifically denied her request made earlier in the day to set the record straight on the clothes issue. The news from Florida came on the heels of another *Politico* exclusive that had damaged the campaign's image. Reporter Ben Smith had written about the divide between campaign aides who defended Palin as a well-intentioned but mishandled political phenomenon and those who were actively spreading word that she was a self-absorbed disgrace. One unnamed Republican told Smith that Palin had decided to "go rogue" in making her own decisions.

CNN's Dana Bash, Peter Hamby, and John King followed up on the report about inner turmoil with a blog post on the network's website reporting that one anonymous aide had called Palin a "diva" who "takes no advice from anyone." The next domino fell when another unnamed staffer, whom *Politico*'s Mike Allen later described as "very senior," described the governor of Alaska as a "whack job."

Palin did not point fingers when the leaks came out. Instead, she channeled her disappointment inwardly, becoming uncommunicative at times but determined to muddle through to the end of a campaign that had now spiraled out of control. Some of Palin's most fiercely loyal aides worried that she might incorrectly think they had been leaking disparaging comments to the media. Suspicion and paranoia became the predominant sentiments in the campaign's final days.

The ill will between Mark Wallace and Randy Scheunemann that had begun before debate prep was now particularly acute. When conservative columnist Bill Kristol e-mailed Scheunemann, his longtime friend, asking who he thought was behind the "diva" comment and specifically questioning if it was Wallace, Scheunemann replied, "My very educated guess is mark wallace defnding [sic] his wife Knows king well, gives [Nicolle] deniability, spent several weeks through debate with her, not there now Real piece of [EXPLETIVE]." Kristol then sent another e-mail to Scheunemann, noting the unusual phrasing of a quotation in the CNN.com story: "Right—very weird quote: 'Divas trust only unto themselves, as they see themselves as the beginning and end of all wisdom.' Kind of pseudo-literary . . . doesn't sound like Schmidt or Salter—is Mark W a little pretentious in this way."

Scheunemann replied to Kristol, "He is beyond pretentious—and knows something about divas, being married to one Mw is arrogant, incompetent, annoying."

Kristol did not report Scheunemann's suspicions, but the *Politico* and CNN reports were damaging. Two days after Kristol and Scheunemann's e-mail exchange, Kristol's *Weekly Standard* colleague Fred Barnes went on *Fox News* and blasted Nicolle Wallace by name over the pricey clothes flap. "The person who went and bought the clothes and, as I understand it put the clothes on her credit card, went to Saks and Neiman Marcus where she was not asked to go by Sarah Palin, where Sarah Palin has never set foot, and bought these clothes and brought them back," Barnes said, getting the facts wrong. "The staffer who did that has been a coward." When *Special Report* host Brit Hume asked who the staffer was, Barnes named Nicolle Wallace. Steve Schmidt, furious that his colleague and friend had been attacked so publicly, put in a personal phone call to *Fox News* chairman Roger Ailes to complain about Barnes's accusations.

After learning that he had been mistaken about the details in question, Barnes apologized to Wallace the next day on Fox.

Schmidt and Rick Davis felt that the now-public internal discord had become serious enough to merit an investigation. With just ten days to go until the election, they instructed the campaign's director of administration and information technology specialist, Brad Loncar, to search through staffers' e-mails specifically for the keyword trifecta of "rogue," "diva," and "whack job."

The e-mail investigation failed to uncover the source of the leaks. It did, however, lead to the discovery of Scheunemann's e-mail to Kristol. When Mark Salter told McCain about what had been found, the candidate expressed his frustration that his longtime foreign policy aide had been engaging in that kind of finger pointing. "Oh, why did he have to do that?" McCain asked.

Steve Schmidt, also furious that Scheunemann had blamed the leaks on the Wallaces, challenged him to offer proof that they were responsible. Scheunemann had none. Still, he did not back down from his conviction that Mark Wallace had been undermining Palin. Incensed, Schmidt told Mark Salter, "We have to do something about this."

Salter and Rick Davis spoke to Scheunemann about the e-mail, and Davis subsequently told Schmidt that he would take care of it, leading Schmidt to believe that Scheunemann would be dismissed from the campaign. Schmidt then instructed Loncar to turn off Scheunemann's BlackBerry and campaign computer credentials.

Next, Schmidt placed calls to both McCain and Palin telling them that Scheunemann had been fired from the campaign because of the e-mail discovery.

When Scheunemann found that he could no longer log in to his campaign e-mail address, he asked Davis, his fellow longtime McCain veteran, what was going on. Davis told Scheunemann he would "fix it," and within an hour, the BlackBerry was working again. Scheunemann never really stopped working for the campaign, but top aides had already begun to spread word that he had been fired. In reality, he stayed at headquarters and continued to work through election day. He did not, however, travel to Phoenix on election night out of concern that no hotel room would have been reserved for him or that he might have to suffer some other indignity.

The other near casualty of the e-mail investigation was Maria Comella, the campaign spokesperson who had initially been assigned to travel with Palin as her press secretary before being sent back to headquarters after the convention. An e-mail conversation between Comella and the *Politico*'s Ben Smith was discovered, though she was not found to have leaked information about the campaign's inner turmoil. Word quickly spread that Comella would be fired, but staffers who knew her reputation as a loyal and competent professional stepped in to defend her, and Comella kept her position. Meanwhile, reports containing new anonymous quotations from "senior advisers" kept coming.

★ ★ ★

"IT'S ALWAYS DARKEST BEFORE IT'S TOTALLY BLACK."
John McCain was fond of repeating the line, which he attributed to Chairman Mao. It could not have been more appropriate during

the final week of the campaign. In stark contrast to the tight-knit, "no-drama-Obama" operation, the factionalism and behind-the-scenes backstabbing within the McCain/Palin campaign gave it the feel of a burnt-out organization with a terminal illness. Staffers with a perverse appreciation for the absurd marveled at how media reports were now dividing their colleagues, all ostensibly working toward the same goal of winning the election, into pro- and anti-Palin camps.

With each day, the prospect of victory seemed less likely. But instead of devoting all their energy to finding a way to come from behind and shock the world, the campaign was caught in a death spiral of paranoia and self-destruction. One high-level aide became so concerned with Palin's makeup artist's idle musings about the possibility of writing a book about the campaign that he dispatched a lower-level staffer to collect information about the prospect.

For her own part, Palin did not allow accusations that she was only concerned with self-preservation to diminish her growing assertiveness. After the bombshell report of Alaska senator Ted Stevens's felony conviction hit on the afternoon of October 27, she delivered a brief announcement to the traveling press in a hastily called news conference under a driving rainstorm in Richmond, Virginia. In a decided understatement, she called the conviction of Alaska's most storied political titan "a sad day" and said she hoped Stevens would "do the right thing for the state of Alaska."

Palin surely knew that the circumstances would eventually compel her to call for Stevens's resignation, but she was not about to rush into doing so. The next morning in Hershey, Pennsylvania, she huddled with aides in her hotel room as a bout of wintry weather forced the cancellation of two of her planned outdoor rallies. Members of Ted Stevens's Senate staff pleaded for her to hold off on a public pronouncement, but the jury had rendered its verdict, and so had she.

Top McCain aides wanted both members of the Republican ticket to put out a joint statement calling on Stevens to quit, but Palin again put her foot down. This time, she had a sound argument on her side. She was the governor of Alaska after all, and a joint statement, she felt, would send the wrong message to her constituents. The McCain aides relented, and Palin sent out her own remarks.

"After being found guilty on seven felony counts, I had hoped Senator Stevens would take the opportunity to do the statesman-like thing and erase the cloud that is covering his Senate seat," Palin wrote in a stinging rebuke e-mailed to reporters. "He has not done so. Alaskans are grateful for his decades of public service but the time has come for him to step aside. Even if elected on Tuesday, Senator Stevens should step aside to allow a special election to give Alaskans a real choice of who will serve them in Congress."

Palin's accusation that Stevens had not acted in a statesmanlike manner was a particularly stinging one. His conviction was later set aside amid stunning accusations of prosecutorial misconduct, and back home in Alaska, Palin would change her tone on the matter dramatically.

In an interview the day after the governor called on Stevens to resign, *ABC News*'s Elizabeth Vargas asked Palin if she would start thinking about 2012 if the Republicans lost on Tuesday. Recognizing the question as potentially damaging if she gave the wrong answer, Palin said she was focused on November 4. When Vargas pressed, asking the governor if the sexism she had experienced on the campaign trail made her want to give up and return to Alaska, Palin replied that she would not surrender to the shots she had taken. "I'm not doing this for naught," she said.

The comment seemed innocuous enough, but in an apparent attempt to reach for some newsworthy significance in the remark, ABCNews.com ran a story previewing the Vargas interview under the provocative headline "Sarah Palin Vows to Remain Player in 2012: 'Not Doing This for Naught.'"

Though it was clear from the transcript that the comment had been taken out of context, several media outlets succumbed to the pressures of the nonstop news cycle and repeated ABC's interpretation. Palin's chief adviser Tucker Eskew was particularly livid. After he placed a phone call to ABC, the network acknowledged the error and worked to correct it, but this, too, was handled clumsily, and the story had to be corrected and recorrected several times.

For the first time in weeks, Eskew ventured to the back of the campaign plane to make a statement to reporters. He was clearly irritated but composed himself enough to deliver a lengthy lecture using the *ABC News* situation as an example of how unfairly the media had treated Palin in perpetuating the "going-rogue" narrative. "I think [it's] beyond the pale," he said. "I think it's a time for us, as this campaign builds an occasionally acknowledged, but real momentum toward a very fast-approaching deadline of election day, that this record get corrected, get corrected very directly, and that some standards of fairness and accuracy be better observed."

Several of the reporters traveling with the Palin campaign had already discussed among themselves ABC's apparent misinterpretation of Palin's remarks. There was a general consensus among the traveling press corps that Eskew's concerns about the hazards of the fast-moving media environment were valid, and a certain amount of self-reflection took hold in the back of the plane. Perhaps the reports of internal discord had been overblown after all. But despite the mainstream media's mistake in this particular case, the events of the following Saturday would prove that reporters were not off base in probing the campaign's internal health.

Palin embarked on her final weekend of campaigning with a trio of rallies across central Florida. The bus was headed east between stops in New Port Richey and Polk City when the governor's cell phone rang. Her personal assistant, Bexie Nobles, answered it and told communications aide Brad Easterbrooks, one of the staffers usually by Palin's side, that the call was for the governor. Nobles took the phone to the back cabin, where Palin was sitting with Todd, and told her boss that the president of France was on the line.

Palin had been expecting the call from Nicolas Sarkozy, though few others knew about it. The request from the French president's office had originally been taken at her Alaska office and made its way to Steve Biegun, the former national security adviser to Senator Bill Frist, who had been brought in from the private sector to advise Palin on foreign affairs. Like Randy Scheunemann and the other policy advisers, Biegun was a staunch Palin loyalist. But he had left the trail the previous day to spend Halloween with his children and had yet to return.

The governor took the phone, and a heavily accented voice on the other end of the line told her that President Sarkozy was not yet on the call.

"Oh, it's not him yet, they're saying," Palin said, as she sat in the back of the bus next to Todd. "I always do that."

Just a couple seconds passed before Marc-Antoine Audette, a member of the French-Canadian comedy duo known as the Masked Avengers, came on the line and introduced himself as the French president. "Oh, it's so good to hear you," Palin said without a hint of skepticism. "Thank you for calling us."

With that, the game was on. For the next five minutes, Audette peppered Palin with a series of increasingly ridiculous statements and questions.

"I just want to be sure," Audette as Sarkozy said. "I don't quite understand the phenomenon Joe the Plumber. That's not your husband, right?"

"That's not my husband, but he's a normal American who just works hard and doesn't want government to take his money," Palin said.

"Yes, yes, I understand. We have the equivalent of Joe the Plumber in France. It's called 'Marcelle the Guy with Bread under his Armpit.' Oui."

This was one of several of the more absurd statements that might have alerted a cynic, if not a vice presidential candidate, that something was amiss. But Palin had no aides listening in or standing by to offer advice. She could not be sure it was a gag, even if she was beginning to hatch suspicions, as she assumed that the call had gone through the proper channels.

"Right, that's what it's all about, the middle class and government needing to work for them," she said.

At the front of the bus, Brad Easterbrooks could hear Palin spouting off talking points and became nervous that something was amiss. He had been tasked with briefing Palin for radio interviews, and he had not spoken to her before this call. He asked Andrew Smith whether he knew the identity of the person to whom Palin was speaking. Smith had no idea.

"She's on with the president of France," Nobles said.

Jason Recher asked which aide was listening in. No one, he was told.

"No principal makes a phone call to another principal without other people listening in," Recher said. "Is anyone taking notes?"

Well, Todd was back there.

Palin then drifted to the front of the bus and signaled, with a twirling finger at her temple, that the man on the other end of the line was out of his mind. One Palin aide later suggested that the governor might have thought Sarkozy had had one too many glasses of wine.

"Oh, we've been pranked," Palin finally said, but only after Audette ran out of material and revealed the gag. "What radio station is this?"

She handed the phone back to Nobles, who immediately hung up. "Guys, I've been pranked," Palin declared to the group, which included Florida governor Charlie Crist, who was sitting on a couch, surrounded by campaign staffers. Crist's jaw dropped, and a blank stare crossed over his face—he knew things were about to get ugly. Palin immediately retreated to the back cabin, and Tucker Eskew followed, trying to glean as many details as possible about the call. As the staffers on the bus went into emergency-response mode, Crist continued to smolder in uncomfortable silence. When the bus finally made it to the next stop, the governor of Florida silently disembarked, eager to leave the disaster zone.

Palin was visibly embarrassed as the seriousness of what had just happened sank in. She had the right to expect that a call from a foreign leader would be properly screened, but it was also careless of her to engage in such a conversation without even being handed a briefing paper on Franco-American relations. The call had been on the official schedule that went out to all campaign aides, but it had merely been labeled "personal phone call," which could have meant a conversation with her mother or son. And she had been far too indiscrete in some of the comments the fake Sarkozy had coaxed out of her. She had even agreed that she could see herself as president, "maybe in eight years."

Palin's demeanor softened a bit when she learned that Biegun, a staunch loyalist, had been responsible for allowing the call to go through. As her stunned aides looked on, Biegun was called and told what had happened. He was mortified and accepted full responsibility for not notifying the proper aides about the phone call and allowing the pranksters to get to the candidate, but Palin was determined to correct the mistake rather than reflect upon it.

"I'm sorry you feel badly this happened, but I don't want an apology right now," she said. "I want to figure out how to fix this. How do we get ahead of this?"

Just as it had done in response to the clothing story, the campaign released a short statement trying to downplay the incident. On the plane and back at headquarters, the reaction was mixed. Some staffers laughed it off. Others rolled their eyes and said, "Here we go again." Steve Schmidt, on the other hand, was apoplectic. Yet again, the chief campaign strategist was being called in to handle another screw up in vice presidential operations. He just could not wrap his mind around the idea that Palin and her handlers had thought nothing of accepting a call from a head of state without notifying the State Department or, for that matter, senior aides. How could she have thought John McCain would benefit from her taking a private phone conversation from the president of France without any meaningful preparation? Schmidt declared that no further item could go on Palin's schedule unless he personally approved it. Any remaining thread of a unified campaign organization had been definitively severed.

A few days after the election, Biegun fired off an e-mail to his fellow ex-Palin aide, Cecil Wallace. The Sarkozy incident had been weighing heavily on him, and he wanted to know whether Wallace thought it would be a good idea for him to hit the send button on an e-mail he had written to explain himself. Though he still accepted full responsibility for the fiasco, Biegun wanted to make sure everyone understood the mitigating circumstances. The setup for the crank call had been routed through a real Paris phone number, passed on by Palin's Alaska office, and it even used Sarkozy's communications director's real name. Since it was a cell phone call, it would have been impossible for anyone to listen in on another line. This was not the White House, with unlimited resources, and John McCain sometimes took calls from foreign leaders with the same minimal screening.

Wallace told Biegun if he wanted to send the e-mail to get it off his chest, he should do so, but it would only add fuel to the fire. Biegun agreed, and the e-mail remained in his drafts folder.

★ ★ ★

HAVING GOTTEN THROUGH THE seemingly unending series of unpleasant incidents, Palin finally received some good news just a few hours before the polls opened on the East Coast. The Alaska Personnel Board had released its finding that she did not abuse her power in allowing her husband and aides to pressure Walt Monegan to fire Trooper Mike Wooten, a direct contradiction of the state legislature's report filed by Stephen Branchflower. Independent counsel Tim Petumenos said that he had more information available to him than Branchflower did, including depositions from Sarah and Todd Palin, which helped to account for the different decision. Most significantly, the governor had flat out denied to Petumenos the existence of two private conversations that Monegan had cited, in which the then public safety commissioner said Palin complained about Trooper Wooten's continued employment. It was impossible for Petumenos to establish whether Palin or Monegan was not telling the truth since there were no witnesses.

Furthermore, Petumenos concluded that Branchflower had misinterpreted the law in concluding that Palin had acted unethically in failing to stop Todd Palin from applying pressure on Monegan. "To find that the Governor violated the Ethics Act by failing to control her husband's behavior would require one to add language to the Ethics Act that does not exist," Petumenos wrote.

The Petumenos report was an enormous weight off Palin's shoulders, but the relief would prove short-lived.

★ ★ ★

AT A FEW MINUTES PAST 6 A.M. the next morning, Palin burst into Wasilla's Kaladi Coffee with a troupe of Secret Service agents, her bleary-eyed staff, and the traveling press corps in close pursuit.

Before the arrival of the campaign entourage, the strip mall coffee shop had been empty, as the candidate's high school friend and former track teammate Chris tidied the place up to make it presentable for the television cameras trailing the woman who could rightfully claim to be the most famous Alaskan who ever lived.

"We've been planning this for a week!" Palin said. "We're coming to see Chris."

The governor gave her old friend the preferred Wasilla greeting—a tight bear hug—then asked for two lattes and five regular coffees for the Secret Service agents to split among themselves. "How's your mom doin'?" Palin asked, on the day when she would find out whether she would become the first female vice president of the United States. While Chris worked behind the counter, steaming the nonfat milk for the two lattes, a reporter asked the governor if she was confident of victory. Palin replied without hesitation, "Yep. I do believe that things will be very good at the end of the day here."

As she waited for her hot drinks, Palin's eyes wandered to a stack of newspapers by the door. She picked up a copy of the *Anchorage Daily News* and held the paper up for the cameras. Channeling the famous photograph of Harry Truman, she pointed to the headline, "Board Exonerates Palin." She smiled at Kris Perry. "Well, nice headline, Kris!" Palin said. "Kris, kudos to you!"

"Let's go vote!" Palin said to no one in particular. And with that, the entire traveling circus was out the door in seconds. After killing some time before the polls opened with a quick stop at her scenic lakeside home, the ringmaster arrived at Wasilla City Hall shortly before 7 A.M. It was still a couple of hours before the arctic sunrise, and the air was dark and cold. Legions of the hometown faithful had already gathered along the streets, tracking footprints in the snow from the many espresso shops around town. "Sarah! Sarah!" they chanted from the sidewalks, fueled as much by the excitement of the moment as by their white chocolate mochas and skim lattes. Many held up homemade signs to passing motorists, proclaiming their support for the Republican ticket and professing their admiration for the "Coldest State, Hottest Gov."

After she and her husband voted, Palin greeted reporters on the icy parking lot outside Wasilla City Hall before getting into her SUV. Next, the motorcade pulled up to the Mocha Moose. The governor stepped out of the SUV to approach the line of cars backed up at the drive-thru window and began shaking hands with drivers and passengers alike. "Oh, nice! Tell your hubby I say hi!" She then walked up to the tiny hut, its walls adorned with "Palin Fever" posters, and peered into the window to find some familiar faces. "Oh, the girls! How are you?"

After another heavy dose of caffeine, it was time for more questions from reporters.

What would she do next if she lost the election?

"You know, if there is a role in national politics it won't be so much partisan. My efforts have always been here in the state of Alaska to get everybody to unite and work together to progress this state. . . . It certainly would be a uniter type of role." It was an admirable goal but one that would soon fall victim to some unpleasant new realities.

The natural majesty of Alaska took over once the motorcade made it onto on the Glen Highway. Beams of sunlight were just beginning to poke through the soaring, icy peaks of the Chugach Range, turning the clouds an impossible shade of deep blue above the orange horizon. Sarah Palin's nine-week journey on the 2008 campaign trail was about to reach its conclusion, but it was merely the end of the beginning of her national political career.

$\star$ $\star$ $\star$

9. Can't Let Go

FOR THE FIRST TIME SINCE the plane became hers, there was plenty of room to spread out aboard Palin's "Straight Talk Air 2" as it made its final campaign voyage back to Alaska on the day after the election. Gone were most of the campaign staffers and the traveling press corps. The Secret Service agents were still on board, but their presence was a mere formality. The vice presidential candidate whom they had codenamed "Denali" was back to being just one of fifty governors.

No one tried to mask the gloomy atmosphere as Palin and members of her extended family who had made the trip to Arizona sat quietly in their seats. Many of them had their television sets turned to the postmortem coverage on *Fox News*. As disappointing as the election defeat was, the exit poll results were almost as disheartening: 60 percent of the people who had voted considered Palin unqualified to be president. Those numbers did not foretell a particularly easy mission to rehabilitate her image.

The mood on the plane darkened even more when *Fox News* correspondent Carl Cameron appeared live from the Arizona Biltmore Hotel. "There was great concern in the McCain campaign that Sarah Palin lacked a degree of knowledgeability necessary to be a running mate, a vice president, and a heartbeat away from the presidency," Cameron said. Palin and the three non-Alaskan campaign aides on board the flight—Jason Recher, Bexie Nobles, and Jeannie Etchart—watched in near disbelief as Cameron reported that anonymous sources had told him Palin did not know which countries were in NAFTA and did not understand that Africa was a continent and not a country. "And that there were times when she was hard to control emotionally," Cameron added. "There's talk of temper tantrums at bad news clippings."

The aides who shared these accusations with Cameron had stipulated that he not report them until after the election, and those ground rules indicated that the anonymous sources had assumed Obama would win. Her now-former senior adviser Jason Recher conferred with Palin's Alaska aides Kris Perry and Meg Stapleton about how to combat the whispering campaign among unnamed sources that was poised to expand. Perry asked if some of the campaign spokespeople could step up to deny the accusations. They could, Recher told her, but they probably wouldn't. The campaign was over. Loyalties were fragile. Some aides would speak out in public in support of Palin, but the detractors would drown them out.

There was a temporary reprieve from the misery of returning home, under the circumstances, when Palin disembarked from her plane in Anchorage. "2012! 2012!" chanted the crowd that had gathered to greet her. "We'll see what happens then," Palin told reporters.

When she arrived at her lakeside home, she retired to her office and began to sort through the boxes of mail that had accumulated over the past two months. Though the governor found solace in the hundreds of supporters who had written to her, Recher, Nobles, and Etchart had a more tedious task at hand. The three former campaign aides began the three-day process of conducting an inventory on all of the clothing purchased for the Palin family. Inside the Wasilla home, they went through every receipt, took a picture of every item, and laid the entire ensemble on the floor.

Palin's ever-concerned mother, Sally Heath, brought over all the clothes that had been given to her and Sarah's father, Chuck. In her eagerness to follow protocol and rid her family of all the fancy attire for which she had never had any real use, Sally accidentally donated one of her husband's own belts—his only good one, according to Chuck. He would laugh about the mix-up for months to come.

While John McCain retreated into relative isolation in the days after the election, Palin embarked on a national media blitz, despite the advice of loyalists from the campaign who told her she should disappear for a while and refocus on the job to which she was returning. Predictably, very few of the questions from the national journalists who interviewed her from her home in Wasilla touched on Alaska state business. When Palin answered *Fox News* anchor Greta Van Susteren's query about her presidential ambitions, she might have been expected to give a coy response, considering the 2008 race had ended just days earlier. But Palin was astonishingly blunt, using an "open-door" metaphor that she would revert back to in the coming months. "If there is an open door in '12 or four years later, and if it is something that is going to be good for my family, for my state, for my nation, an opportunity for me, then I'll plow through that door," she said.

In an interview with NBC's Matt Lauer, Palin seemed to struggle with coming to terms with the Katie Couric interviews that were in many ways the turning point of her candidacy. Palin told Lauer that she found Couric's now-famous question about the newspapers and magazines she read "a little bit annoying" and suggested that Couric had belittled Alaskans by assuming they did not have access to the same reading materials that people in Washington and New York did. But in a satellite interview with CNN's Larry King that aired the following night, Palin changed her tone. Now she said, "There was nothing off base [or] unfair about" Couric's questions, adding, "Certainly I should have done the interview and to attribute I think that interview to any kind of negativity in the campaign or a downfall in the campaign, I think is ridiculous."

Having left the teleprompter and talking points in the Lower 48, Palin was back to speaking off the cuff, but there did not seem to be any clear strategy or reason for the media blitz, other than to soak up as much postcampaign attention as she could. It would become clear in subsequent weeks and months, however, that Sarah Palin had joined a short list of celebrities who did not need to try to get noticed. She continued to garner more media coverage than any other Republican politician, and even the mundane task of pardoning a turkey before Thanksgiving turned into a YouTube moment. While the governor was being interviewed on camera, a farmworker could be seen in the background going about the bloody task of slaughtering turkeys. It was the kind of off-the-wall situation that seemed to occur wherever she went.

When Palin agreed to sit down for an interview in early January with conservative filmmaker John Ziegler, she had a new opportunity to sound off on the media's treatment of her during the campaign that had ended two months earlier. Ziegler caused a stir when he released advance clips of his film, *Media Malpractice*, which argued that biased coverage of the 2008 campaign had been a determinative factor in the election of Barack Obama and the destruction of Palin's reputation. Though Palin agreed with Ziegler that she was not "whining" about her press treatment, she spent the better part of the forty-three-minute interview unloading on the media and its campaign coverage. At one point, Palin wondered aloud whether political bias, sexism, or classism had been the determining factor. When Ziegler asked if she thought she would have gotten different treatment had she been Obama's running mate rather than McCain's, Palin was unequivocal. "I think they would have *loved* me as a candidate," she said.

Even former campaign aides who agreed that the media had treated Palin unfairly thought that agreeing to do the Ziegler interview was a big mistake. As a national politician, they thought, continuing to complain about her press treatment two months after the fact made her seem like a minor-league player. Though attacking the media was a sure way to fire up the conservative base, those voters would continue to support her regardless. At the beginning of the campaign, Steve Schmidt had told Palin to "never, ever, ever complain about the media" and instead to leave that task to the aides. "You need to be tough and strive to have the steeliness of Margaret Thatcher, Indira Gandhi, Golda Meir, Hillary Clinton," he had told her. Several of Palin's former aides who remained intensely loyal to her agreed that most Americans are turned off by high-profile politicians who play the victim card. "Our advice was, 'Turn the page. Let Sean Hannity, Rush Limbaugh, and Laura Ingraham beat up on the media. You are an elected official,'" says one former aide who still speaks highly of Palin. "But we never really succeeded at that."

According to Ziegler, members of Palin's inner circle in Alaska also advised the governor not to do the interview. She overruled them, he said in an interview for this book, because she felt so strongly about clearing the air. After Palin's communications director Bill McAllister complained when Ziegler released some clips from his interview before the movie's release, the filmmaker said that the governor phoned him to reiterate her support for his project.

"She did make it clear that she wasn't upset with anybody and that she clearly wasn't upset with me," he said. "We talked about how the media was attacking her on this issue of whining about the news media, which she was not doing. That was really her number one thing that she wanted to get across, was that she was not whining."

But whether she was whining or merely elucidating a point of view, many Alaskans wished she would stop talking about a campaign that should have been old news and focus on governing the state. Democrats who had worked closely with Palin on oil and gas legislation in particular were quickly tiring of the seemingly endless diatribes against the press in interviews, speeches, and even official press releases. "She really does think that the media is wrong, and she's right," Mike Doogan, a Democratic representative and former *Anchorage Daily News* journalist, said. "And she really does think that everybody would be better off if we just all did what she told us to do, and I credit her with sincerity there."

Though few Alaskans wanted to drag out the Troopergate issue even further, the McCain campaign's self-titled "Truth Squad," led by Palin's press secretary turned campaign spokesperson Meg Stapleton and McCain/Palin campaign lawyer Ed O'Callaghan, had left a lasting negative impact on public perceptions of Palin and her administration. As the politicization of the Troopergate issue heated up during the campaign, the Truth Squad had held a series of press conferences in Anchorage during which Stapleton, in particular, had been especially vitriolic in her comments about Walt Monegan—a well-respected former marine and Anchorage police chief—accusing him of "egregious insubordination" and a "brazen refusal" to abide by proper procedures. The charges seemed like quite a reach to many of the journalists who covered the Truth Squad press conferences and had known Monegan as a decent and respectful man. Stapleton's attempt to condemn him as an insubordinate was especially implausible since Palin, through Chief of Staff Mike Nizich, had offered Monegan a new position as head of the Alcoholic Beverage Control Board when he was told he could no longer be public safety commissioner.

Palin needed only to look at her still relatively high, yet indisputably declining, approval rating in Alaska to see that she had a lot of work to do to recapture her image as a pragmatic, nonideological leader. But she seemed more interested in maintaining her conservative base in the Lower 48 than with repairing relationships with Democratic state lawmakers with whom she had worked so well before the campaign. The rancor between Democrats and Palin emanated not only from the governor's side. Democratic representative Bob Buch, for instance, was among those who still had not gotten over Palin's claim that Obama "pals around with terrorists."

"When you think about that in the context of a black man running for office, she was inciting somebody to take the law into their own hands," he said in Juneau, three months after the campaign had ended. "And it only takes one bullet in this country. I gotta tell you, it was something that I was absolutely horrified to hear anybody say."

Reconciliation with legislators as incensed as Buch seemed unlikely at best, but when the new year rolled in, Palin did seem to make an earnest effort to refocus her attention on Alaska and the impending twenty-sixth state legislative session. She was well aware that every move she made would be met with intense scrutiny, as Alaskans and national political watchers were eager to see how she dealt with some of the more mundane aspects of running the state after having enjoyed several months as an international celebrity.

In early January, members of the bipartisan Alaska Senate governing coalition gathered at a retreat in the town of Girdwood to discuss their goals for the upcoming session. Seizing on the opportunity to apply her personal touch, Palin decided to make a surprise visit to the powerful governing bloc that included sixteen of the state's twenty senators (the four conservative Republican senators who formed the minority coalition were excluded from the majority for issues ranging from personal clashes to political differences). Her presence at the meeting was surprising enough, but in an earnest effort to demonstrate the high level of involvement she strove to showcase in the upcoming session, she also brought with her a half dozen of her commissioners and several members of her support staff.

The state senators were pleasantly surprised, but the warm feelings ended rather quickly once the governor opened the floor to questions. Asked to name the state infrastructure projects for which she intended to request funding from the Obama administration's stimulus package, Palin replied tersely that the information was "confidential." She was working on the details with the state's congressional delegation, the governor added cryptically.

"Well, if you are working with the congressional delegation on submitting requests, why can't you share it with us?" one senator asked.

Palin could not come up with a satisfactory response. She began to take a defensive posture, even as the senators insisted they were merely seeking information. Democratic senator Bill Wielechowski decided to try to ease the tension by lobbing a softball that he figured Palin would knock out of the park. "Governor, what are your priorities for the session?" he asked.

Palin tensed up at Wielechowski's question, which was later misattributed to Senator Gary Stevens in news reports about the incident. "You guys are always putting me on the spot!" she said.

After the awkward moment passed, Palin's chief of staff Mike Nizich took his turn. He insisted that the Palin team had come to the retreat to spark a new era of transparency and open communication between the executive and legislative branches. But more than one senator at the Girdwood retreat wondered how that sentiment jibed with Palin's refusal to answer simple questions about the direction in which she intended to take the state.

Their concern that the governor's top priority was no longer the state of Alaska would only escalate when she jetted off to the nation's capital for a weekend in late January. Though her Saturday-night dinner at the exclusive Alfalfa Club generated most of the headlines since President Obama was one of the guests, even more intriguing was Palin's arrival at a private dinner on the previous night at the northern Virginia home of Fred Malek, a longtime Republican fund-raiser and the former national finance cochairman of the McCain campaign. A few days after the election, Malek had lamented with the Arizona senator about the anonymous comments impugning Sarah Palin's character, which former campaign aides had been offering up by the handful. McCain and Malek agreed that the leaks were grossly unfair and reflected poorly on the senator and the campaign he had run. Malek suggested that he help try to make amends by connecting Palin with some well-heeled Washingtonians, and McCain agreed with the plan.

Malek invited about thirty guests from the political, business, and media worlds to his home, and it was quite a list indeed. Dick Cheney and his daughter Liz, John McCain, Madeleine Albright, Alan Greenspan, Andrea Mitchell, Barclays Bank president Bob Diamond, author Walter Isaacson, Charlie Crist, Diane Feinstein, and Senate Minority Leader Mitch McConnell and his wife, former secretary of labor Elaine Chao, gathered for the event, but no guest was in more demand than Palin. Malek granted the request of Senator Feinstein's husband, prominent businessman Dick Blum, who had asked to be seated next to the Alaska governor, but Palin seemed to win over everyone in the room equally. She had never before met former vice president Cheney, but after exchanging greetings with him, she immediately turned to his daughter and engaged her in conversation about how they were both mothers of five. As much as Palin had always disdained the "Washington cocktail circuit," she was suddenly milking it for all it was worth. "I think everybody was impressed with her," Malek recalls. "Andrea Mitchell, who's a tough and seemingly partisan on the other side reporter, said to me afterward, 'Boy I've sure turned around on Sarah Palin. She is very smart and very nice.'"

★ ★ ★

BEFORE THE CAMPAIGN, when Sarah Palin delivered her second State of the State speech in January 2008, she was just beginning her second year as Alaska's youngest governor ever, still trying to navigate the state's complicated web of personalities. Some legislators had privately derided her as a naïve political neophyte, but they dared not cross the woman whose approval ratings had crowned her America's most popular governor. A year later, when she entered the Alaska House chambers on January 22, 2009, the atmosphere could not have been more different. She had become one of the most famous women in the world, but Palin's arrival was greeted not with the adulation accorded a returning heroine but rather with tepid applause.

In drafting her remarks with the help of unnamed advisers from outside state government, Palin had reworked some of what Matthew Scully had penned for her in the concession speech she had been barred from delivering on election night. With the excitement of Barack Obama's inauguration still hanging in the air, she took a cue from Scully's playbook to sound a graceful note in acknowledging the new era of national government under the man she had accused of befriending terrorists. "His work is cut out for him, but if President Obama governs with the skill, grace and greatness of which he is capable, Alaska's going to be just fine," she said.

After her brief reference to national politics and the campaign from which she had just returned home, she was careful to focus on Alaska. She sprinkled her address with an array of similes and metaphors about "the great North Star" that were flowery enough to match the oversized corsage pinned to her chest: "Today, when challenges may seem as high as Mt. McKinley, and change as constant as the mighty Yukon flows, and political events send shockwaves through our foundation like the '64 quake—what do Alaskans do? We climb Denali, we forge the river, we rebuild a stronger foundation on higher ground."

Despite acknowledging a possible revenue shortfall in excess of $1 billion, Palin highlighted a series of ambitious projects on her agenda, including an in-state gas line, the construction of a road to Nome, and the ultimate goal of generating half of the state's electricity through renewable sources. Though she offered few details, no one could accuse her of not thinking big as she began the second half of her first term. Still, the only point in the speech in which legislators responded with a standing ovation was when Palin alluded to Ted Stevens's "long and distinguished senate career." Despite her newly achieved superstar status, the governor was left with no question about who remained the most revered Alaskan politician in state legislators' eyes.

The lawmakers' public reaction to the speech was generally positive. "I think that if there was any doubt in anyone's mind, it's clear that the governor is back in town," Senate President Gary Stevens (no relation to Ted) told the *Anchorage Daily News*. But in private, many legislators shared their concerns that the governor who had stood before them was no longer the same person they had known before she left for the Lower 48. Two House Democrats independently commissioned informal polls after the speech to find out whether their colleagues had noticed the same thing they had: that Palin had not made eye contact with anyone in the room. The results were unanimous. Everyone who weighed in agreed that the governor had been looking past everyone in the chambers.

The lack of visual communication might not have been particularly notable under normal circumstances. But to lawmakers, the State of the State speech was an important test of where Palin's attention was focused. Here was an opportunity to demonstrate that all the glitz and glamour she had enjoyed during the national campaign had not gone to her head and she was still just Sarah from Alaska. Instead, the consensus was that she was not really speaking to the people sitting in front of her. Democrat Mike Doogan, who joined his colleague Representative Lindsay Holmes as a recreational pollster, was particularly unimpressed. "It was clear to all of us sitting there that we were just props in this TV program, and she was talking over our heads to a national audience," he said.

In several dozen interviews conducted in Juneau during the 2009 legislative session and afterwards, lawmakers recounted many personal anecdotes that lent credence to Palin's distrustful views of many of her colleagues in the legislature and their leeriness of their returning governor. They also elucidated the clear struggle she had with returning to her old job. Though no one could have predicted her abrupt resignation a few months later, it was wildly apparent that the governor was not readjusting well and would have preferred to be spending her time anywhere but Juneau.

During the presidential campaign, Democratic representative Harry Crawford had spoken to the media about Palin only once, and it was to convey how happy he was for her. Once the legislative session began, however, Crawford was not so shy. He recalled an incident in which he found himself sharing an elevator with the governor, but instead of engaging in what had been her usual friendly banter, Palin did not even acknowledge his presence. "And that never, ever happened before," the brawny native southerner said. "It didn't matter where I saw her. When I saw her, she would make an effort to come and talk to me, to acknowledge me. A long time ago when I had run for office, but I hadn't been elected to anything, she would search me out whenever she was in a room full of people. She'd say, 'Oh, hi, Harry!'"

Lawmakers on both sides of the aisle complained about Palin's increasingly hands-off approach to pushing her legislation and brokering compromise. Republican representative John Harris, the former House Speaker and 2010 gubernatorial candidate who hired John Bitney and Christopher Clark as legislative aides after Palin fired them, echoed many legislators' view when he said that if he were governor, he would have put in more face time. "I'd make a point of periodically during the session trying to drop into legislators' offices unannounced," Harris said. "I would try to figure out when they didn't have a committee hearing or whether they weren't in this and that, and I'd go down to their offices and drop in and say, 'How are you doing? You got some issues that I can help you with?'"

Several legislators complained that they had found it impossible to get even a single meeting with the governor. Lawmakers in leadership positions had more luck, but many of them found her to be disengaged during important discussions about legislation, much of which her own administration had been pushing. When asked for her opinion, Palin would typically defer to the commissioners who accompanied her, and she had an annoying habit of focusing on sending and receiving e-mails in the middle of meetings, several lawmakers said.

"She'll get involved from time to time, but mostly you can see that she just tunes out on detail and pays more attention to playing with her BlackBerries," Republican Senate Finance Committee cochairman Bert Stedman said in February. "All of us pack either BlackBerries or iPhones, but it's rude to sit in meetings if people are playing around with their text messaging and their e-mails. We all get piles of e-mails to deal with."

Not every lawmaker we talked to spoke negatively about the governor. Palin's few staunch supporters in the legislature disputed the prevailing view that she had become disengaged. Republican Fred Dyson from Eagle River, a member of the four-person Republican minority caucus in the Senate, questioned whether some of the men in the state house suffered from jealousy over Palin's achievements. "I wonder if on some level, for some of these guys, if a bright woman being successful is upsetting," he said. "I don't know that, but it feels like it's something visceral like that."

"Visceral" was an apt word to describe the reactions of Alaska's political class to Palin upon her return home, just as it had been fitting to describe voters' reactions to her during the national campaign. Several of the state's top political players were quick to take their criticisms of the governor to a highly personal level in their conversations with us. One well-known Republican was not shy about comparing the Palin clan to a family of "half-wits." A prominent state Democrat seemed to cross the line of decency in disparaging the governor's family and even her decision to fly home from Texas so that her baby Trig could be born in her hometown. "You talk to people in Wasilla, this is not a normal, functional family," the Democrat said. "Personally, I don't really give a rat's ass. There's a thousand different ways to be a good family and loving parents. But don't trot yourself out as this mononuclear family and do all the bullshit that she's doing. Don't tell me you're a great mom when your water breaks and you get on a fucking airplane." It was not difficult to sympathize with Palin's growing certainty that a diverse group of people and interests had consolidated forces to line up against her or to understand why she would want to escape such a toxic environment.

Her personal life remained a topic of furtive conversation within the halls of the state house, but her political record was more openly disparaged. "It's absolutely weird," Democratic representative Les Gara explained of the strange bedfellows in Juneau who had coalesced against Palin. "You've got some of the legislators who their big interest is coming down here and getting capital projects for their districts, and they don't like her because she vetoed some of their projects. And you've got the 'chamber of commerce Republicans' who don't like her because they think she committed treachery by joining us on oil-tax reform last year. You've now got Democrats who tried to work with her who have seen a whole new side of her during the campaign."

Some of Palin's most persistent Alaskan adversaries with offices outside the capitol building were the leaders of the state's powerful energy companies that she had confronted during her first year in office. A representative of the oil industry, who agreed to be interviewed for this book under the condition of anonymity, began the meeting with an earnest assurance. "If you screw me, I'll screw you," he said, doing little to lessen the perception of the brass-knuckle tactics that Palin had stood up against early in her term.

The oil industry representative said that Palin had essentially nonexistent relationships with him and others in similar positions in the industry that drives the state's economy and fills the government's coffers. He acknowledged the political success the governor had achieved in combating what was widely seen as an entrenched culture of corruption but insisted that she had been perpetually unwilling to compromise. "I think her view is that it's going to be my way or the highway, and in that respect she is not at all different from, in many cases, Frank Murkowski—the person that she, I think, has stated over and over again is not representing the interest of the state of Alaska," he said. "There doesn't seem to be a lot of room for an intellectual debate on the merits of the issue. You sense that when you go into a meeting, she's already made up her mind, and there's not a negotiation."

The oil industry representative was particularly miffed by Palin's campaign trail rhetoric on energy issues, which he found disingenuous. "'Drill, baby, drill!' But what does that mean?" he asked. "Her tax policy here doesn't lead people to drill."

As she had throughout her career, Palin continued to find lukewarm support from the leadership of the Republican Party of Alaska. Even though her efforts to expose his ethical breaches at the oil and gas commission later became one of her most frequent campaign talking points, party chairman Randy Ruedrich continued to insist that any old wounds from that time had healed. But a February visit to the tiny party headquarters off Fireweed Lane in Anchorage revealed hints that the relationship between the state party and its celebrity governor was far from peachy. The main office prominently featured a wall of framed photographs of George W. Bush, Dick Cheney, Ted Stevens, Don Young, and Lisa Murkowski, but it took a closer inspection of the makeshift Republican Wall of Fame to reveal the small cutout picture of Rosy the Riveter's body with Sarah Palin's face that hung off to the side and below the other esteemed GOP leaders.

Despite her clear discomfort with the unaccommodating political environment in Juneau, Palin did make at least one more attempt to show some good will toward the legislature a couple of weeks into the session. This time, she invited the twenty-six members of the bipartisan House governing caucus, composed of twenty-two Republicans and four Democrats, to a meeting in Speaker Mike Chenault's chambers. During the question-and-answer session, freshman Democrat Bob Herron asked the most memorable question of the meeting: "What's it like being a national celebrity?"

Palin answered that it was a big responsibility to be a positive role model but that national politics merely served as a distraction to the task of governing Alaska. Fairbanks Republican Jay Ramras happened to be next in line for a question. Ramras had long harbored a particular distaste for Palin's cult of personality and what he saw as her tendency to lower the political discourse into sound bites more befitting a talk radio host than the governor of a state. An orthodox fiscal conservative, Ramras had had an antagonistic relationship with Palin since he helped lead the unsuccessful fight against her push to increase the oil companies' tax burden. When he cast his ballot in November, he had voted enthusiastically for John McCain but could not bear to check a box next to Sarah Palin's name. In a nod to his view of the Joe the Plumber phenomenon as a sheer absurdity, Ramras wrote in McCain's name for president and Rocky Pavey, his own plumber in Fairbanks, for vice president.

"Well, governor, my constituents are not at all distracted by national politics," Ramras said in a matter-of-fact manner that everyone in the room knew was designed to get on Palin's nerves. "They need in-state gas, they need affordable energy, and they need it now. Where's the enabling legislation?"

Palin answered that her administration was focused on developing policies that they would soon unveil publicly and that she felt as strongly about building an in-state gas line as he did. After a few more exchanges, the room went silent. "No more questions?" Speaker Chenault asked.

Ramras raised his hand again. "I got a question," he said. "What are we going to do about these hungry people out in western Alaska? They are hungry; they are hurting. What are we going to do about getting food to them?"

"Well, we are working on it," Palin said. "We've sent a team onto the ground."

Palin asked her chief of staff Mike Nizich to delve into specifics, and Nizich deferred to Deputy Chief of Staff Randy Ruaro, who listed the steps the government was taking to deal with the burgeoning crisis in the bush. But Representative Ramras was not convinced that the administration was doing enough to react to the western Alaskan emergency, where a combination of high fuel prices, a poor fishing season, and a particularly harsh winter threatened to leave thousands of Alaska Natives without enough food. The situation had begun to receive significant media attention a few days earlier, after a letter written by Nick Tucker, of the village of Emmonak, was published in a local newspaper, circulated around the blogosphere, and ultimately picked up by the national media.

The Palin administration had initially said the situation did not meet the legal criteria for declaring an economic disaster, but that only fueled the anger of those who accused the governor of both inaction and a lack of foresight. Several critics noted that Walt Monegan had predicted the crisis in western Alaska in an e-mail to some of his administration colleagues in July 2008 to tell them he was being fired as public safety commissioner: "Given the gathering storm of a questionable fishing season and the escalating price of fuel in our state, there will be serious stress placed upon communities and residents who will struggle with the coming winter's challenges," Monegan had written in his farewell letter, five months before the food crisis hit.

Following the tense exchange in the Speaker's chambers, Ramras and Palin retreated to their battle positions, and a series of dueling press releases ensued. The Fairbanks Republican fired first, accusing Palin of putting her national political ambitions ahead of her stewardship of the state. "The governor's horizon includes dinner at the Alfalfa Club and who is the best Republican candidate for governor in Texas," he said, referring to her trip to the exclusive Washington event and endorsement of Rick Perry in the Texas GOP primary. "She's active in pursuing those interests, but extraordinarily passive to the bureaucratic mess when it comes to the plight of Alaskans out in western Alaska, and I have no tolerance for that point of view."

Palin responded by calling Ramras's accusations "incomplete and misleading" and accused her most vocal critic in the legislature of playing politics with the issue. "This is particularly concerning since he knew I would be attending a meeting with his entire caucus that evening," Palin said. "Representative Ramras did not mention the specific issue of using state assets to me personally at the meeting. Instead, I read about it later in the press release."

More than two weeks later, Palin joined with Christian evangelist Franklin Graham's charitable organization and traveled to the bush to help deliver food donations to two of the impoverished villages along the Yukon River. But Ramras, who had organized his own food drive weeks before Palin made her trip, could not resist the opportunity to twist the knife a little further with a backhanded compliment. "I applaud her for following in the footsteps of what Alaskans and nonprofits and churches have already been doing over the last four to six weeks," he said.

The back-and-forth with Ramras was a precursor to several other highly charged public battles Palin would engage in with state officials and private citizens. She and her communications team had apparently decided that they would respond to every insult, large or small, rather than leaning on her role as the leader of the state to rise above such pettiness.

Ramras's accusation that the governor had taken her eye off Alaska during the food crisis came on the heels of Palin's establishing a political action committee called SarahPAC, with its headquarters in the Washington, D.C., suburb of Arlington, Virginia. Unlike most politicians' political action committees, SarahPAC was not initially designed to support other candidates who might one day be called on to return the favor. Instead, it was mainly intended to raise money for Palin's own travel, primarily to events in the Lower 48. Though political action committees are common among politicians with high national profiles, the establishment of SarahPAC angered the growing list of Palin critics who were all the more convinced that she was no longer interested in the job of being governor. Ramras was particularly incensed. "If you go on SarahPAC, I can show you [House Finance Committee Cochairman] Mike Hawker's accomplishments because they are all listed on SarahPAC as her accomplishments," he said in an interview from his Juneau office in February. "It's not a thread and it's not a stream. It's a river of disingenuousness that runs through this administration and runs through SarahPAC, and she is a political sociopath in the way that she conducts herself."

The frequency with which Ramras unleashed his diatribes against Palin had the effect of mitigating their effectiveness. Still, as the legislative session wore on, the sneaking suspicion among lawmakers that Palin's decisions were being made through the filter of her national ambitions grew into an assumption that was taken for granted. In an interview from his senate office, Senator Bert Stedman framed his remarks as if Palin were already running for president. "I wish Sarah all the luck in the primaries of the next presidential election," the Republican from Sitka said during the middle of the legislative session and months before Palin resigned the governorship. "And if I have the opportunity, I'll vote for her again."

In Juneau, odd-numbered years like 2009 are typically more noted for deliberation and long debate than for tangible accomplishments, as newly elected legislators join long-serving lawmakers to embark on the arduous process of drafting and debating bills in committee. Pieces of legislation often do not receive full votes until the second year of the session when reelection battles loom again. Especially during the coldest days of January and February, the process moves at a tedious pace before the first signs of spring seem to remind everyone in the capitol that there are only ninety days allotted to complete the state's business.

The culture of the Alaska House of Representatives's floor sessions can be reminiscent of a high school classroom, and after being the center of attention during every minute of every day amid the lightning-fast pace of the national presidential campaign, Palin must have found the legislature's proceedings rather tiresome. The defining characteristics for someone watching from the outside are the inside jokes, note passing, and apparent anxiousness on the part of many participants to get the proceedings over with. On February 11, for instance, House members began a floor session by standing and reciting the Pledge of Allegiance and listening to an invocation. Next, House Speaker Mike Chenault invited lawmakers to introduce guests sitting in the two viewing galleries that flanked the small chamber. Representative Charisse Millet stood to acknowledge her "very first boyfriend," who had made the trip to Juneau. Her colleagues laughed as Speaker Chenault shrugged. "Alrighty then," he said. "Any messages from the governor?"

"No messages from the governor," the administrator sitting next to the Speaker replied.

"Any messages from the other body?"

"No messages from the Senate."

Any other communications?

Nope.

Representative Nancy Dahlstrom asked the House to honor the military. There were no arguments. Representative Les Gara then delivered a short yet passionate speech on the state's foster-care program, noting that 40 percent of Alaska's foster-care children end up homeless, but several of his colleagues seemed not to be paying very much attention. After Gara finished with the only policy-related remarks of the thirty-minute session, Representative Richard Foster, a Vietnam veteran turned public servant from Nome, rose slowly from his seat wearing his favorite American-flag tie. "*I* want to talk about my kids," Foster said, as his friends in the crowd chuckled at their beloved colleague's joke about his last name. "I'm just sick of everyone talking about my kids all the time."

After the laughter died down, Representative Peggy Wilson stood to express her concern that the ninety-day legislative session was not long enough. The old 120-day session was superior, she said, because it gave legislators more time to communicate with one another, whereas the 90-day version put too much stress on everyone. House Majority Leader Kyle Johansen closed out the day's events by noting that there were two birthdays in the building. "I'm going to talk about the one in our body," he said. "Someone else can talk about the other person if they want to." Johansen then roasted Representative Millet, reminding everyone that her first boyfriend was still in their presence and relating the story of how she once killed a caribou with an axe. Everyone sang to Millet, but no one took Johansen up on his offer to acknowledge the other birthday in the building, Governor Palin's.

Two days later, the House convened again. After each representative pressed the button on his or her desk to confirm attendance, the chaplain delivered a lengthy invocation, and the Pledge of Allegiance was recited. Introductions came next, and almost every representative stood and applauded to acknowledge the slew of family, constituents, and other guests who came in to witness the proceedings. Even lobbyists were given their due recognition. After Governor Palin's message condemning the federal stimulus package was read, a "brief at ease" was called, at which point Representative David Guttenberg took the opportunity to ask some of the guests in the viewing galleries about their concerns, while other lawmakers discussed their weekend dining plans. The Island Pub was a possibility for at least two members.

Members employed the young House pages, dressed in identical navy-blue suits with yellow ties, to help them pass a steady stream of notes to one another. It was impossible to escape the distinct feeling that more than a few of these notes had little to do with state business. Johansen again took the floor and broke the "at ease" by bringing to a vote House Bill 100, which would ensure that the entirety of a recently lengthened nature trail in his home district would be named the Joseph C. Williams Sr. Coastal Trail. Representative Doogan rose from his seat. "I support this bill because I actually want to see him do some work," he said, referring to the pledge Johansen had made to help out on the project. Laughter ensued, and the bill was passed by a unanimous vote. Next, it was Representative Harry Crawford's turn to speak. He wanted to take the opportunity to praise his son Trevor for winning his school's seventh-grade spelling bee. "Takes after his mom," Speaker Chenault joked, causing another bout of laughter. The session was adjourned after forty-two minutes.

After firing up massive crowds from Maine to California, hobnobbing with world leaders, and receiving celebrity treatment wherever she went, Sarah Palin must have felt as though reimmersing herself in the proceedings of the Alaska State Legislature was a giant step backwards. After all, she was used to achieving progressively higher goals in what had been, until then, a charmed political career. In an April press conference, she stated that her office still had a good working relationship with the legislature—"as far as we know." It was a telling caveat. "It's tough to judge the happiness quotient in this building," she added.

$$\star \quad \star \quad \star$$

10. Only in Alaska

OBSERVERS OF SARAH PALIN'S political career have often wondered whose voices in her inner circle carry the most weight. Considering the fast-moving revolving door of advisers that marked Palin's time in elected office and her enthusiastic embracing of new media that has allowed her to communicate with the public directly, some have wondered whether she truly trusts *anyone* beyond herself. Kris Perry is her closest counselor outside of her family, having been with her every step of the way from Wasilla City Hall through the vice presidential campaign and beyond her resignation from the governorship. But Perry is much more a friend and confidante than an adviser equipped to navigate the wilds of national politics. Aside from the vice presidential run and Palin's forays into the Lower 48 afterwards, Perry's political experience has been confined to Alaska. It seems clear that Palin still values her advice, but not even Perry can match the clout that Todd Palin enjoys.

In some ways, Todd Palin's life represents the Alaskan ideal. Part Alaska Native, he has spent his entire life in the state, working with his hands to achieve a comfortable lifestyle even before his wife hit the big time. When his family had earned enough money from Sarah's government salary and his jobs on the North Slope oil fields and Bristol Bay commercial fishing vessels, he did not just move into a bigger house; rather, he built his beautiful lakeside home himself, along with "a few buddies." Though a former member of the Alaskan Independence Party and currently a registered Republican, Todd has never pushed a political agenda other than his wife's. His utter lack of pretension made him perhaps the most popular figure on the vice presidential campaign trail among the staffers who spent time around him. "No matter how hard you wanted to call him Mr. Palin, you finally just gave up and called him Todd," recalls campaign photographer Shealah Craighead.

Washington politicos used to dealing with demanding personalities and fragile egos found Todd's straightforwardness and disdain for extraneous fuss refreshing qualities indeed. And in a campaign dogged by allegations of wasteful wardrobe purchases, the most extravagant item the candidate's husband purchased for himself after that first week of September was a pair of blue jeans from Macy's, which he paid for with his own credit card. After the election, Todd was far more proactive about keeping in touch with former staffers than his wife was.

"What you see is what you get with him," an aide who traveled with Todd on the campaign trail says. "He's very comfortable in his shoes. He knows who he is. He is never threatened by a successful, powerful wife, not threatened whatsoever. He is very, very proud of what she has accomplished."

But just as it is not entirely fair to assign simple adjectives to Sarah Palin's character and motives, Todd is also far more complex than the portrayals of him have suggested. During his wife's time in office, Palin critics accused her husband of being a "shadow governor," a charge his defenders considered both sexist and inaccurate. But the Troopergate case in particular provides clear evidence of a "First Dude" who was highly engaged in his wife's political life. Revelations that Todd, ostensibly a private citizen, had called Walt Monegan into the governor's state office to discuss firing Trooper Wooten were particularly damaging to the governor's insistence that she did not allow her husband to apply pressure in making the case for Wooten's termination. It would require quite a leap of faith to accept the premise that Sarah Palin was oblivious and powerless to intervene against her husband's clearly inappropriate use of the governor's office to push a personal grievance.

During his wife's vice presidential campaign, Todd took a leave of absence from his job with British Petroleum and divided his time between appearances with his wife, going off to stump on his own, and manning the fort back home in Alaska. On the trail, he spent much of his time in states like Maine and New Hampshire, where his reputation among outdoor sportsmen preceded him. Todd would often share with his traveling aide his amusement that the campaign thought him important enough to give speeches on his own. "I'm just the provider for the family and a support for her," he would say.

As the campaign's deficiencies became increasingly apparent, Todd took an active role in trying to get things running more smoothly. He regularly placed phone calls to senior adviser Jason Recher to discuss the governor's schedule and tried to ensure that briefings were well organized and that events ran on time. Todd was unafraid to let aides know when he sensed that his wife was being overworked, reminding them that she still had to take care of Alaska business on top of her duties as the vice presidential candidate.

Despite his ruggedly laid-back persona, he is by all accounts more sophisticated and tuned in to complicated political dynamics than he lets on in public. John Green, the Washington lobbyist who helped manage the Troopergate matter for the national campaign, found him particularly helpful. "Todd had an encyclopedic memory of every legislator—friend, foe, what they're doing," Green says. "It was amazing. It was like the *Almanac of American Politics* pulled down to the state legislature."

In contrast to Sarah, who tends to operate on instinct and is not averse to straying from the plan if the situation merits it, Todd is doggedly methodical in dealing with both his wife's concerns and his own. Less meticulous snowmachine racers ("snowmobile" is a word confined to the Lower 48) marvel at his organizational skills, which have helped him narrow the gap with faster competitors in more than a few Iron Dog competitions. "If you go to Todd and say, 'Where's your spare socks?' he'll say, 'In the second bag, to the left, at the bottom wrapped in a blue bag,'" says Jim Wilke, one of the founders of the now-famous Iron Dog race.

One trait that Todd shares with his wife is his single-minded competitiveness. Just as Sarah found remaining a minor player in local government unfulfilling, Todd has never been satisfied with being just another snowmachiner. The physical courage, mental tenacity, and unbridled ambition it takes to reach the level of success in the sport that Todd has achieved were all on display at the twenty-fifth annual Tesoro Iron Dog race he participated in that winter, as his wife navigated the perhaps equally icy and challenging terrain of the state legislature.

Snow-covered pine trees towered over the narrow road leading into Big Lake in the predawn hours of February 8, 2009. They glistened under the moonlight as a few light flakes fluttered gracefully to the icy surface. The thermostat had already climbed to a merciful eight degrees Fahrenheit—a refreshing improvement over the previous year's start, when the temperature had hovered around minus thirty. Once the racers headed up north and began to approach Nome, the temperature could drop to a sadistic sixty below zero. That was part of the allure for Todd Palin, his partner Scott Davis, and the twenty-nine other pro class teams who had entered this year's 1,971-mile snowmachine race, the world's longest and toughest, as any of its riders would have you know.

On this winter morning, incoming vehicles were directed toward a makeshift parking lot on the frozen lake where "No Wake" signs and wooden docks stuck out of the ice. Pilots who would soon be called upon to assist the fortunate racers who could afford their services circled their tiny biplanes around the lake and periodically came in for landings along the sheet of ice that served as a makeshift runway. Not every team had a plane to help resupply and update them at the various checkpoints on the weeklong trip through Nome and on to Fairbanks, but only those who did had any chance of winning the thing. A Caribbean-themed establishment called The Islander was perched on the edge of the frozen lake, with fake palm trees adorning the snow-covered "beach." Inside the bar and restaurant, three men decked out in racing gear washed down plates of eggs and breakfast potatoes with a round of Coronas—an unusual pregame drink considering the grueling journey upon which they were about to embark.

But the members of Team #22, Todd Palin and Scott Davis, were certainly not downing any beer in the hours before their start time. They were by far the most decorated team in the race: Palin was a four-time Iron Dog winner, Davis had a record seven victories. At forty-four and forty-nine years old, respectively, Palin and Davis had more experience between them than any other partnership. But it was their self-assured aura, more than their age, that put the other teams in their shadow. From their eye-catching black and orange Arctic Cat uniforms to their custom-made helmets with their names splashed artfully across the back, they exuded professionalism and confidence. Even their impeccably polished snow-machines seemed to shine a bit brighter than everyone else's. Sarah Palin was not the only one in Alaska's "First Family" who understood the importance of looking the part.

Though their top-notch equipment and the attention they generated made it clear that they were among the elite, Palin and Davis exhibited none of the pretensions common to world-class athletes. As the clock ticked closer to the 11:00 A.M. start time, they chatted warmly with competitors and well-wishers inside the heated tents in the middle of the lake. Though many Iron Dog teams break up after a year or two, succumbing to arguments generated by the race's rigors, the Palin and Davis partnership had lasted through six years of ups and downs. Davis attributed their longevity to his ability to get along with Todd. "A lot of it is his personality," he said. "You know, [he's got a] level head and a lot of determination and drive."

The rigors of the campaign had left him little time to participate in early training for the 2009 event, but Todd insisted that he had caught up after November 4 and was actually more prepared than he had ever been. Still, he acknowledged that this year's outing was unlike any of the previous races. "Oh, it feels different," he said. "It was different after Sarah became governor as well, so this is just another step up. We keep ourselves grounded every day. You don't let the attention go to your head."

A few minutes before the start, Governor Palin emerged from the Suburban where she had been keeping warm and out of sight. She and her seven-year-old daughter, Piper, were dressed as if they intended to make a last-minute entry into the race themselves, wearing matching green and black Arctic Cat gear from head to toe. Despite the biting cold, the only protection the governor wore for her head was a pair of designer sunglasses.

Had she been in any other state, Palin's presence at a well-attended public event would have created a much bigger stir. But here in Alaska, she was merely the center of attention, rather than the generator of a mob scene. The team of Secret Service agents and aides who perpetually surrounded her on the campaign trail were gone, and just two staffers trailed Palin as she strolled along the frozen lake. Young children sporadically approached her for pictures and autographs, but there was no visible security and not a single television camera in sight as the governor blended with the other fans and family members. Instead of wild cheers and sustained applause, there was only the occasional, "Hi, Sarah," as she made her way through the crowd. Her constituents were here for a snowmachine race, not a celebrity sighting.

Just as its organizers had predicted, the 2009 start drew the largest crowd in Iron Dog history. The race had come a long way in the twenty-five years since president and race director Jim Wilke helped found it. Back in 1984, he had huddled with some Alaska bush pilots and racing friends to design the route using wall maps and magic markers. Then the most pressing concern had been the need to reach an understanding with the leaders of the already well-established Iditarod dog-sled race, many of whom considered snow machining a mechanical abomination. To get approval for the first race, Wilke and the other founders had to agree to hold off the start date of the Iron Dog until after the Iditarod had ended in late March. But by that time, the ice had already begun to melt in Anchorage—where the race was slated to begin—so the manufacturing sponsor chartered a couple of airplanes and moved the whole operation further north.

"We flew twenty two-man teams, forty snowmobiles, and the riders to McGrath," Wilke recalls, "and then did a loop up there trying to make sure we got enough mileage so we could call ourselves the world's longest snowmobile race."

Todd did not compete in that inaugural race, but he had become a fixture of the event by the early 1990s and was about to embark on his sixteenth start. With just a few minutes to go before the teams began leaving the starting line in two-minute intervals, he kissed his infant son, Trig, good-bye and made his way to his colorful snowmachine set on two orange skis, with Sarah and the kids' names in script beneath the windshield. Palin's two teenaged daughters, Bristol and Willow, approached him one last time before he would cross the finish in Fairbanks on the following Saturday, barring any unfortunate incidents, of course. "Love you, Dad," Bristol said.

No one in the family seemed particularly worried about the treacherous journey their patriarch was embarking on. They had been through this many times before. Asked about her state of mind before her husband set out across the arctic frontier, mercilessly exposed to the elements, Governor Palin's body language matched her calm demeanor. "Not so much nervous, just curious to see how conditions are, how they are doing," she said. "They know what they are doing, you know? They are pretty hardcore."

Not many would argue with that assessment. But hardcore and experienced as they were, Todd and his fellow racers faced very real dangers. The requirement that racers take designated breaks along the way helps reduce the risk of exhaustion, and the two-person teams ensure that no one is completely alone. But teammates do not ride side by side and are sometimes separated by as much as a mile as the rider in the back tries to avoid some of the snow dust kicked up by his partner.

The advent of reliable GPS systems has helped ease some worries, but the most important safety advance has been the invention of electrical hot grips on the snowmachines' handles. Still, frostbite remains as common as bumps and bruises are in other sports. The duct tape that Todd and other competitors use to protect the patches of their faces most vulnerable to exposure can help, but it rarely eliminates frostbite. Racers wear layers beneath their outerwear, including Gore-Tex shells and polypropylene fabric. Rubber "bunny boots," designed by the military to withstand temperatures of sixty below, protect their feet. As counterintuitive as it may be, overheating can sometimes pose the greatest threat, especially for the less experienced riders, who tend to overdress. Yes, veterans insist, it is possible to overdress for the Alaskan wilderness in February.

No one has been gravely injured or killed in the race's twenty-five-year history, a record more attributable to good luck than anything else. Todd Palin knew as well as anyone that diligence and innovation could never eliminate the dangers completely. In the 2008 race, he was somewhere along the Yukon River when his snowmachine hit a barrel beneath the snow. His chest protector might very well have prevented him from becoming the Iron Dog's first fatality, as he flew several feet into the air. Davis saw the crash out of the corner of his eye, went back to retrieve his partner, and took him to a clinic in Galena. Afterwards, Davis told the *Fairbanks Daily News-Miner*, "It looked like he hit a roadside bomb." With a mangled snowmachine, Palin refused to quit. He held onto his pride as a defending champion (as well as his broken arm) and completed the race with Davis towing him across the finish line. The story was a favorite with John McCain, who liked to retell it when introducing his running mate's husband at rallies. Indeed, there was no better anecdote to capture the essence of Todd Palin.

As he revved his engine at the start of the 2009 race, Todd had to put aside the danger and channel his nervous energy as he listened to some final words of encouragement from his wife, who was acting in her role as governor. "I know enough of you to know too that the last thing you want to hear is a politician talking to you right now," she said. "So I just ask for God's protection to be all around you guys. Come back safe, sound, ride hard, ride fast, have a blast. We love you guys. Go, Iron Dog!"

Palin and Davis were assigned to hit the trail directly after Andy George and Dwayne Drake, the team to whom they had just barely lost in 2006. In that race, Palin and Davis used their patience and experience to take advantage of some of the worst conditions the Iron Dog had ever seen and led most of the way. But on the race's final morning, they lost ground, and George ended up colliding with Davis and knocking him off stride. George and Drake won the nearly two-thousand-mile race by a mere second. "It still burns a hell of a lot when you lead the whole entire race and lose by one second by somebody running into you when you're on the trail," Davis said. For his part, Todd Palin publicly blamed the astoundingly narrow defeat on a faulty fuel pump and says he harbors no hard feelings toward Andy George. But others in the sport say that Todd has not really let the incident go so easily and shares Sarah's tendency to hold long-standing feelings of resentment toward those who cross him. "If he feels he's been wronged, it takes a long time for that to go away," says Jim Wilke, who knows all four racers well. "It was a grudge. He ranted and raved about it."

Just before they were sent off, Palin, Davis, George, and Drake all stepped off of their snowmachines and exchanged handshakes. But the moment of sportsmanship soon passed, and after George and Drake were released on the trail, it was time to focus. Davis shared some last-minute strategizing with Palin before retreating to his machine and pulling it up to the starting line. At precisely 11:28 A.M., Piper Palin waved a ceremonial green flag, and Team #22 was off, a cloud of snow dust in their wake as the Palin family cheered along with the other spectators.

For the next week, Palin and Davis carved their way through the topographical odyssey that had grown very familiar to them over the years. From the suburban Mat-Su Valley, they headed north into Alaska timber country before dropping into a featureless white expanse that stretched into the distance as far as the eye could see. Next they passed through the majestic Alaska Range before arriving at the tiny interior settlements of Nikolai and McGrath, where temperatures hover near sixty below. The biggest adrenaline rush came along the Yukon River where racers can hit speeds of over one hundred miles per hour. The favorable conditions that prevailed throughout the week benefited some of the younger, flashier racers but worked to the detriment of Palin and Davis, who relied on their steady pace and formidable mechanical skills to compensate for their relatively advanced age. As the Palin family kept track of Todd's progress from their Wasilla home using an online GPS system on the race's website, they saw Team #22's chances for another win slip slowly away. By the time Davis and Palin headed back out after the temporary reprieve provided by the annual "halfway banquet" in Nome, they knew the race was already out of reach. Their competitive juices still flowing, the teammates made a gentleman's bet over whether their 2007 course record of thirty-eight hours, seven minutes would be broken. Ever the optimist, Palin said it would stand, while Davis said it would fall.

In anticipation of the big crowd expected at this year's finish, officials had moved the ceremony to downtown Fairbanks, where racers would roll in under a twenty-five-mile-per-hour speed limit after crossing the official finish line at Pike's Landing across town. Sure enough, a crowd of several hundred people had gathered by mid-morning and spread throughout the downtown area, including across a footbridge spanning the frozen Chena River. Once again, just a couple of staffers flanked Governor Palin as she waved and greeted spectators. Despite the absence of a media scrum, the governor's press aide, Sharon Leighow, was on her toes, looking out for troublemakers. "No interviews!" she snapped at the one reporter who was scribbling notes several feet away. Even at the festive Iron Dog, the media was treated as a dangerous threat, rather than an opportunity for the governor to talk about something other than her problems in Juneau.

Todd Palin and Scott Davis approached the ceremonial finish line shortly before 2 P.M. The crowd applauded respectfully, knowing full well that the race had been a disappointment for the team. Palin climbed off his machine, took off his goggles, and ripped the tape off his cheeks, revealing some minor cuts and discoloration. Davis looked much worse. Two large splotches on his neck had turned a nasty shade of brown. Of course, the seven-time champ acted as if it were no big deal. The frostbite would heal in a few days, at which point he would simply shave the dead skin off with a razor. Just another day at the office.

The first thing Todd wanted to know was the winning time, and he was told that the new champions, Todd Minnick and Nick Olstad, had clocked in at thirty-seven hours, nineteen minutes. Palin and Davis's record had been shattered. Doing little to mask his disappointment over his sixth place finish, he accepted a pink vitaminwater from his partner and downed it in two gulps. Todd Palin does not like to lose.

After her husband exchanged conciliatory hugs and kisses with his family, Sarah Palin participated in a quick interview with *Fox News*'s Greta Van Susteren, who was on hand at the finish line. Van Susteren was at the center of the Palins' postcampaign media strategy. The reporter's husband, former Hillary Clinton supporter John Coale, had advised Palin on setting up her political action committee, SarahPAC, and continued to play a prominent role in running it. He too was present in Fairbanks.

Van Susteren had made the trip to Alaska primarily to interview eighteen-year-old Bristol Palin, who had decided to begin a national media blitz after becoming a new mom. Having spent the months during and immediately after the campaign lambasting the media for addressing Bristol's pregnancy at all, Palin's implicit consent to her daughter's decision to place herself in front of the cameras marked a notable change.

In the interview from her Wasilla home, Bristol struggled to offer a coherent viewpoint on the issue of abstinence, which she encouraged teens to embrace while also declaring it to be "not realistic at all." As she stumbled through her answers, more or less as any unseasoned eighteen-year-old would be expected to do, Sarah Palin suddenly appeared on the set cradling her infant grandson, Tripp.

"I wasn't expecting you," Van Susteren said to the governor as the video cameras swung around. "We were down on the river, had to come up just for a second, wanted to say hi," Palin said, giving a strong impression that this "spontaneous" moment had actually been far more calculated than she was letting on. Palin said she was proud of her daughter for taking on an advocacy role on the issue of teen pregnancy. "Many, many, many young parents have been successful in raising their children and have raised healthy, happy, contributing members of our society," she said. "Bristol will, and Levi, they will be parents like that. We're real proud of them."

Bristol agreed that the baby's father, Levi Johnston, was a good father. "He's just in love with him as much as I am," she said.

But the Palin family's tone would change just a few weeks later when Bristol and Levi broke off their relationship. In April, Johnston appeared on *The Tyra Banks Show* with his mother, Sherry, and sister,

Mercede, and answered questions revealing intimate details of his relationship with Bristol. He also alleged that Bristol would not let him take his son out of the Palin's house very often and suggested he might start a custody battle.

Instead of ignoring Levi's personal accusations and keeping her public statements confined to state business, Palin dispatched Meg Stapleton, her political spokesperson. Stapleton released to the media an extraordinarily abrasive statement for a sitting governor to make against a teenaged father and his family, especially considering how passionately and eloquently Palin had spoken out about the media's obligation to leave her own children alone. "Bristol did not even know Levi was going on the show," the statement said. "We're disappointed that Levi and his family, in a quest for fame, attention, and fortune, are engaging in flat-out lies, gross exaggeration, and even distortion of their relationship. Bristol's focus will remain on raising Tripp, completing her education, and advocating abstinence." Sort of. But that was just the beginning. Next, Stapleton ramped up her public evisceration of the teenaged father of Sarah Palin's grandson: "It is unfortunate that Levi finds it more appealing to exploit his previous relationship with Bristol than to contribute to the well-being of the child. Bristol realizes now that she made a mistake in her relationship and is the one taking responsibility for their actions."

Predictably, the blogs, tabloids, and cable news shows could not get enough of the escalating saga in which Palin had now fully engaged herself. But a few days after the statement's release, the governor seemed to recognize that the charges against Levi had been counterproductive. "He's a young kid," she said during an interview with Alaskan radio show host Eddie Burke. "Every kid that age, they've all got a lot of growing up to do. But forever and ever, he's gonna be Tripp's father and he's gonna be part of our family. And we will love him and help him through this also."

But, when Levi again took to the media to weigh in on Palin's resignation months later, the governor could not resist dispatching Stapleton once again to treat the teenager as if he were a worthy political opponent, rather than a kid looking to drum up some attention. "It is interesting to learn Levi is working on a piece of fiction while honing his acting skills," Stapleton wrote.

Whether Levi's comments were true or false, Palin lacked the discipline and self-assuredness to ignore them. Todd and Sarah had clearly decided to respond to any perceived slanders against their family, no matter where they emanated from and how irrelevant in the long run they might be. They are both natural fighters, and their gut instincts scream for them to protect their kin from anyone who would challenge them. But someone with Sarah Palin's innate political skills should have realized that fighting a family feud out through press releases would not help a potential presidential hopeful who has struggled with her well-deserved reputation for mixing her public and private lives. The Palins' instinctive combativeness, a trait that Sarah and Todd share, has gotten them further than most would have thought possible. But it has also led them to behave in self-destructive ways that a political partnership anchored by more deliberative dispositions might have avoided.

* ★ ★ ★

11. Alaska Outgrown

O N MARCH 17, 2009, the halls of the capitol building were abuzz with word of the surprising phenomenon that had been occurring all morning. Speculating about Sarah Palin's methods and motives had become a favorite Juneau parlor game, and no one was quite sure what to make of this latest hand she had dealt the players.

Until that day, the governor had been acting as if she had developed an allergy to the building and had quarantined herself on the third floor. Legislators and aides had agreed that she had come back from the campaign trail having learned an unconstructive lesson from the persecution she felt she had suffered. She had apparently concluded that she could no longer trust anyone entirely but herself and Todd. However, Palin had spent this morning casually strolling through the halls of the capitol, particularly resplendent in her eye-catching black-and-blue plaid suit and matching purse. She was sticking her head into lawmakers' offices as she passed by, calling out in a cheerful tone, "Hey everyone!" or "How's it going?"

Some of the very people who had spent much of the legislative session lambasting her for being aloof were now the ones most greedily lapping up this unexpected personal attention from the governor. She suddenly reminded them of the "old Sarah" who used to pop in on legislators throughout the session. Her personal touch was still there, after all.

Palin's most notable appearance of the morning came at about 8 A.M. when she wandered into the press room on the ground floor. Only two reporters were present: Rena Delbridge from the *Fairbanks Daily News-Miner* and KTUU's Rhonda McBride, whose relationship with the governor remained uncomfortable due to the lingering fallout from McBride's former employment as Palin's rural adviser. McBride had left her job in the Palin administration and returned to the media after becoming frustrated with the governor's relative lack of interest in addressing pressing rural issues. Palin had not offered McBride any face time and had not responded to her e-mails on the sky-high sexual-assault rates in the bush. McBride had also become convinced that the job should belong to an Alaska Native.

After exchanging pleasantries with Delbridge and McBride, Palin gazed around the mostly empty room, appearing surprised by the lack of reporters present. The governor set her purse down on the floor and pulled up a chair. "I understand your questions aren't getting answered," she said.

The two reporters were surprised by Palin's words. Sure, they did not always receive immediate responses to their questions and requests for comment, but neither of them had complained about any particular communications issues. Perhaps Palin's concern stemmed from the magazine article that had just been published online in Condé Nast's *Portfolio*, which took a highly critical look at the natural gas–pipeline project and suggested that the governor herself was the biggest obstacle to its construction. Or maybe she had simply woken up that morning and decided to try to recapture her pre-campaign relationship with the Juneau press corps.

"I don't know if there's some kind of communications glitch," Palin continued, "but I want you guys to be able to get to me directly if you have questions."

The governor asked for and received each of their e-mail addresses and plugged them into one of her two BlackBerries. She then sent test messages to Delbridge and McBride. Both reporters now found themselves with better access to the superstar governor than anyone in journalism. Palin asked that they contact her directly whenever they needed an official comment or clarification.

Her reference to a "communications glitch" seemed, to them, to acknowledge that her press office had proved ineffective at mitigating the damaging media reports that continued to pile up. Palin wanted more control. Whether it was handling the basketball in the final seconds of a high school game, plotting her own campaign strategy, or responding to critics, she had always trusted her own instincts above all else, and she felt that she could not even depend on the filter of her own press office. But given the kind of scrutiny she was now under, her belief that she had the time and wherewithal to act as her own communications shop was simply unrealistic, and the decision would quickly come back to haunt her.

Initially, the reporters who benefited from this new access were as pleased about the situation as Palin was. The afternoon of the day the arrangement was made, Rena Delbridge e-mailed Palin to ask for a comment on a story, and the governor responded almost immediately. The *Daily News-Miner* reporter began to reach out to Palin frequently as part of her reporting, and the governor would usually respond within an hour or two, no matter what the time of day. Palin seemed pleased to have the ability to communicate directly, especially on energy issues—an area in which Delbridge specialized. When Delbridge asked if she could give Palin's e-mail address to other state journalists who were asking for equal access, the governor joked that the reporters were really going to push her to the limit but said it would be fine if she shared it.

To Palin, there was nothing particularly unusual about granting journalists this level of access. After all, back in her days in local government, it had been a normal occurrence for reporters from the *Mat-Su Valley Frontiersman* to dial up Mayor Sarah with a question about the new sports complex or a recent road repair. Furthermore, she had learned a tough lesson during the vice presidential campaign about the consequences of cutting off the media. But she still did not fully appreciate the changes in the game that came with the new league she was in. For Sarah Palin, the most intensely watched Republican in the country, interacting with the media was not a one-person job.

Two weeks after their initial e-mail exchange, Delbridge began working on a story about Palin's public support for Ted Stevens, which had become emphatic after his felony conviction was thrown out. Another factor that had made Palin's return to Alaska politics exceedingly difficult was the aftershock of her appeal in October for Stevens to resign. Many political watchers still see Palin's abandonment of Stevens as the determining factor in his narrow reelection defeat to Democrat Mark Begich. It is difficult to overstate how beloved Stevens remains among Alaska state legislators from both parties, most of whom refer to him in conversation as "Ted." Even before his felony corruption conviction was set aside, many state Republicans saw Palin's denouncement of Stevens as a betrayal.

Though Palin had expressed her sympathy and outrage over the way Stevens's case had been handled, she had not signed on to Randy Ruedrich's call for the newly elected Begich to resign from

the Senate so that a special redo election could be held. Though undoubtedly bold, the state GOP chairman's proposal was unlikely to
convince the Democrat that he had not won his Senate seat on his
own merits. Even Republican senator Lisa Murkowski said that
throwing out the November election results was "not an option."

Delbridge wanted to know what Palin thought about the proposal, so she e-mailed her on April 2. The reporter worded her question fastidiously, asking if Palin agreed that Stevens should get a new
election and if she agreed that Begich should step down until then.
"I absolutely agree," Palin responded a mere twenty minutes later.

Many more reporters than not would have deemed that answer
clear enough to insert it into their story immediately. But Delbridge
wanted to be particularly thorough, considering the significance of
the three words Palin had just written. After all, a governor doesn't
issue a statement to the press every day calling for a freely elected
senator to resign. Delbridge wrote back immediately and asked her
to be very clear. Did she agree with the Republican Party's release?
Did she really think that Begich should step down so there could be
a special election?

Yes, Palin responded two minutes later; she agreed with all
of that.

After the *Daily News-Miner* ran its blockbuster scoop featuring
her call for Begich to resign, Palin was asked about her stunning
statement at a news conference in her Juneau office. By this point,
she had taken the time to consider more deeply the implications of
a governor's asking for a sitting senator's resignation. "I didn't call
for Begich to step down either," she said. "I said I absolutely agree
that Alaskans deserve a fair, untainted election for the United States
Senate seat."

Except, that was only part of what she said, as she knew quite
well. Palin also knew there was evidence, in the form of an e-mail
exchange with a reporter, that she *had* called on Begich to resign,

but that did nothing to dissuade her from presenting what she wished she had said rather than what she actually did say. It was another example of her tendency to refuse to acknowledge any error in judgment and to offer instead a version of events that could easily be proved false.

This infallibility syndrome would only push her back into her corner. Still, Palin had not completely given up on reestablishing a bond with the reporters who covered her. One morning, she left in the press room a container filled with cupcakes and a handwritten note: "Left over from Piper's birthday party. Enjoy! Sarah." But the experiment with direct e-mail communication was waning. She was running out of tactics to try to change the increasingly poisonous dynamic in the capitol, and she still lacked a coherent strategy to do so.

During this period, Palin's communications shop embraced a new, rather unorthodox tactic in dealing with the local media. Instead of responding to potentially damaging stories by providing statements to reporters, they tried to preempt the reports. When journalists submitted inquiries about matters including the food crisis in western Alaska, legislators' condemnation of the gas-pipeline project, and Palin's new energy proposal that appeared light on details, the governor's communications shop sent out preemptive press releases before the stories could make it to print. The pattern became so obvious that reporters in Juneau began to joke among themselves that they should start keeping track on a wipe board of how many times their private inquiries led to public statements. Palin's decision to mitigate the role of the press rather than working with it to communicate her agenda reflected the bunker mentality once again in full effect inside the governor's office. She had tried to reach out, and it hadn't worked. Now the media was back to being the enemy.

As the session wore on, Palin suffered a seemingly endless series of political setbacks. The stress of it all was clearly getting to her, as the already svelte governor had lost a considerable amount of weight since the campaign ended. In her public statements, she increasingly struck the tone of a besieged leader whose enemies continued to come at her from all directions. She could not move on from the disappointment of the campaign and seemed to be struggling with the realization that she no longer enjoyed the job to which she had been elected. Her sense of victimhood showed particularly in her responses to the myriad of ethics complaints filed against her, which were in part facilitated by the ethics-reform legislation that Palin herself had worked with lawmakers to pass and by her repeated calls to hold her administration accountable. Any Alaska citizen could submit allegations of ethics violations to the attorney general, and for a small group of state residents, the filing of such complaints became something akin to a full-time job. Though the complaints were designed to be issued anonymously, great fanfare accompanied the announcement of formal allegations ranging from improper use of government aides' time to Palin's dressing inappropriately at the Iron Dog race (she was accused of serving as a walking billboard for her husband's sponsor, Arctic Cat).

In the months after the presidential campaign, new complaints against Governor Palin became regular occurrences. At least twenty were filed between August 2008 and July 2009, six of them by one woman: Anchorage resident Andree McLeod, a former Alaska House of Representatives candidate and self-described government watchdog. In an interview at an Anchorage coffee shop, McLeod said her ethics crusade against Palin had caused the state of Alaska to blacklist her. She had applied for about one hundred government jobs, she said, but been rejected for every one. McLeod was not shy about revealing her ultimate goal in filing the incessant complaints and promised more in the future. She wanted Palin impeached. Though the *Anchorage Daily News* and other media reported each complaint against Palin, the manifestly frivolous nature of many of the charges gave them a cumulative "boy-who-cried-wolf" effect. Palin could surely have been excused for becoming annoyed by the incessant stream of accusations and the toll they took on her and her staff, but by responding publicly to each and every one, she and her communications team were once again brought down to the level of the critics, who were often flailing around for anything that might stick. Furthermore, if the complaints were so absurd and trivial, Palin might have shown real leadership by rising above them and focusing on governing, rather than spending most of her working hours immersed in them and releasing triumphant public statements every time a new complaint was dismissed.

In response to the complaint about her Arctic Cat clothing at the Iron Dog race, which was issued by blogger Linda Kellen Biegel, Palin resorted to a tone more befitting the "anonymous blogosphere" she professed to detest. "This would be hilarious if it weren't so expensive for the state to process these accusations and for me to defend against these bogus harassments," Palin wrote in an official press release. "Yes, I wore Arctic Cat snow gear at an outdoor event, because it was cold outside, and by the way, today, I am wearing clothes bearing the names of Alaska artists, and a Glennallen Panthers basketball hoodie. I am a walking billboard for the team's fund-raiser! Should I expect to see an ethics charge for wearing these, or the Carhartts I wear to many public events? How much will this blogger's asinine political grandstanding cost all of us in time and money?"

Palin's exasperation might have been understandable had she been responding off the cuff in a live interview, but she was not. She had all the time she needed to consider it before hitting the "send" button, but she could not help but let her raw emotions show.

It wasn't just frivolous ethics complaints that caused Palin and some of her staff to overreact to perceived menaces. In December 2008, we put in a phone request to the governor's closest aide, Kris Perry, to interview Governor Palin for this book. Within minutes, Perry called back with Palin by her side and extended an open invitation to come to Alaska for an interview. "What's in it for me?" Palin jokingly shouted into the phone. But the arrangement was revoked a couple of weeks later when Stapleton e-mailed us to say that the governor would no longer agree to be interviewed. We were disappointed but pleased that several of her friends and family in Alaska did agree to participate. One afternoon, while conducting interviews in Juneau, we decided to take a short walk to catch a glimpse of the governor's mansion, which is located on a busy street in the heart of downtown. On our way back to the capitol, we crossed paths with Piper Palin and two of her friends, who were evidently returning home from school. We had known Piper as a frequent guest in the back of the plane during campaign flights between cities. Her energy and humor made her a favorite among the ever-exhausted members of the traveling press corps, and she seemed excited to chat briefly with us about her return to Alaska.

We thought little of the unexpected encounter until about an hour later when a voicemail arrived from an irate Sharon Leighow, the governor's deputy press secretary. Leighow explained that a security official had notified the governor that Piper had stopped to talk to a pair of strangers on the street and that we matched the description. Palin, of course, knew quite well who we were and that we were well acquainted with her daughter on a friendly basis. In fact, one close aide told us that Palin frequently used to encourage Piper to venture to the back of the campaign plane to butter up the press corps. But that didn't stop the governor from dispatching an intermediary to attempt to intimidate us with a series of absurd accusations. Leighow accused us of "cornering Piper at her bus stop for comment." Then she added for good measure, "We don't appreciate you being here, and we don't appreciate you stalking the governor as you have been."

It was quite jarring to be accused simultaneously of cornering a seven-year-old and stalking the governor of Alaska, so we called Leighow back to explain the harmless circumstances and make it known that we took issue with her attempt to bully us. Leighow apologized for having been "terse" in her voicemail and promised to pass our message on to the governor. She did not respond to an e-mail we sent her the next day, which raised our concern that she had tried to use this harmless incident to try to chase us out of Alaska.

As Palin's disposition continued to reflect the cold Alaskan winter, she found another extraneous opportunity to lash out at her critics when Juneau state senator Kim Elton announced that he was resigning his seat to take a job in Washington as the director of Alaska Affairs at the Department of the Interior. A Democrat, Elton had been one of Palin's chief antagonists in his role as chairman of the bipartisan Alaska Legislative Council that voted to investigate Troopergate. Still, his departure from state government did not seem an appropriate occasion for anything other than a simple well-wishing from Palin's office. Instead, she could not resist the opportunity to get in the last word. "Senator Elton pledged his allegiance to President Obama last summer," her press release began. It was difficult to fathom what Palin had to gain from this jab, other than the satisfaction of making sure that Elton knew she had not forgotten the past.

Filling Elton's now vacant Senate seat soon became one of the most dramatic battles of the legislative session. If all had gone according to tradition, the local Democratic Party in Juneau would have submitted three names for Palin's consideration, and the governor would have chosen one of them to replace Elton. But, consistent with the vitriolic exchanges taking place daily between state Democrats and the executive branch, the process did not go so smoothly. The Juneau Democratic Party submitted only one name to Palin: State Representative Beth Kerttula, the House minority leader and a respected lawmaker who had long been considered Elton's heir apparent. A ten-year veteran of the House, Kerttula should have been a shoe in. But there was one small problem. And like many of the conflicts that arose during the session, it stemmed from something that had happened during the campaign.

On August 29, the day Palin was named to the Republican ticket, Kerttula's office had received a call from the McCain campaign. They wanted her to be ready to be interviewed by the national press in an hour. Kerttula was one of the many Democrats in the Alaska House of Representatives who had worked closely with Palin on the governor's two most important accomplishments: the natural gas pipeline and oil-tax reform. The two women had a good personal rapport, and Palin assumed that Kerttula would be a strong surrogate to highlight her bipartisan approach to governing. But Kerttula refused to go along with the plan. She liked Palin on a personal level and was proud of what they had accomplished together, but she was a Democrat and a firm Obama supporter. She was not about to go on national television to promote John McCain's candidacy. Two days later, Kerttula did agree to talk to the *Juneau Empire*. But the interview did not go exactly as Palin might have hoped. "I've worked real well with the governor, but she's not ready for this step," Kerttula told the newspaper. "She's not ready to be a heartbeat away from the presidency."

That unexpected blow was apparently still ringing in Palin's ears five months later when she refused to appoint Kerttula to Elton's Senate seat. Instead, the governor asked for any interested candidates to apply for the job. Thirteen Juneau Democrats, including

Kerttula, took her up on the offer, but Palin selected Tim Grussendorf, a legislative aide. Though Grussendorf was the chief of staff for Democratic state senator Lyman Hoffman, his party allegiance was somewhat suspect. He had only recently changed his affiliation from Republican to Democrat, thus meeting the legal requirement that Elton's replacement be a member of the same party. The Senate Democrats rejected Grussendorf and the Juneau Democrats then submitted an expanded list of four names for Palin to choose from. The governor in turn ignored each of those submissions and nominated college admissions director Joe Nelson, who quickly became the second Palin pick rejected by the Senate Democrats. The standoff devolved further when Palin submitted her own list of three names for the Democrats to consider, two of which they had already turned down. The political posturing continued, and the era of bipartisan cooperation that Palin had helped foster two years earlier was officially a distant memory.

After a flurry of public charges and countercharges, a deal was finally brokered to appoint Democrat Dennis Egan, the former mayor of Juneau and son of Alaska's first governor. Clearly disappointed not to be chosen, Kerttula expressed her support for Egan and said she harbored no ill will toward Palin. Though she tried not to take personally the governor's refusal to appoint her to the seat, Kerttula couldn't help but wonder about Palin's motives when she reflected on the saga in an interview for this book two months later. "I'm the minority leader of the Democratic Party in the state house, [and] I was also very firmly for Barack Obama," she said. "It's very hard for me to even understand how you could hang on to that and act out of spite for a state Senate seat. I mean that's also something that's also kind of mind-boggling, but I have certainly had people tell me things that lead to the conclusion that that may have been what it was."

The saga surrounding the appointment to the vacant Senate seat also provided the impetus for Palin's most crushing political defeat of the 2009 legislative session: the failure to confirm Anchorage attorney Wayne Anthony Ross, her nominee to replace the recently resigned attorney general Talis Colberg. While Colberg was known for his unassuming nature and disdain for the limelight, Ross was easily recognized around Anchorage as the driver of a bright red Hummer with a vanity license plate showing off his initials, "WAR." A former columnist for the now-defunct *Anchorage Times*, he could always be counted on to make provocative pronouncements railing against gun regulation, abortion, and giving Alaska Natives preference over urban residents in hunting laws. W. A. R. just might have been the only living Alaskan considered more divisive than Sarah Palin, which was why her decision to nominate him for the job of chief law enforcement officer demonstrated her strategy of doubling down on her hard-right conservatism and embracing conflict.

Surprising no one, W. A. R. did not shy away from past controversial comments during his Senate confirmation hearing. When asked how he would view cases involving gay Alaskans, in light of having previously referring to them as "degenerates," he offered up the following line of reasoning to try to put legislators' minds at ease: "I hate lima beans. I've never liked lima beans. But if I was hired to represent the United Vegetable Growers, would you ask me if I liked lima beans? No. If I disliked lima beans? No. Because my job is to represent the United Vegetable Growers."

W. A. R. suffered a serious accusation from a woman known to be a Palin critic who said she once heard him defend men's right to rape their wives—a charge he vigorously denied. He also said that he had been falsely accused of being the guest of honor at a "machine gun shoot" in Seward, in which participants set off dynamite charges using automatic weapons. Though Governor Palin also mentioned this accusation, it was never discussed in the floor debate. Nonetheless, W. A. R. insisted that this allegation had impugned his reputation. After his failed confirmation, he said that the only time he had ever discharged a firearm in Seward was when he shot a seventy-pound halibut with his revolver while fishing in the harbor. He had been concerned, he explained, that the fish might damage his boat if he tried to reel it in.

Though he certainly had his fair share of fierce detractors, W. A. R.'s larger-than-life personality attracted legislators who admired his ardent support for Alaska's sovereignty and Second Amendment rights. A few days before the vote, he appeared to have the support he needed for confirmation—until, that is, he decided to weigh in on the Juneau Senate seat appointment controversy. "It seems to me the most important thing that can be done by the Senate is not argue with legal or illegal, but to appoint somebody to represent Juneau," he said to two reporters who captured the remark with their tape recorders.

The casual approach to the law that the comment seemed to imply created immediate controversy in light of the nature of the job for which he was applying. W. A. R. later explained that he had not meant to suggest that legislators should ignore the law in filling the appointment but rather that they should focus on getting it done while the attorney general's office researched the legal ramifications. Still, he had gone too far this time in many lawmakers' eyes. His nomination was rejected by a vote of 35–23, as he looked on helplessly from the viewing gallery. "It was like going to your funeral without having to die first," he said. W. A. R. was convinced that he had been rejected in retaliation for Kerttula's being passed over for the Juneau Senate seat. And so the vicious cycle of antagonism in Juneau continued to spiral downward.

W. A. R. had earned the dubious distinction of becoming the first nominee to head a state agency to fall short of confirmation in

Alaska's history. Though she could not have anticipated the exact manner in which he would go down, Palin's nomination of such a controversial figure in the first place had been a dare that the legislature gladly took her up on. Even though she voted in favor of confirming him, Anchorage Republican Lesil McGuire echoed the common sentiment that Palin's nomination of W. A. R. had lacked the spirit of accord that she had so expertly promoted earlier in her term. "Wayne Anthony Ross, I believe, was selected by her to make a statement," McGuire said.

After the defeat, Palin placed the blame on the now-familiar straw men of "anonymous bloggers" and the lies she alleged had been told about W. A. R. She also told the *Anchorage Daily News* that the failure to confirm him was rife with "hypocrisy," given that the legislature had once passed a citation to honor his sixty-fifth birthday. She did not elaborate on how a birthday greeting should have made his confirmation as the attorney general of Alaska a forgone conclusion. On the day W. A. R. went down in flames, Palin was publicly criticized by Sitka Republican Bert Stedman for choosing to attend a Right to Life event in Indiana, rather than working to round up votes for her attorney general nominee. And truth be told, her timing could not have been worse.

In response to all the complaints that she was aloof and unenthusiastic about pushing her legislative goals, she and her staff tried to hammer home in almost every press release and media comment that her focus was fully, exclusively, and unconditionally on Alaska. By the last week of the session, Palin had only left the state once, turning down what Meg Stapleton described as "thousands" of invitations and speaking engagements. After her round of immediate postcampaign national interviews, the governor had regularly shunned events like the Conservative Political Action Conference in Washington and the National Governors Association winter meeting. Her apparent lack of interest in attending these high-powered

Republican gatherings was perplexing since she showed no desire to diminish her national profile in other ways. Palin had indeed made sustained forays into issues having nothing to do with Alaska per se, from her endorsement of Rick Perry in the Texas gubernatorial Republican primary to the soap opera involving Miss California's thoughts about gay marriage. She even weighed in on President Obama's commencement address at Notre Dame, declaring how disappointed her favorite grandfather, who was Catholic, would have been to witness the esteemed university's invitation to a politician who harbored "an anti-life agenda."

Before she realized how jeopardized her attorney general nomination would become, the Vanderburgh County Right to Life Banquet in Evansville struck Palin as a perfect event for her to attend. It promised to attract thousands of her most devoted supporters and would give her a chance to talk about her unequivocally pro-life stance, which she had promoted earlier in the legislative session by backing a ballot measure requiring parental consent for teenagers to have abortions. Attending the Indiana event would also give her the opportunity to take part in a separate function in the state benefiting families who have children with Down syndrome—another cause close to her heart. But Palin's decision to skip town during the final week of the session, the most critical time of the year for state business, frustrated more than a few legislators.

One early spring day, Tom Wright, the chief of staff to Alaska House Speaker Mike Chenault, printed out a copy of an online *Anchorage Daily News* story about the governor's planned trip to the Lower 48 and legislators' concerns about it. He planned to show it to his boss. But before he did, Palin's legislative liaison, Jerry Gallagher, happened to walk into Wright's office and see a copy of the article. Previously unaware that the *Anchorage Daily News* had published a story on the matter, Gallagher asked Wright to print out another copy for him.

The next morning, Wright was sitting at his desk in his side of-fice when he heard a familiar female voice near the front desk. "Is Tom Wright in?"

Wright shot up and made his way out to the main entrance where Governor Palin was standing. She did not look pleased.

"I understand you're distributing brochures about my leaving town and going to this rally," she said, according to someone who was there.

Distributing brochures? Wright had merely made two copies of a newspaper article. He explained that he had given her legislative liaison a copy upon request and made one for his boss, since it was his job to keep the Speaker informed. Palin was not satisfied.

"Do you have a problem with me leaving?" she asked in a sarcas-tic tone that only augmented the increasingly tense standoff.

"Governor, I could care less if you leave," Wright said. "That's your business. But you've got some detractors around here who are going to make an issue out of this because you are leaving within the last week of session."

"Well, I have my cell phone, and I'll only be gone for thirty-six hours," Palin said, attempting to somehow convince Wright that his concerns were entirely unjustified.

But Wright did not concede the point. Instead, he reiterated that the trip would not look good to people in the building who ques-tioned her priorities. After a couple more minutes of back-and-forth arguing, the governor realized she was not getting anywhere. She turned around and walked away.

Later that day, Wright told Chenault, his boss, about what had happened. The Speaker was incensed that Palin had taken it upon herself to berate a member of his staff and falsely accuse him of dis-tributing "brochures." Furthermore, if she had a problem, she should have gone to the Speaker himself.

As word of the encounter began to spread, the consensus in the capitol was that the governor's decision to confront a legislative staffer instead of going to his boss directly had indeed been a tremendous breach of protocol. Even after all the political firestorms and ceaseless scrutiny she faced every day of her life, Palin's skin had not thickened one millimeter.

Her April 21 speech to the banquet was a study in contrasts and emblematic of her ongoing struggle to address perceived injustices of the past while simultaneously trying to move forward. She dedicated the first part of the address to topics from the campaign that had ended almost six months earlier, including the controversy over her wardrobe, her interviews with Katie Couric, and her by now stale joke about having provided job security for Tina Fey. Palin seemed almost wistful in rehashing these campaign lowlights, as if they reminded her of the time when she was at the forefront of national discourse. But later in the speech, Palin enraptured the crowd with an honest, deeply personal account of the struggles she faced in becoming pregnant with a Down syndrome child. "I knew for sure that my prayer was answered," she recalled of Trig's birth, as she fought a losing battle to choke back genuine tears. "And my heart overflowed with joy, and I tell you this for a reason. I felt a love that I had never felt before and compassion that I didn't even know was there." This was Sarah Palin at her best: warm and sincere without a tinge of the bitterness that often dominated her postcampaign political persona.

The Indiana speech, however, came amid a series of embarrassing communications mishaps that reignited the narrative that her handlers lacked the political expertise to navigate the complexities of their boss's closely scrutinized moves. Communications director Meg Stapleton came under particular attack from two people

who have played prominent roles in SarahPAC and several other former Palin aides and associates who lament the way she has handled
the governor's messaging, antagonized journalists, and annoyed
supportive organizations by ignoring attempts at outreach."You
wouldn't believe how many people have come up to me and called
me. You know, 'How can I get a hold of Palin or somebody? Because
Meg Stapleton refuses to answer my calls, return my e-mails,'" says
one adviser who was involved in SarahPAC. "She lashes out. You
know, there's nothing wrong with telling a media person, 'Look, I
got your call, but we're not gonna talk to anybody.' I mean, people
in the media get that every day and they go, 'Ok, they were polite.
Next time.'"

In March, Palin had been invited to headline the June fund-
raiser for the National Republican Senatorial Committee (NRSC)
and the National Republican Congressional Committee (NRCC).
SarahPAC's Washington-based aides reported to Stapleton that they
needed to know whether Palin would attend and give the keynote
address at the marquis dinner, since committee officials were pressing them for an answer. According to John Coale and another Sarah-
PAC adviser who was on the conference calls, Stapleton declared to
the group that Palin would, in fact, attend the event. When an aide
asked if that was the confirmation they needed to report to the congressional Republicans holding the dinner, Stapleton said that
it was.

Once the Washington-based SarahPAC officials confirmed that
Palin would attend the fund-raiser, the NRSC and NRCC issued a
joint press release heralding her appearance. The committees, however, failed to notify Palin staffers about their intention to send out
the press release beforehand. Bill McAllister, Palin's official
spokesman at the time, told the Anchorage Daily News that he and his

boss were dumbfounded. "I communicated with the governor directly, and she did not know anything about it," he said.

Stapleton apparently felt that the committees had wronged the Palin camp by failing to give them a head's up about the press release, and in light of the predictable push back from Alaskans concerned that she was neglecting her in-state duties, the governor expressed reservations about attending the event in Washington. Instead of taking responsibility for the mishap.herself, Stapleton claimed to the *Daily News* that the aide who wrongly confirmed that Palin would attend the event was "someone helping me out on the East Coast," placing the blame squarely on others instead of herself. When Palin realized she had already planned to be on the East Coast at that time and could, in fact, attend the event, she had Fred Malek reach out to the NRSC to try to convince the group to reinvite her. But the event's organizers were angry that the governor's team had given them the runaround and concerned that Palin would overshadow Newt Gingrich, whom they had asked to keynote after Palin declined. They balked at extending her another invitation.

Stapleton then publicly chastised an NRSC official over the embarrassing series of mishaps that she herself had apparently initiated. "Why, at a time when we're trying to build the party, would you pull a move like that on somebody who earlier in the day just attracted twenty thousand people?" she said to *Politico*, recounting her conversation with the official, in which she was referring to an event Palin had attended in upstate New York to honor William Seward. The congressional committees ended up working out a compromise with SarahPAC whereby Palin attended the event but ceded the keynote speaker's slot to Gingrich, but SarahPAC's reputation for incompetence and penchant for finger-pointing had become cemented.

"How do you keep just Alaska-centric and then do cover stories for *People* magazine?" asked one frustrated political operative with knowledge of the inner workings of SarahPAC. "I'm not sure who has the ears of the governor. I don't get the sense that any staffer is that close to her."

In the weeks before her blockbuster announcement that she would step down as governor, the issue that most defined Palin's postcampaign national profile was her reaction to the economic stimulus package that President Obama signed into law. It does not take a particularly cynical person to suggest that Palin had her political future in the back of her mind when the federal government's offer of stimulus money for Alaska landed on her desk. She was one of several Republican leaders who spoke out early and often against the stimulus, arguing emphatically that the "free money" would lead to unsustainable federal mandates. It was a stance that contradicted the long-standing precedent set by Ted Stevens (and followed by almost every statewide politician in his wake, including her) to attract significant federal funding for Alaska.

On March 19, Palin issued a press release with the headline "Governor Accepts Half of Stimulus Funds." The release stated that she intended to take "just 55 percent" of the $930.7 million that Congress had allotted to Alaska and expressed her concern over the growing national debt and "program expansion." But she also indicated that she knew her actions would be met with severe resistance in the Alaska legislature. "Our desire is to foster a discussion about what is true stimulus and what is just more federal interference in Alaskans' lives through the growth of government," she said at the time.

Sure enough, Palin's declaration that she would not accept almost half the funds generated a public outcry from state lawmakers on both sides of the aisle who complained that she was selling out Alaska's interests in order to brandish her fiscally conservative bona fides in advance of a future presidential run. At a time when her approval rating in the state had dropped below the 60 percent threshold and before she had decided to resign, Palin seemed to take the criticism to heart. After weeks of debate in the legislature, a spokesperson announced on April 28 that the governor would accept all of the funding, except for $28.6 million allotted to help increase energy efficiency. Palin said the energy money was tied to the adoption of building codes that intruded on local government and were not practical in a state as geographically diverse as Alaska.

Though her acceptance of most of the funds was a clear retreat from her original hard line, many legislators believed that Palin's rejection of the energy dollars was a rank attempt to save face after caving on everything else. Once again, state Republicans were not shy about questioning the governor's motives in decrying the "strings" attached to the money. "When you look at the stimulus package as it applies to Alaska, the kinds of strings really aren't there," said State Senator and Resources Committee Cochair Lesil McGuire. "And so it sounds good to say that politically, and it really bolsters up your place as a Republican candidate, but in reality when you break it down and look at the facts, they don't bear out."

Undeterred, Palin announced on May 21 that she would use her veto to trim $80 million from the budget the legislature had passed, including the $28.6 million for energy assistance. The legislators reacted swiftly and consistently, and several seemed scarcely able to contain their anger. After all, the governor presided over the state with the highest energy prices in the nation, and she had vowed to embark on an ambitious and expensive alternative energy plan using state funds. Many rural Alaskans deemed Palin's move particularly offensive since some of them had spent the winter on the brink of choosing between feeding their families and heating their homes. The federal money that Palin rejected would help weatherize and insulate their villages.

Though Palin had long been skeptical of federal intrusion, going back to her days in local government in Wasilla, her clumsy handling of the stimulus issue exemplified her ongoing struggle to balance the needs of her state with national considerations. Her final decision to reject the energy money threatened to make her look like just another ambitious politician who was playing the very "politics-as-usual" game that she so consistently decries. "I think the governor had a mind-set this year that she was going to snipe instead of govern," says Democratic state representative Les Gara. "And she really spent three months this session sniping instead of governing." Alaska lawmakers voted to override Palin's veto of the stimulus funds in a special session held on August 10.

Though relatively few Alaskans supported Palin's rejection of the stimulus funds, fiscal conservatives nationwide strongly backed the move. Some of Palin's most reliable and increasingly influential allies could be found on the website Conservatives4Palin.com. In early 2009, one of the site's founders purchased its domain name for the more-than-reasonable fee of $10, and it quickly overtook all other unofficial blogs, groups, and draft committees to become the go-to online community for Palin's most ardent supporters. With just a handful of editors posting regularly, the blog has generated an impressive volume of timely news and well-written opinion about all things Palin. Rebecca Mansour, a screenwriter by training who blogs on the site from her home in Los Angeles (none of the regular contributors live in Alaska), says the site tripled its readership every month in early 2009. Mansour is in constant online contact with the other editors, who met virtually during the presidential campaign at HotAir.com. They stay up to the second on Palin-related news through RSS feeds, Twitter, and old-fashioned trial and error when it comes to figuring out the timing of Palin's press releases. "We get tips from our readers all the time in our e-mails saying, 'Hey guys, post this,'" Mansour says. "It's like this whole giant movement."

Among their primary goals, the Conservatives4Palin editors aim to dispel the stereotype that Palin supporters are uneducated and unsophisticated. While their reactions to events have a predictable pro-Palin slant, their blog posts are often well informed and meticulously reasoned. Most of the editors have advanced degrees, and Mansour says that three of the site's contributors are MENSA members: "We like to think of ourselves as intellectuals, not elitists."

Though scattered around the world, the Conservatives4Palin contributors tuned intensely into Alaskan issues during Palin's last few months in office and familiarized themselves with the state's political players.

Conservatives4Palin has also played an important role in drumming up outrage over incidents in which the group felt Palin had been wronged. When David Letterman put his foot in his mouth by making an off-color joke about Palin's daughter "getting knocked up by" Yankees slugger Alex Rodriguez, the website led the charge in the ensuing backlash. Palin and her defenders did not buy Letterman's explanation that the joke had referred to eighteen-year-old Bristol Palin, not fourteen-year-old Willow, who had been the lone Palin daughter to attend a game the previous day at Yankee Stadium, and the governor released a statement decrying Letterman's "sexually-perverted comments" and claiming that jokes like his contribute to sexual abuse of minors. Todd Palin added a statement of his own, condemning Letterman for making light of "raping my 14-year-old."

The forceful response garnered sympathy from Americans of all political persuasions who felt that the comedian had crossed the line, and as the controversy continued to dominate the news and entertainment world, Letterman was compelled to apologize publicly for the joke. He also invited Palin to come onto his show to put the matter to rest once and for all, but the governor was in no mood to make amends, and she dispatched Meg Stapleton to issue one of her typically scathing statements: "The Palins have no intention of providing a rating's [sic] boost for David Letterman by appearing on the show. Plus, it would be wise to keep Willow away from David Letterman."

By insinuating that Letterman might himself be a sexual predator, Palin jeopardized the moral high ground that she had earned over the previous few days. At the time of the Letterman/Palin standoff, general wisdom held that the incident benefited both parties, boosting Letterman's ratings while generating sympathy for Palin. But even though the public at large was on her side on this one, the Letterman saga was yet another instance in which Palin dominated headlines because of a personal feud. As she worked behind the scenes to usher in progress on the oil pipeline and brandished her foreign policy resume with a trip to visit National Guard troops in Kosovo, her decision to engage with Letterman ensured that she would continue to be discussed as a tabloid-friendly celebrity, just as she was striving to attach her name to more substantive issues.

Palin's compulsion to respond to every minor slight manifested itself in one of the most baffling ways soon after the Letterman incident, this time in response not to a world-famous comedian but to one of those Alaska bloggers who have always irritated her the most. The blogger had taken a photograph from the Republican convention of Palin holding her infant son, Trig, and Photoshopped a picture of conservative Alaskan radio host Eddie Burke's face over Trig's, in order to make the point that Burke's fawning coverage of Palin had become obsessive. Once again, Stapleton unleashed, calling the Photoshop job a "malicious desecration of a photo of the Governor and baby Trig that has become an iconic representation of a mother's love for a special-needs child." The statement added that "babies and children are off limits" and noted that the "Obama administration sets the moral compass for its party," an apparent reference to the conviction within the governor's inner circle that an associate of the president of the United States had engaged in a campaign to undermine Palin.

Palin had little to gain by getting dragged into the mud with a liberal Alaskan blogger, but her disgust with, and exasperation over, the doctored photo were sincere. She would go on to include the episode in her list of reasons why she had decided to resign the governorship, demonstrating once and for all the extent to which she had allowed her critics in Alaska to get to her. The woman who had steadfastly faced down powerful oil companies two years earlier had now become preoccupied with bloggers.

12. The Next Chapter

SHORTLY AFTER 9 A.M. LOCAL TIME on July 3, 2009, Sarah Palin's gubernatorial office sent out a press release that compelled reporters from Wasilla to Washington to suspend their holiday breaks and pick up the phones to find out what exactly was going on. The release stated that Palin would make an "announcement" at her home in less than two hours. It was barely enough time for local media in Anchorage to make it to the event, and the news networks lacked the technical capability to broadcast it live on such short notice. Almost immediately, speculation swirled that Palin would announce that she would not seek reelection, though it seemed odd that she would make such a declaration with so much time left in her term.

With Lake Lucille composing the quintessentially Alaskan backdrop, the governor stood behind a podium in front of the tiny media contingent, while geese honked in the background. Todd, Piper, and baby Trig were by her side, but Meg Stapleton was over three thousand miles away on vacation in New York, lending further credence to the impression that this announcement had not exactly been planned meticulously. Palin began her speech in a familiar way, speaking about her love of Alaska, listing her accomplishments as governor, criticizing the media coverage of her administration, and going into great detail about the time and effort that responding to the ethics complaints filed against her had required. Not until more than twelve minutes into the speech, which she wrote herself, did she finally announce that she was resigning (though she carefully avoided using the word) at the end of the month. The ensuing press release carried the headline "Palin Announces No Second Term," as if her decision to step down almost immediately, with a year and a half left in her first term, were a mere afterthought.

Palin's media team appeared to have crafted no strategy for how to deal with the inevitable onslaught of questions that followed her stunning announcement and could not even seem to settle on a reason for why she had decided to, in her words, "pass the ball for victory" instead of going with the flow like a "dead fish." Any remaining doubts about whether the country's infatuation with Palin remained as strong as it had been during the campaign were dispelled in the ensuing hours and days when the media fed round-the-clock Palin coverage to a country eager to speculate about why she had made such a shocking move. Though her surrogates settled on the talking point that she was declaring her independence on Independence Day (or the day before it, at least), the immediate reaction, even among many of her most ardent supporters, was one of bafflement and concern.

"I first was a little bit surprised and initially didn't think it was a good idea," said Fred Malek, who remained one of her strongest and most powerful backers in Washington. "But after thinking more about it and kind of analyzing it, I came to the conclusion that it was a very good decision."

Palin cited as reasons for her decision the onslaught of ethics complaints, her desire not to become tempted by out-of-state junkets as a lame-duck governor, the tactics of "mean-spirited" bloggers, and the lessons on courage she had learned from a visit to wounded troops. Malek and other Palin backers contend that these explanations should be taken at face value. "You've got to put it in the perspective not in the grand strategy for 2012—if you put it against that strategy I would argue that it wasn't a good decision—but I don't think that was the basis which she was making the decision," Malek said, adding that her priorities were "one, the impact on her family, and two, the financial strain that staying in office was causing, and three was the ability to execute on her agenda, fourthly to perpetuate that agenda, and fifthly, and only fifthly, would be the impact on the longer-term possibilities."

The particular emphasis Palin placed on the ceaseless ethics complaints filed against her showed the extent to which they had gotten under her skin. There had indeed been a remarkable change in tone in the two years since she had begun her administration with a promise to make Alaska government more transparent and repeatedly called on its citizens to hold her accountable. As she stated her intention to reenter the realm of national politics, many observers in Alaska and beyond wondered how she would handle the additional scrutiny that would come her way once she left the relatively low-intensity worlds of Juneau and Anchorage and again faced the full wrath of the best-equipped political opponents in the country.

Some of her earliest supporters felt the most let down. "I feel really disappointed," said Representative Nancy Dahlstrom, one of the three Alaska House members who endorsed Palin's uphill gubernatorial primary campaign. "If somebody would have told me when she was running that this was gonna happen, I would have just said, 'You are out of your ever loving mind. There is no way. There is just no way she would quit before her term is up.'"

John Bitney said that nothing about his former boss surprised him anymore, but his disillusionment with the politician he had once dedicated his career to was evident. "These ethics complaints, they were frivolous, they were stupid, so ignore them," he said. "Just ignore that crap and stick to the working hard, and you'll be fine. But she really took a rise out of the bait way too easy."

On the Monday after her resignation announcement, Palin agreed to conduct interviews from a fishing boat in Todd's home-town of Dillingham with four of the five major television networks (CBS, the home of David Letterman, was conspicuously omitted.) Her interview with NBC's Andrea Mitchell, whom she had previously met at dinner at Fred Malek's home, was particularly contentious. When Mitchell asked Palin, who was decked out in fishing waders on the shores of Bristol Bay, about her reaction to those who said that she hadn't finished the job she was elected to do, Palin snapped back, "You're not listening to me!"

When she returned to her home in Wasilla, Palin was greeted by a photographer from *Time* magazine who was there to conduct a cover shoot. Nowhere in sight was the contingent of aides who, during the campaign, would have made sure that every last hair was in place and the light directed at its most flattering angle. Instead, Palin directed the photographer on her own in front of the lake, moving a paddleboat out of the way of the shot and dragging it around the dock. She expressed concern that she might have had fish scales stuck in her hair.

After the daylong national media campaign that had been needed to try to clarify her reasons for stepping down, Palin once again built up a wall between herself and reporters. Perhaps more than any prominent politician, she had embraced wholeheartedly the emergence of Twitter as a means to bypass the press and communicate directly to the public. Since she first started using the social-networking service in the spring of 2009, she had consistently posted everything from press releases and details about her official schedule to personal notes about her family and triumphant reactions each time a new ethics complaint was dismissed. As Palin's distrust of the media became complete, her decision to work around it using Twitter and Facebook became an innovative concept. After all, her success in getting her "tweets" and Facebook posts cited frequently in mainstream media accounts was impressive.

As was the case in her botched experiment with e-mailing Juneau reporters directly during her final legislative session, she again ran the risks inherent in not having her communications team vet her messages. Many Americans who appreciate a down-to-earth leader might have some concerns about a potential presidential candidate who sometimes uses emoticon smiley faces on her Twitter page. Her free-flowing thought process can also open her up to dramatic inconsistencies that she might otherwise have avoided. On July 19, for instance, she tweeted, "Time DOES fly! Work hard so u can genuinely enjoy every recreation minute! Avoid time spent tearing down, whining, complaining; WORK & ENJOY." The very next day, she proceeded to grumble about the strains that the latest ethics complaint had placed on her, adding her standard critique of media coverage, in a succession of eight tweets over the course of nearly three hours.

Though Palin and her supporters framed her decision to resign as a response to all the negative forces that had combined to make governing impossible, her move seemed at least as opportunistic as it did reactive. Presiding over Alaska had become difficult, dull, and unfulfilling. Resigning to travel the country without the burden of a day job would be relatively easy, invigorating, and both personally and financially rewarding. Even if Palin's more analytical side understood that it would be to her long-term benefit to tough it out, her gut must have told her that an immediate change was the preferable course, and she had learned never to ignore her instincts. Furthermore, the word around Juneau, Anchorage, and Wasilla was that Todd Palin had been particularly adamant in encouraging his wife to step down for the good of the family.

Just over three weeks after her resignation announcement, Palin spent a farewell weekend attending the annual governor's picnics around the state, culminating with her final speech in office in Fairbanks. The interior city where Palin had been sworn in had long held sentimental value for her, but little was sentimental about the combative twenty-minute speech she gave before her successor, Sean Parnell, was sworn in.

Before reflecting on her administration's accomplishments, she unleashed a diatribe against the media that was at turns condescending and contemptuous. "You represent what could and should be a respected, honest profession that could and should be a cornerstone of our democracy," she said. "Democracy depends on you, and that is why—that's why our troops are willing to die for you. So how about in honor of the American soldier, you quit makin' things up."

It was the biggest applause line of the afternoon among the highly supportive crowd that had gathered to see her in her last public appearance as governor. Though the event was billed as the transfer of power to Parnell, Palin only mentioned her successor briefly. For a few more minutes, it was still her stage, and she leaned forward into the microphone, adding in a reprimanding tone, "One other thing for the media, our new governor has a very nice family, too, so leave his kids alone." It was a far cry from the good old days of her honeymoon with the press that had ended just a year earlier.

Palin's blistering rhetoric was a winner with the Fairbanks crowd, but whether it can be an effective long-term strategy is far less certain. Though she has not stated so explicitly, it seems clear that she harbors aspirations of becoming president of the United States. Given her unwavering answer to John McCain's stunning offer to be his running mate, her postcampaign interviews in which she was remarkably frank about crashing through any "open doors" to the presidency, and the steps she has since taken to sustain her national profile after her resignation, no clearheaded assessment could conclude otherwise. Palin's lofty ambition is unlikely to subside, and she is now essentially free to campaign as a full-time job in advance of the official start of the 2012 race. Having thrown off the shackles of a position that would have required a full day of travel to get her to most places in the continental United States, she can now make frequent jaunts to early-voting states and congressional districts where there are Republican friends to be made. Despite polls that have shown her overall support taking a downward turn, Palin's resignation amid the perception that nefarious forces chased her out seemed only to strengthen support for her among the white evangelical conservative base that holds a disproportionate sway over the Republican primary process.

After her resignation, Palin laid low for a few days before appearing at a National Rifle Association event in Anchorage and then taking to her Facebook page on August 7 to chime in on the health-care debate going on in Congress at the time. She had previously promised to be "less politically correct" after resigning from office, and she did not disappoint in this instance, writing, "The America I know and love is not one in which my parents or my baby with Down syndrome will have to stand in front of Obama's 'death panel' so his bureaucrats can decide, based on a subjective judgment of their 'level of productivity in society,' whether they are worthy of health care. Such a system is downright evil."

Enthusiastically taking up the task of accusing the president of having palled around with terrorists was one thing, but charging him with favoring a national passive-euthanasia program—an allegation that had been spread among conspiracy theorists but lacked any semblance of truth—was an over-the-top distortion that put many of her previous misleading claims to shame. Not only that, her decision to use the theoretical killing of her parents and infant son to make a political point tested the boundaries of good taste in a way that seemed at least as repugnant as David Letterman's joke about her daughter. The statement made it clear, if it was not already evident enough, that Palin had fully abandoned her once-successful pursuit of the political middle ground and was now intent on feeding the visceral furor of a relatively small, but vocal, minority of voters.

Even so, the "death panel" comment impacted the national debate and showed how much clout Palin continues to have. As she settles on what's next in her political life, it is feasible that she will take time to reflect and calculate that her chances of becoming the nation's first female president would be significantly greater in 2016, when she would have had even more time to familiarize herself with national policy and would be running in an open-seat election, rather than waging an uphill battle against an incumbent president with memories of her 2008 stumbles and controversial resignation relatively fresh. But throughout her career, Palin has seized opportunities as they come, instead of holding back patiently and waiting for the kinds of ideal situations that rarely, if ever, present themselves. What if the economy takes another dive, and President Obama's popularity plummets? Surely she would regret passing up an opportunity to strike while the iron was hot in 2012. One lesson she will have learned from Obama is that running the right presidential campaign at the right time can overcome relative youth and inexperience. It will be impossible to predict with any accuracy as the campaign begins in earnest in early 2011 just how vulnerable Obama will be in November 2012. Palin will be guided by her own faith and intuition, and she is more likely than not at least to test the 2012 waters.

Above all the other controversies that she has been immersed in, the negative ramifications of her decision to resign the governorship with a year and a half left in her term will be her most daunting challenge to overcome. After she returned from her vice presidential run, the single-most important thing she needed to do to prepare for a future national campaign was to demonstrate skill in handling complex issues that affect the country. Without the benefit of her elected position, it will be much more difficult for her to assuage the reservations that many independents and moderate Republicans harbor about her experience and heft. Even more problematic is how salient the "quitter" label figures to become, as other Republican candidates will point out again and again their own records of hunkering down when the going got tough.

"It does raise questions about her ability to stick to something, and it also raises the longer-term questions about the resume and the experience," says Mike Huckabee's 2008 Iowa campaign manager Eric Woolson. "People will say, 'She's an unconventional candidate, and so the rules don't apply to her.' But the fact is basic rules do apply to most everybody, and I think it creates a bigger problem for her than an opportunity." In a preview of the potential line of attack that Huckabee might take against Palin should they both decide to run in 2012, Woolson adds, "Frankly, I would think that experience and results would be an issue in the comparison that people would make. Here's a governor who got stuff done versus a governor who had a great potential, but left too soon."

Palin's still theoretical natural gas pipeline is the issue that will most define her record of achievement as governor. A defining moment will come during the 2010 "open season," when the major oil companies must declare whether the gas they own can be transported by the state-sponsored TransCanada pipeline. In what was seen as a major sign of progress, Exxon announced in June 2009 that it would work with TransCanada to go forward with the process, but many questions about the project's viability remain. Palin may have left the governor's office, but the Alaska Gasline Inducement Act figures to be either her crowning achievement or most embarrassing failure. Former state senator Kim Elton was one of the many lawmakers who backed Palin's gas-pipeline deal yet sees trouble ahead. "I think anybody that says we have found the answer to the gas pipeline, that's very, very optimistic," he said during the 2009 legislative session.

No matter what happens with the pipeline, Palin's most fervent supporters will continue to see her as Ronald Reagan in high heels— a throwback to the rugged American West whose conservative ideals represent the fulfillment of the Founding Fathers' dream. Like Reagan, Palin has borne the wrath of that vague, yet unmistakably nefarious, entity known as "the elites," many of whom belong to her party and supposedly lash out at her because they fear her power and ability to connect with voters. Just as Reagan's defeat in the 1976 primaries was merely the warm-up act for his triumphant reemergence, Palin is destined to take her place as the next political comeback kid, or so this line of thinking goes, astonishing the Washington punditocracy along the way with her unimpeachable appeal to the "real" people.

But to her critics, Palin summons memories of Dan Quayle rather than the Gipper. Just like the former vice president, they say, Palin's appeal is almost entirely confined to a small group of right-wing activists, while the more reasonable masses have seen the evidence and deemed her insufficiently equipped to utter a grammatically correct sentence, let alone have her finger on the nuclear button. The Katie Couric interviews were her "potatoe" moment, they say, the final verdict in the case against a telegenic, yet intellectually vapid amateur, made all the more conclusive in an era when YouTube would ensure it would not soon be forgotten. As with

Quayle's truncated run for president in 1999, the country at large would greet a future Palin campaign as a running joke. Or so the story goes.

If a politician's ideal makeup combines innate appeal with a solid philosophical core based on years of study and experience, Palin already has the first, more difficult half taken care of. And therein lies the most glaring difference between the Alaska governor and George H. W. Bush's vice president. In a variation on the barb used by his 1988 debate opponent, Dan Quayle is no Sarah Palin, at least when it comes to star quality. Quayle may have been a darling of the base, but he never attracted the enraptured crowds that greeted Palin from coast to coast, whereby she often upstaged her running mate. The media liked to poke fun at Quayle, but they never dissected and debated his every utterance and movement as they do Palin's. Only the lives of the president and Hollywood A-listers rival Palin's in terms of public interest. Sarah Palin has "it," and "it" cannot be learned.

In truth, Palin's political prospects are not as cut-and-dried as either her fiercest supporters or her harshest antagonists claim them to be. There is no doubt that she can be Reaganesque in her communication skills and her ability to connect on a deeply personal level. But by the time he first ran for president, Reagan had made his name as a two-term governor of the state that became the nation's most populous during his tenure and as a longtime advocate of a brand of conservatism for which he had cultivated a solid philosophical grounding. The *Weekly Standard*'s Fred Barnes, who had been one of Palin's strongest advocates inside the beltway, wrote after her resignation, "Forget about Sarah Palin as the Republican presidential candidate in 2012 and probably ever." In an interview from his downtown Washington office in January 2009, Barnes remembered one particular conversation with Palin that left him with some reservations well before her resignation. "I asked her, 'Who among conservative thinkers and writers, who are your favorites?' She said, 'Of course, you!' [but] I knew that wasn't the case," he recalled. "I'm not sure she's curious about that at this point. There's a lot of great stuff that's been written that's not that hard to read."

But Barnes's colleague Bill Kristol thinks many of his conservative intellectual friends who dismiss the Alaska governor miss the point. "Some politicians have a natural gift and talent for exciting people and interesting people and connecting," Kristol said. "And it's not something one merely can understand. I'm not sure anyone can. A lot of it is instinctiveness. Some of it is superficial things: looks and background. But some of it is personal charisma, and she does have it. That is a huge advantage and shouldn't be underestimated."

Attempting to predict the outcome of primaries still years away is not much easier than guessing which team is going to win the Super Bowl two seasons in advance. But that does not mean the likely participants have not begun jockeying for position. They have. In the campaign before the campaign, Mitt Romney has enjoyed a somewhat unlikely reemergence as a very early favorite to win the nomination. Like Palin, he certainly does not lack determination. A millionaire many times over, he also has no need to worry about holding down a day job as he continues to build goodwill with members of the Republican establishment who might have initially doubted his conservative bona fides, and he has already proved himself a highly skilled fund-raiser. Romney has become one of the most respected voices on the right to counter the Obama administration's economic policies, and the former Massachusetts governor could benefit from the Republican Party's tradition of embracing its second-place finishers the next time around.

When it comes to their attributes as candidates, Romney shares Palin's sunny demeanor and physical attractiveness, and both are impressive in their own ways when standing behind a lectern. But the similarities end there. While Romney is the son of a millionaire former presidential candidate and graduated from Harvard Business School near the top of his class, Palin changed colleges four times before earning her degree and proudly drops the *g*'s at the end of her gerunds. But just as it is nearly impossible to imagine Romney struggling through an interview as badly as Palin did with Katie Couric, the Alaska governor is much better equipped to handle the unpredictable moments that arise in face-to-face interactions on the trail.

In the end, a potential Palin versus Romney battle could hinge on the former's retail politicking mastery versus the latter's organizational expertise, a skill that the Obama campaign proved remains critical, even in the high-tech age. Though it is tempting to see the potential matchup as a clash between the conservative and moderate wings of the party, Romney has shown no sign of backing down from the hard-right positions he emphasized during the beginning of the 2008 campaign, before deemphasizing them somewhat to rediscover his roots as a nonideological problem solver. Though Romney will once again hammer home his private-sector experience and status as a Washington outsider and undoubtedly stress his track record of seeing his own gubernatorial term through to its completion, Palin's best hope might be to make the contest another referendum against "the Establishment."

One former senior Romney advisor who figures to play a prominent role in the 2012 campaign offered an early preview of the line of attack the former Massachusetts governor might take against Palin. He argues that of the two, only Romney could attract a wide enough net of general election supporters to beat the incumbent president. "If she goes down the path she is now, I mean, it's a pretty damn small party," the advisor said. "It's a small party of real fervent supporters, which might get a nomination, but it won't get her the

White House. . . . You can't confuse [attracting] rabidly enthusiastic crowds with being ready to be president."

Of course, several other Republicans have already given strong indications that they are seriously considering the race. Mike Huckabee, Minnesota governor Tim Pawlenty, and former House Speaker Newt Gingrich are among the most mentioned would-be contenders. Almost all of the early-buzz potential candidates hail from the conservative wing of the party, but in a potential field crowded with white males who look and sound about the same, Palin could carve a formidable niche, especially among right-leaning women.

The nominating calendar remains nearly as unpredictable as the field and will likely not be settled until early 2011. As Michigan and Florida demonstrated in 2008, states can always break the rules of the Republican National Committee and hope to get away with it, but Iowa, New Hampshire, and South Carolina appear poised to retain their traditional roles as the earliest-voting states. Iowa, with its rural, evangelical dominance, would be an ideal state for Palin to seek an early, resounding victory in. Unlike some of the other potential Republicans in the field, she would not have to get an early start to build name recognition there and could focus instead on remaining strong nationally while simultaneously building her ground game.

An informal survey of some of the most influential conservative leaders in Iowa conducted soon after her resignation announcement suggested that Palin's decision to step down might not have affected her support there profoundly. "She has a built in base that would be ready to support her immediately," said Kraig Paulsen, the Republican minority leader in the Iowa House of Representatives. "Whether or not that would be enough to get her over the top, time will tell, but it's not like she would have to start from zero in Iowa."

While Paulsen said that he could see himself supporting Palin for president, Ed Failor, the president of Iowans for Tax Relief, went a step further. "She would be the person I would be most likely right now to say, 'Yeah, that's a person that I can support for 2012,'" he said. Failor added that pundits who ruled her out based on her resignation overlooked the reality of what most Republican caucus goers look for in a candidate. "It makes her potentially a populist icon, and that's how I believe we move forward, that's how we win," he said. "I'll tell you, grassroots Republicans, particularly in Iowa, are dead tired of political insiders, are dead tired of elected officials, dead tired of Republicans and Democrats alike." Asked if, as a leader of a free market group, he was concerned about Palin's push to raise taxes on oil companies and distribute $1,200 oil-revenue checks to every Alaskan, Failor frankly admitted that it was her persona, rather than her record, that drew people to Palin: "No, to be completely honest with you. For the average American, the people that are going to be voting, the people that are going to caucus and then general election voters if she were to be the nominee, the hardest thing to do is beat somebody up on a confusing issue."

Steve Scheffler, the president of the heavily influential Iowa Christian Alliance, remained supportive but added some words of caution for Palin to dissuade her from relying more on her celebrity appeal than on hitting the ground hard. "People here in Iowa are used to being talked to not just once, but again and again and again," he said. "Even though she's very popular with the average caucus goer here in Iowa, I still think she would have to work very hard, come here a lot, convince people why she is the best candidate."

Chuck Larson, a former Iowa state senator and senior adviser to John McCain, took a contrarian view. His take on Palin's resignation serves as a reminder that not every prominent Republican in the state is willing to let her midterm resignation slide. "In Iowa, we believe in completing the mission, and here she clearly did not, and if she thinks the kitchen is too hot as the governor of Alaska, it's going to be even hotter at the national level, so I have to presume that she is no longer looking at running for president," Larson said. "The presidency without a doubt is the most difficult job in this country, and all one has to do is look at the gray hair on George W. Bush's head or Bill Clinton's head to understand what it does to that individual. And I believe it is a hundred times worse, if not a thousand times worse, than what she probably saw in Alaska."

Even were she to come out on top in the Iowa caucuses, the victory would mean little unless she could build on the momentum with the vastly different voting blocs in the states that follow, as Mike Huckabee can well attest. New Hampshire, for instance, figures to be as challenging for Palin as Iowa is advantageous. New Hampshire's Republican primary voters have a proud tendency to shun candidates who run media-heavy campaigns at the expense of face time with voters (see: Rudy Giuliani and George W. Bush), and they take collective pride in making the front runners for the nomination work especially hard. New Hampshire's voters and the local media are not inclined to shy away from tough questions requiring long, thoughtful answers, and they typically shun the sound bite–ready generalities that have served Palin well in past campaigns. Democrats and Independents in the state may cross over in greater-than-usual numbers to vote in the open primary since the Democratic side is unlikely to be contested, and Romney figures to do well. He maintains a home on Lake Winnipesaukee and continues to build good will after his second-place finish in 2008, which might have been a victory had the Giuliani campaign not collapsed so completely, causing many of the former mayor's national-security-focused supporters to flock to McCain.

If Palin were able to reconnect effectively with her independent streak, she could beat expectations in New Hampshire. But in a

New England state that has trended dramatically Democratic in recent years, that proposition is more likely a losing one. Palin's best bet, it seems, would be to skip New Hampshire altogether and compete heavily in the state with a heavily conservative, evangelical tilt that figures to vote next: South Carolina. The dance she will have to dance to attract enough moderates while running as a Christian Right candidate will be a difficult one to master, but as Ronald Reagan proved, it can be done if the circumstances are right, and the campaign is skillfully run.

Despite the old adage that they do not exist in American lives, second acts in American politics have actually been commonplace. Richard Nixon and Ronald Reagan are just two examples of presidents who had been written off after early defeats. Anyone who dismisses out of hand the possibility that Palin could reemerge as a viable presidential contender ignores not only her extraordinary visceral appeal complimented by her natural political talents but, perhaps more importantly, the unpredictability of the national political winds. Still, there is no doubt that she faces an uphill climb to overcome doubts stemming from her resignation, and she has not made things easier on herself since. There is nothing she can do about her 2008 flubs and the Tina Fey caricature, but she can still make a concerted effort to demonstrate that she has become well versed on issues outside her comfort zones of energy security, ethics reform, and special-needs education. But that will require her to exhibit a deeper understanding of nuance, a tactic that she has thus far shunned in favor of talk-radio-ready sound bites.

Many find Palin's reticence around the Republican establishment at home and at the national level an endearing trait. But in a serious presidential campaign, there is no way around the cocktail-party circuit, a fact that Palin demonstrably recognized when she attended the dinner at Fred Malek's home. If she is serious about winning, she will at times have to swallow her pride and stand on stage beside politicians she may not agree with on every issue. She will also have to learn how to channel more productively her unbridled contempt for the media. On that front, she might take a page from the book of someone like Romney, who in the 2008 campaign was questioned incessantly about his religion, ridiculed for being an unrelatable stiff, and labeled an incorrigible flip-flopper, yet refused to dwell on the largely negative media narrative. One former Romney strategist explained why. "Presidential campaigns have too many moving parts, and if you spend all your time being a victim, you don't get done what you have to get done," the strategist said. "Who's a victim who has actually won? People don't like that. They don't feel comfortable with it."

Even if she chooses not to run for president in 2012, Palin will be an enormous factor in the race and quite possibly a kingmaker on the Republican side. She believes that she has the leadership qualities needed to take the country on a rightward course, and she is ambitious enough to try. The most conservative Republicans will always see her as one of them and will continue to back her because they can relate to her on a personal level. As one Palin supporter said to a coauthor of this book at a 2008 campaign rally, "If she can run a home, she can run the government." The appeal of the limelight remains as strong as ever for Sarah Palin, and there is no job in the world that better satisfies the craving for stardom than the presidency.

Palin will never be urban America's preferred candidate, but in the 2008 campaign, she let slip a comment at a closed fund-raiser that sheds some particularly unflattering light on her image of vast swaths of the country. In Greensboro, North Carolina, her off-the-cuff remark that it was good to be in "what I call the 'real America,' being here with all of you hard-working, very patriotic, very pro-America areas of this great nation" seemed all too sincere. Though she apologized for it and no doubt wished she could take it back, the attitude that only some areas of the country are pro-America really does seem engrained in her consciousness. Perhaps it is a product of being raised and spending the majority of her political career in a homogenous environment. But the days when Republicans can win elections merely by holding their base appear to be over, and Palin will have to find a way to relate to many voters who have written her off as the epitome of a mentality that is foreign to them.

Sarah Palin was initially drawn to local government as a young mother in Wasilla for the noblest of reasons: She saw problems in the system and thought she could do better than the men in power. Her astonishingly rapid rise to the forefront of national politics resulted from a combination of her innate skill, burning ambition, and, yes, more than a few lucky circumstances. She now enjoys a platform and has become more influential than perhaps anyone but she herself thought possible. Despite her prominent role in the national discourse, however, Palin would likely have been better off if her rise had not been quite so rapid. Republican state senator Lesil McGuire from Anchorage laid out how Palin's hasty ascent may have affected her present circumstances negatively:

> I am proud of her for entering the fray, for coming out and being strong with a full family and all of those obligations that she struggles with. And I am very proud of the person that she was when she entered the race. She was very real and plain spoken. But what I see as having happened now is that you had a really good person thrust way up ahead of where their experience level was. Maybe it would be like asking someone who had observed or read medical textbooks to go and perform a surgery. No matter how competent you are as a person and your character and what you stand for, it doesn't mean that you have the experience necessary to govern. People take that for granted. I think they think that when

*they are voting for someone, it's a personality contest. Well, if I
like them, if they are attractive to me, if they seem like a good person, maybe I want them to be my neighbor, but that doesn't necessarily mean they are qualified to govern. And it may mean they are
qualified to govern later on in their life, not at that particular
point. So she got ahead of her experience. Because of that, in my
opinion, her self-confidence deteriorated. She stopped having one-
on-one meetings because, frankly, the conversations would get into
details that she wasn't able to answer. That then begets a whole
other series of problems. People feel like you are not respecting
them because you are not meeting with them. You are evasive; you
are aloof. You're not doing it necessarily because you're mean, because you are rejecting the public; it's because you're maybe out of
your league and then now you compound this with this national
exposure, and she never got an opportunity to define to the world
who she was prior to that.*

Though many Americans refuse even to consider the idea, Sarah
Palin truly is a likable person. She handles face-to-face interactions
so well because she genuinely cares about the concerns of others, a
trait that other politicians struggle to convey with sincerity. As we,
the authors, went through the process of interviewing former campaign staffers for this book, it did not take long to realize that the
people who liked her the most tended to be the ones who had spent
the most time around her.

But although she remains empathetic in many respects, Palin's
lightning-fast political rise has fundamentally changed her in some
unflattering ways. The insurgent gubernatorial candidate with the
positive message of reform is unrecognizable in the postcampaign
Sarah Palin, who has been more drawn to the appeal of celebrity
than good governance. She dwells constantly in an attack stance and
seems to relish the task of inflaming people's worst instincts. Palin is

not an angry person by nature, yet her resignation speech in Fairbanks showed the extent to which she has now become a politician who thrives on anger.

Palin has a proven ability to absorb and digest complicated information, but the 2008 exit polls and other surveys since have shown that the majority of Americans are not convinced that she has the depth of knowledge required to perform the most challenging job in the world. She has since done little to assuage those doubts or to counter the caricature that Tina Fey successfully ingrained into the national consciousness. Even her always-blunt father, Chuck Heath, seemed to acknowledge concerns about her readiness when asked if his daughter would make a good president. "Oh, yeah," he said. "You know, this is like Obama. He didn't know what he was doing, but if you surround yourself with the right people, she would definitely surround herself with the right people."

Sarah Palin is no different from any other potential White House hopeful in that she has flaws that she can mitigate if she addresses them forcefully. Her captivating life story and exuberant personality give her a huge advantage over all of the others, but is she willing to buckle down and immerse herself in learning what she needs to learn in order to get more people to take her seriously? The first step toward success in that endeavor would be to acknowledge its necessity, which she has not yet done. If she refuses to address her own shortcomings and continues instead to point fingers at others, casting into the void all who dare to challenge her, she will not have matured as a leader. She will no doubt continue to succeed in generating national attention and riling up the passions of her base. But if she does decide to apply herself to mastering the issues and takes some good advice from people who want to help her, she might just yet join the long list of politicians who took advantage of being underestimated to succeed beyond what the doubters dreamed feasible.

★ ★ ★

Acknowledgments

WE ARE ETERNALLY GRATEFUL for the love and support that our families and dear friends have provided throughout this yearlong process. Estelle and Mick Walshe and Lynn and Jim Conroy were always on call to offer just the right words of encouragement, as they have been throughout our lives. In addition to that, Jim Conroy's red pen was a merciless, yet indispensable, weapon that chiseled the cumbersome first draft of this book into something more to the point, one "the fact that" at a time. Heartfelt thanks are also in order to Dalia and Adam Goby, Louise and Arnold Magid, Jodi Buckman, Emily Cole, Lauren Kratz, Sean Kaplan, Kimberly and Jason Wynn, Isabella and Allen Fitzgerald, Erin Hennessy Conroy, John Hennessy, Justin Shuster, Shannon Semler, George Tully, Mike Mahoney, Dave Waytz, Eamon Monahan, Pete

Brancale, and Jared Berenter. We would also like to recognize our grandparents who are no longer with us: Bernard and Marguerite Conroy, Martina and Joe Walshe, and Bessie Fish. We know how much they would have enjoyed seeing this book in print.

Steve Chaggaris never seems to get the credit he deserves, which is why it is so gratifying to thank him for providing a life-changing opportunity. Alice Martell is quite simply the hardest-working and finest literary agent in the business, and this book would never have been written without her. Dan Collins knows what an immeasurable debt we owe him for introducing us to her. Alice found the ideal home for us at PublicAffairs, where we were guided by Lisa Kaufman's first-rate vision, along with the team effort helmed by Clive Priddle, Peter Osnos, Susan Weinberg, Whitney Peeling, Melissa Raymond, and Jen Kelland. Robert Draper was a generous friend and mentor who offered his sage advice and much- needed encouragement.

Jason Recher was particularly generous with his time, and his memory for detail was matched only by Matthew Scully's. Some of the former campaign staffers we spoke to wished not to be named, but Jeannie Etchart, Chris Edwards, Mark Salter, Cecil Wallace, Shealah Craighead, John Green, Douglas Holtz-Eakin, and Jordan Hostetter were particularly helpful in elucidating the historical record, and Lisa A. Kline was generous enough to speak to us exclusively.

There is no place quite like Alaska in the wintertime, and its inhabitants are rightfully proud of their unique way of life. We arrived at Sally and Chuck Heath's home in Wasilla as strangers, yet they treated us like old friends. We deeply appreciate their kindness and hospitality and the wonderful stories they shared of their daughter's youth. Special thanks are in order to the many Alaskans who were ready to lend a hand (or a well-insulated glove) every step of the way, including Tom Kizzia, John Bitney, Christopher Clark, Rhonda McBride, Rena Delbridge, Paul Fuhs, Ashley Brown, Larry Persily, Charles Fedullo, John Tracy, Rebecca Braun, Gregg Erickson, Dani

Carlson, Mike Carey, Jason Moore, Andrew Halcro, Randy Ruedrich, Dave Ditman, Bob Poe, Walt Monegan, Cody Rice, Lyda Green, Bob Weinstein, Wayne Anthony Ross, and Irl Stambaugh.

We particularly enjoyed our time spent in Juneau and want to thank some of the elected officials and staffers who educated us about their state's history and political culture, including Rep. Les Gara, Pat Galvin, Rep. Nancy Dahlstrom, Rep. John Harris, Rep. Mike Doogan, Matthew Moser, Shoshana Seligman, former senator Kim Elton, Sen. Lyman Hoffman, Rep. Carl Gatto, Rep. Bob Buch, Rep. Jay Ramras, Sen. Gary Stevens, Sen. Fred Dyson, Sen. Lesil McGuire, Rep. Beth Kerttula, Speaker Mike Chenault, Rep. Wes Keller, Rep. John Coghill, Rep. Harry Crawford, Sen. Gene Therriault, Rep. Bob Herron, Rep. Woodie Salmon, Rep. Berta Gardner, Rep. David Guttenberg, Rep. Scott Kawasaki, Rep, Chris Tuck, Rep. Bob Lynn, Dirk Moffatt, Mike Sica, Sen. Bert Stedman, Sen. Tom Wagoner, Rep. Cathy Munoz, and Sen. Bettye Davis.

It was especially fun to sit down with members of the Wasilla Warriors' 1982 state championship basketball team, including Don Teeguarden, Susan Oakley, and Katy Allers, and Iron Doggers Jim Wilke, Scott Davis, John Faeo, and Evan Booth. Thank you for sharing your moving experiences and death-defying tales, many of which would not fit onto these pages but nonetheless deserve their own book. Thanks are also in order to John Coale, Fred Malek, Rebecca Mansour, Bill Kristol, Fred Barnes, Jeb Bradley, Sarah Huckabee, Ken Green, Chuck Larson, Eric Woolson, Ed Failor, Kraig Paulsen, Dave Roederer, Steve Scheffler, and Dotty Lynch.

Finally, we owe a special debt of gratitude to Peter Hamby, Tim Albrecht, Elizabeth Holmes, Matt Stuart, Erin McPike, Katie Connolly, Michael Luo, Abby Brack, Will Ritter, Michael Levenson, Alex Marquardt, and everyone else with whom we spent some of the most challenging, yet incomparably rewarding, months of our lives on the 2008 campaign trail.

✯ ✯ ✯

Sources

THE BULK OF OUR REPORTING for this book came from the 190 interviews we conducted over eight months with McCain/Palin campaign staffers, Alaska state legislators and staff, Governor Palin's friends and family, journalists in Alaska, and political experts and consultants in the Lower 48. We have recognized many of these people in our acknowledgments, and others did not wish to be named. We also consulted the following sources.

INTRODUCTION
In this chapter we used *Fox News*'s election night coverage, specifically the conversation between Brit Hume and Karl Rove when Hume called Ohio for Barack Obama. Palin was listening to their coverage when she found out that her ticket had lost the state of Ohio.

CHAPTER ONE
Becker, Jo, Peter S. Goodman, and Michael Powell. "Once Elected, Palin Hired Friends and Lashed Foes." *New York Times*, September 23, 2008, www.nytimes.com/ 2008/09/14/us/politics/14palin.html (last accessed August 9, 2009).

Benet, Lorenzo. *Trailblazer: An Intimate Biography of Sarah Palin.* New York: Simon and Schuster, 2009.

Grove, Gary. "Sarah Heath Profile." *Mat-su Valley Frontiersman*, March 11, 1982.

Klott, Kevin. "Wasilla Girls Deny Juneau Douglas." *Anchorage Daily News*, March 25, 2007, C1.

Outside the Lines. "Outside the Lines Looks at Palin's Basketball Days," first broadcast October, 26, 2008, by ESPN.

Singler, Brian. "Wasilla Fans, Team Bask in a Double Glow." *Anchorage Daily News*, March 26, 2007, C1.

Wilmot, Ron. "Valley Represents as Wasilla Celebrates Two Championships." *Anchorage Daily News*, March 25, 2007, AA1.

CHAPTER TWO

"Alaska Ear." *Anchorage Daily News*, August 13, 2006, B2.

"Alaska Gov. Murkowski Concedes Defeat in GOP Gubernatorial Primary." Associated Press, August 23, 2006, www.foxnews.com/story/0,2933,209918,00.html (last accessed August 9, 2009).

Burns, Alexander. "On Small Stage, Palin Scored Big Debate Wins." *Politico.* October 1, 2008, www.politico.com/news/stories/1008/14158.html (last accessed August 9, 2009).

"FBI Raids Legislative Offices." *Anchorage Daily News*, September 1, 2006.

"First Dance; Having an Inaugural Ball in Juneau." *Anchorage Daily News*, January 22, 2007, A1. Photo by Chris Miller, Associated Press.

Henning, Sarah. "Rare Alaska Glamour Arrives with Governor Galas; Parties: They Range from Punch in a School Gym to Black-tie Optional." *Anchorage Daily News*, January 19, 2007, A1.

Morris, Will. "Palin Adds Glamour to Gala." *Juneau Empire*, January 21, 2007, www.juneauempire.com/stories/012107/loc_20070121013.shtml (last accessed August 9, 2009).

"Poll Shows Palin, Knowles in Lead; Race for Governor: Binkley Running Second and Murkowski Third for Republican Nomination." *Anchorage Daily News*, July 23, 2006, A1.

"Seward's Icebox Heats Up." *Wonkette.* August 11, 2006, http://wonkette.com/193613/sewards-icebox-heats-up (last accessed August 9, 2009).

Volz, Matt. "Palin's Split with Alaska GOP Opened Opportunity." Associated Press, September 10, 2008, http://abcnews.go.com/Politics/wireStory?id=5767780 (last accessed August 9, 2009).

CHAPTER THREE

"Alaska QuickFacts." US Census Bureau, http://quickfacts.census.gov/qfd/states/02000.html (last accessed August 9, 2009).

"Alaska Special Session Report: ACES." *Alaska Budget Report*, November 19, 2007.

Alaska State Legislature. "Bill History/Action for 25th Legislature: HB2001." Alaska State Legislature. December 19, 2007, www.legis.state.ak.us/basis/get_bill.asp?bill=HB2001&session=25 (last accessed August 9, 2009).

———. "Journal Text for HB2001 in the 25th Legislature." Alaska State Legislature. November 11, 2007, www.legis.state.ak.us/basis/get_jrn_page.asp?session=25&bill=HB20001&jrn=1645&hse=H (last accessed August 9, 2009).

"Anchorage: Population Profile." City-Data.com, www.city-data.com/us-cities/The-West/Anchorage-Population-Profile.html (last accessed August 9, 2009).

Bradner, Tim. "Lawmakers Cringe Over Governor's Deep Budget Cuts." *Alaska Journal of Commerce,* July 8, 2007, www.alaskajournal.com/stories/070807/hom_2007070 8005.shtml (last accessed August 9, 2009).

Cockerham, Sean. "Special Session Ends with 25% Oil Tax." *Anchorage Daily News,* November 17, 2007, www.adn.com/oil/story/211548.html (last accessed August 9, 2009).

Forgey, Pat. "House Looks to Join Challenge to Palin's Vetoes." *Juneau Empire,* March 13, 2008, www.juneauempire.com/stories/031308/sta_257548706.shtml (last accessed August 9, 2009).

Halcro, Andrew. "Bill McAllister: A Question of Timing and Bias." AndrewHalcro.com, www.andrewhalcro.com/bill_mcallister_the_job_the_timing_the_question (last accessed August 9, 2009).

"He's Looking for Love, and Mobility." *New York Times,* December 4, 1997, www.nytimes .com/1997/12/04/nyregion/he-s-looking-for-love-and-mobility.html (last accessed August 9, 2009).

Hopkins, Kyle. "Same-Sex Benefits Ban Gets Palin Veto." *Anchorage Daily News,* December 29, 2006.

"Juneau: Population Profile." City-Data.com, www.city-data.com/us-cities/The-West/ Juneau-Population-Profile.html.

Loy, Wesley. "House OKs Gas Pipeline Plan." *Anchorage Daily News,* July 23, 2008, www.adn .com/money/industries/oil/pipeline/story/472490.html (last accessed August 9, 2009).

———. "Legislature Adjourns on Time." *Anchorage Daily News,* April 13, 2008, www.adn .com/news/alaska/story/374722.html (last accessed August 9, 2009).

———. "Palin Picks Canadian Company for Gas Line." *Anchorage Daily News,* January 5, 2008, www.adn.com/money/industries/oil/pipeline/story/255462.html (last accessed August 9, 2009).

———. "TransCanada Gets Senate's OK." *Anchorage Daily News,* August 2, 2008.

Mauer, Richard. "Feds Eye Stevens' Home Remodeling Project." *Anchorage Daily News,* May 29, 2007, www.adn.com/news/politics/fbi/stevens/story/242982.html (last accessed August 9, 2009).

"Maze of Injustice: The Failure to Protect Indigenous Women from Sexual Violence in the USA." Amnesty International. Spring 2007, www.amnestyusa.org/women/maze/ Jurisdiction-Focussheet.pdf (last accessed August 9, 2009).

McAllister, Bill. "Fagan Co-host Departs for Job with Palin Administration." KTUU.com. December 22, 2006, www.ktuu.com/Global/story.asp?S=5852590 (last accessed August 9, 2009).

Office of Alaska Governor Sarah Palin. "Frequently Asked Questions Regarding the Alaska Gasline Inducement Ace ('AGIA') and the AGIA Process." Alaska.gov, www.gov.state.ak.us/agia/agia_faqs_11808.pdf (last accessed August 9, 2009).

"Palin a Hit at Holiday Open House at Governor's Mansion." *Juneau Empire* (via Associated Press and local wires), December 12, 2006.

"Palin on Energy." *Anchorage Daily News,* October 11, 2008, www.adn.com/opinion/ story/553653.html (last accessed August 9, 2009).

Petty, Andrew. "Palin Addresses Juneau Jitters on Capital Move." *Juneau Empire,* August 27, 2006, www.juneauempire.com/stories/082706/sta_20060827001.shtml (last accessed August 9, 2009).

Press Release from the Office of Alaska Governor Sarah Palin. *AFN Speech.* October 25, 2007.

"States Ranked by American Indian and Alaska Native Population." Census.gov. July 1, 1999, www.census.gov/population/estimates/state/rank/aiea.txt (last accessed August 9, 2009).

Toomey, Sheila. "The Alaska Ear: On the Move." *Anchorage Daily News*, April 6, 2008.

CHAPTER FOUR

Branchflower, Stephen. "Report to the Legislative Council." Alaska State Legislature. October 10, 2008, http://download1.legis.state.ak.us/DOWNLOAD.pdf (last accessed August 9, 2009).

Cockerham, Sean. "Palin Staff Pushed to Have Trooper Fired." *Anchorage Daily News*, August 14, 2008, www.adn.com/monegan/story/492964.html (last accessed August 9, 2009).

Holland, Megan. "Monegan Says He Was Pressured to Fire Cop." *Anchorage Daily News*, July 19, 2008, www.adn.com/politics/story/469135.html (last accessed August 9, 2009).

Hopkins, Kyle. "The Bailey Phone Call." *Anchorage Daily News*, August 13, 2008, http://community.adn.com/adn/node/128967 (last accessed August 9, 2009).

"Legislative Director Resigns." *Juneau Empire* (via the Associated Press), July 11, 2007, http://juneauempire.com/stories/071107/sta_director001.shtml (last accessed August 9, 2009).

Loy, Wesley. "Palin Accuses Monegan of Insubordination." *Anchorage Daily News*, September 15, 2008, www.adn.com/troopergate/story/527346.html (last accessed August 9, 2009).

Moore, Jason. "McCain Campaign Questions Motives in Monegan Inquiry." KTUU.com. September 15, 2008, www.ktuu.com/global/story.asp?S=9014325 (last accessed August 9, 2009).

Phillips, Michael M. "In Palin's Past, the Personal Got Political." *Wall Street Journal*, September 9, 2008, http://online.wsj.com/article/SB122092043531812813.html (last accessed August 9, 2009).

Quinn, Steve. "GOP Lawmakers Sue to Stop Palin Investigation." *Anchorage Daily News* (via the Associated Press), September 16, 2008, www.adn.com/palin/story/528049.html (last accessed August 9, 2009).

Ross, Brian, Justin Rood, Anna Schecter, and Megan Chuchmach. "Palin Backstab? Commissioner Praised Then Fired." *ABC News—The Blotter from Brian Ross*. September 11, 2008, http://abcnews.go.com/Blotter/Story?id=5778856 (last accessed August 9, 2009).

Volz, Matt. "Murkowski Volunteer Wounded in Shooting." *Juneau Empire* (via the Associated Press), August 23, 2006, www.juneauempire.com/stories/082306/sta_20060823014.shtml (last accessed August 9, 2009).

CHAPTER FIVE

Dilanian, Ken. "Palin Backed 'Bridge to Nowhere' in 2006." *USA Today*, September 1, 2008, www.usatoday.com/news/politics/election2008/2008-08-31-palin-bridge_N.htm (last accessed August 9, 2009).

Draper, Robert. "The Making (and Remaking) of McCain." *New York Times Magazine*, October 22, 2008, www.nytimes.com/2008/10/26/magazine/26mccain-t.html?_r=1&scp=1&sq=draper%20and%20mccain&st=cse (last accessed August 9, 2009).

Hopkins, Kyle. "11th-Hour Selection Was a Surprise Even to the Palin Family." *Anchorage Daily News*, August 30, 2008, www.adn.com/politics/story/510777.html (last accessed August 9, 2009).

Kizzia, Tom. "Palin Touts Stance on 'Bridge to Nowhere,' Doesn't Note Flip-Flop." *Anchorage Daily News*, September 31, 2008, www.adn.com/sarahpalin/story/511471.html (last accessed August 9, 2009).

Luo, Michael, and Cathy Horyn. "3 Palin Stylists Cost Campaign More Than $165,000." *New York Times*, December 5, 2008, www.nytimes.com/2008/12/06/us/politics/06palin.html (last accessed August 9, 2009).

Luo, Michael, and Leslie Wayne. "GOP Consultant Reimbursed for Palin Shopping Spree." *New York Times*, October 22, 2008, http://thecaucus.blogs.nytimes.com/2008/10/22/gop-consultant-reimbursed-for-palin-shopping-spree (last accessed August 9, 2009).

Mauer, Richard. "Palin to Back Miller for U.S. Senate." *Anchorage Daily News*, April 24, 2004.

"McCain Introduces Palin as Running Mate." *Washington Post* (via CQ Transcripts Wire), August 29, 2008, www.washingtonpost.com/wp-dyn/content/article/2008/08/29/AR2008082901882.html?sid=ST2008083000375&s_pos=top (last accessed August 9, 2009).

Palin, Sarah, Gov. Interview by Sean Hannity and Alan Colmes. *Hannity & Colmes*. Fox News Channel. September 18, 2008.

"Palin Triggers RNC Ratings Spike." Neilsen Wire, September 4, 2008, http://blog.nielsen.com/nielsenwire/media_entertainment/palin-triggers-rnc-ratings-spike (last accessed August 9, 2009).

"Poll: McCain Takes Post-Convention Lead." CBSNews.com. September 8, 2008, www.cbsnews.com/stories/2008/09/08/opinion/polls/main4427157.shtml (last accessed August 9, 2009).

"Post-Democratic Convention Poll." CBSNews.com. September 1, 2008, www.cbsnews.com/htdocs/pdf/Aug08bPostDemConv.pdf (last accessed August 9, 2009).

CHAPTER SIX

"Frontiersman Exclusive: Palin Responds to Questions." *Mat-Su Valley Frontiersman*, September 30, 2008, www.frontiersman.com/articles/2008/09/30/breaking_news/doc48e1e1294d418713321438.txt (last accessed August 9, 2009).

Ross, Brian, and Len Tepper. "'October Surprise' Over Palin Investigation." *ABC News The Blotter from Brian Ross*, September 2, 2008, http://abcnews.go.com/Blotter/Story?id=5702697&page=1 (last accessed August 25, 2009).

CHAPTER SEVEN

Anchorage Daily News Editorial Board. "Palin Vindicated?" *Anchorage Daily News*, October 13, 2008, www.adn.com/opinion/view/story/555236.html (last accessed August 9, 2009).

"Cambria County, PA Voter Registration Statistics." Pennsylvania Department of State, www.dos.state.pa.us/elections/lib/elections/055_voter_registration_statistics/currentstats/currentvotestats.xls (last accessed August 9, 2009).

CNN Newsroom with Rick Sanchez. "Palins and the Fringe," first broadcast October 15, 2008, by CNN.

Dowd, Maureen. "Sarah's Pompom Palaver." *New York Times*, October 4, 2008, www.nytimes.com/2008/10/05/opinion/05dowd.html (last accessed August 9, 2009).

Harris, John F, and Mike Allen. "Palin Clears Bar, Still Falls Short." *Politico*. October 3, 2008, www.politico.com/news/stories/1008/14235.html (last accessed August 9, 2009).

Kristol, Bill. "The Wright Stuff." *New York Times*, October 5, 2008, www.nytimes.com/2008/10/06/opinion/06kristol.html (last accessed August 9, 2009).

Martin, Jonathan. "McCain Pulling Out of Michigan." *Politico*. October 2, 2008, www
    .politico.com/blogs/jonathanmartin/1008/McCain_pulling_out_of_Michigan.html
    (last accessed August 9, 2009).

Rainey, James. "CNN Bid to Tie Palin to Secessionists Is a Stretch." *Los Angeles Times*, Octo-
    ber 15, 2008, http://articles.latimes.com/2008/oct/15/nation/na-onthemedia15
    (last accessed August 9, 2009).

Shane, Scott. "Obama and 60's Bomber: A Look into Crossed Paths." *New York Times*,
    October 3, 2008, www.nytimes.com/2008/10/04/us/politics/04ayers.html?_r
    =1&oref=slogin (last accessed August 9, 2009).

CHAPTER EIGHT

Bash, Dana. "McCain Aide Disputes Sources, Denies Firing." CNN.com. November 6,
    2008, http://politicalticker.blogs.cnn.com/2008/11/06/mccain-adviser-disputes-
    campaign-i-was-not-fired (last accessed August 9, 2009).

———. "Sources: McCain Aide Fired for 'Trashing' Staff." CNN.com. November 5, 2008,
    http://politicalticker.blogs.cnn.com/2008/11/05/soruces-mccain-aide-fired-for-
    trashing-staff (last accessed August 9, 2009).

Bash, Dana, Peter Hamby, and John King. "Palin's 'Going Rogue,' McCain Aide Says."
    CNN.com. October 26, 2008, www.cnn.com/2008/POLITICS/10/25/palin
    .tension (last accessed August 9, 2009).

Bumiller, Elisabeth. "Internal Battles Divided McCain and Palin Camps." *New York Times*,
    November 5, 2008, www.nytimes.com/2008/11/06/us/politics/06mccain.html
    (last accessed August 9, 2009).

Cox, Ana Marie. "A Q and A with Nicolle Wallace, Palin's Chaperone." *The Daily Beast*. Oc-
    tober 28, 2008, www.thedailybeast.com/blogs-and-stories/2008–10–28/a-q-and-a-
    with-nicolle-wallace/1 (last accessed August 9, 2009).

Cummings, Jeanne. "RNC Shells Out 150K for Palin." *Politico*. October 22, 2008, www
    .politico.com/news/stories/1008/14805.html (last accessed August 9, 2009).

Hemingway, Mark. "Who's the Palin Leaker from the McCain Campaign?" *National Review
    Online—The Corner*. July 1, 2009, http://corner.nationalreview.com/post/
    ?q=YWNhZjNjMDBiMDk4MGFiMmU1MGU4NmZmZDMwMmZiZjM
    (last accessed August 9, 2009).

Kurtz, Howard. "After Taking Some Shots, She Fires Back." *Washington Post*, November
    13, 2008, C1.

McMahon, Robert. "McCain's Brain Trust." *Newsweek*, June 3, 2008, www.newsweek
    .com/id/139898/page/3 (last accessed August 9, 2009).

Petumenos, Timothy. "Report of Findings and Recommendations." *State of Alaska Person-
    nel Board*. AnchorageDailyNews.com. November 3, 2008, http://media.adn
    .com/smedia/2008/11/03/12/report-sept12008-complaint.source.prod_
    affiliate.7.pdf (last accessed August 9, 2009).

Smith, Ben. "Palin Allies Report Rising Camp Tensions." *Politico*. October 25, 2008,
    www.politico.com/news/stories/1008/14929.html (last accessed August 9, 2009).

CHAPTER NINE

Cockerham, Sean. "Palin Calls for Hiring Freeze, Big Projects." *Anchorage Daily News*, Janu-
    ary 22, 2009, www.adn.com/news/government/legislature/story/664609.html
    (last accessed August 9, 2009).

Delbridge, Rena. "Palin, Ramras Spar over Aid to Alaska Villages." *Fairbanks Daily News-
    Miner*, February 5, 2009, www.newsminer.com/news/2009/feb/05/palin-ramras-
    engaged-flap-over-aid-alaska-villages (last accessed August 9, 2009).

"Exit Polls: Age v. Race." CNN.com. November 5, 2008, http://politicalticker.blogs.cnn
.com/2008/11/05/exit-polls-age-v-race (last accessed August 9, 2009).

Forgey, Pat. "Legislators Blame Palin for Deteriorating Relationship." *Juneau Empire*, April
12, 2009, www.juneauempire.com/stories/041209/loc_428496963.shtml (last accessed August 9, 2009).

"Fox Report with Shepard Smith." Carl Cameron report first broadcast November 5, 2008,
by Fox News Channel.

Hopkins, Kyle. "Palin Heads to Villages with Christian Group." *Anchorage Daily News*, February 19, 2009, www.adn.com/news/alaska/story/696338.html (last accessed August
9, 2009).

Hopkins, Kyle, and Tom Kizzia. "Western Alaska Villagers Ask for Help from State." *Anchorage Daily News*, January 16, 2008, www.adn.com/news/alaska/story/
657452.html (last accessed August 9, 2009).

McAllister, Bill. Interview by Eddie Burke. *Eddie Burke Show*. KBYR Radio. January 9, 2009.

Palin, Sarah, Gov. Interview by Greta Van Susteren. *On the Record with Greta Van Susteren*.
Fox News Channel. November 10, 2008.

Palin, Sarah, Gov. Interview by Larry King. *Larry King Live*. CNN. November 12, 2008.

Palin, Sarah, Gov. Interview by Matt Lauer. *Today*. NBC. November 11, 2008.

Quinn, Steve. "GOP Lawmakers Sue to Stop Palin Investigation." *Anchorage Daily News* (via
the Associated Press), September 16, 2008, www.adn.com/palin/story/528049
.html (last accessed August 9, 2009).

"'We'll See,' Palin Says of 2012." CBSNews.com. November 6, 2008, www.cbsnews.com/
stories/2008/11/06/politics/main4577409.shtml (last accessed August 9, 2009).

Ziegler, John. *Media Malpractice: How Obama Got Elected and Palin Was Targeted*. DVD. John
Ziegler Productions, 2009.

CHAPTER TEN

Johnston, Levi. Interview by Tyra Banks. *The Tyra Banks Show*. CW. April 6, 2009.

Medred, Craig. "Familiar Faces on the Verge of Iron Dog Victory." *Anchorage Daily News*,
February 18, 2006.

Mowry, Tim. "Palin Suffers Broken Arm in Iron Dog." *Fairbanks Daily News-Miner*, February 17, 2008, www.newsminer.com/news/2008/feb/17/palin-suffers-broken-arm-
iron-dog (last accessed August 9, 2009).

Palin, Bristol. Interview by Greta Van Susteren. *On the Record with Greta Van Susteren*. Fox
News Channel. February 16, 2009.

CHAPTER ELEVEN

Cockerham, Sean. "Lawmakers, Governor Miss Connections over Stimulus." *Anchorage
Daily News*, March 26, 2009, www.adn.com/news/politics/story/738094.html (last
accessed August 9, 2009).

———. "Lawmakers, Palin Bicker to the Finish." *Anchorage Daily News*, April 18, 2009,
www.adn.com/news/government/legislature/story/764532.html (last accessed
August 9, 2009).

———. "Lawmakers reject Ross as AG." *Anchorage Daily News*, April 16, 2009, http://www.
adn.com/news/politics/story/762037.html (last accessed August 25, 2009).

———. "Palin Vetoes Include Some Stimulus Money." *Anchorage Daily News*, May 21,
2009, www.adn.com/189/story/803952.html (last accessed August 9, 2009).

———. "SarahPAC Said to Have Jumped Gun on GOP Dinner." *Anchorage Daily News*,
March 17, 2009, www.adn.com/palin/story/726702.html (last accessed August 9, 2009).

————. "Stimulus Funds Pending as Legislature Winds Down." *Anchorage Daily News*, April 11, 2009, www.adn.com/news/government/legislature/budget/story/756967 .html (last accessed August 9, 2009).

"Consolidated List of Ethics Complaints Filed against Alaska Governor Sarah Palin since August 2008." *Alaska Pride.* July 25, 2009, http://alaskapride.blogspot.com/2009/05/consolidated-list-of-ethics-complaints.html (last accessed August 9, 2009).

Delbridge, Rena. "Palin Says She Never Asked Begich to Resign." *Fairbanks Daily News-Miner*, April 11, 2009, www.newsminer.com/news/2009/apr/11/palin-says-she-never-asked-begich-resign (last accessed August 9, 2009).

Forgey, Pat. "Palin blames 'public lies' for Ross rejection." *Juneau Empire*, April 21, 2009, http://www.juneauempire.com/stories/042109/sta_431404858.shtml (last accessed August 25, 2009).

"Ethics Complaints Filed against Palin" *Anchorage Daily News* (via the Associated Press), June 21, 2009, www.adn.com/palin/story/838912.html (last accessed August 9, 2009).

"From $514.1 Million to $29 Million: Palin and the Stimulus." GOP12.com. April 29, 2009, www.gop12.com/2009/04/from-5141-million-to-29-million-palin.html (last accessed August 9, 2009).

Martin, Jonathan. "Sarah Palin In, Then Out, Back In—and Now Again Out of Fundraising Dinner." *Politico.* June 7, 2009, www.politico.com/news/stories/0609/23454.html (last accessed August 9, 2009).

McBride, Rhonda. "Senate Democrats Reject Palin's Second Choice for Empty Seat." *KTUU* and Associated Press Wire Reports, April 10, 2009, www.ktuu.com/global/story.asp?S=10164604 (last accessed August 9, 2009).

Robichaud, Holly. "University wrong place prestige over principle." *Boston Herald*, May 17, 2009. http://www.bostonherald.com/blogs/news/lone_republican/index.php/2009/05/17/university-wrong-place-prestige-above-principle/ (last accessed August 28, 2009).

Thiessen, Mark. "Aide Says Palin Will OK Most Stimulus Funds." *Anchorage Daily News* (via the Associated Press), April 28, 2009, www.adn.com/palin/story/776620.html (last accessed August 9, 2009).

————. "Last-Minute Deal Seals Senate Seat for Former Juneau Mayor." *Anchorage Daily News* (via the Associated Press), April 20, 2009, www.adn.com/news/government/legislature/story/766537.html (last accessed August 9, 2009).

CHAPTER TWELVE

Cockerham, Sean. "Johnston Says Palin Had Eye on the Money." *Anchorage Daily News*, July 9, 2009, www.adn.com/palin/story/859720.html (last accessed August 9, 2009).

Palin, Sarah. Interview by Andrea Mitchell. *Today.* NBC. July 6, 2009.

————. "Statement on the Current Health Care Debate." Posted on Sarah Palin's Facebook page, August 7, 2008, www.facebook.com/note.php?note_id=113851103434&1&index=0 (last accessed August 9, 2009).

White, Bill, Sean Cockerham, and Elizabeth Bluemink. "Exxon Joins TransCanada in Push to Build Gas Pipeline." *Anchorage Daily News*, June 11, 2009, www.adn.com/money/industries/oil/story/827548.html (last accessed August 9, 2009).

Index

Abortion issue, 39, 52–53, 160, 161,
  248
ACES. *See* Alaska's Clear and
  Equitable Share
AGIA. *See* Alaska Gasline
  Inducement Act
Ailes, Roger, 180
AIP. *See* Alaskan Independence Party
Alaska Conservation Voters forum,
  52–53
Alaska energy assistance, 254–255
Alaska Executive Branch Ethics Act,
  159
Alaska Gasline Inducement Act
  (AGIA), 74–75, 268
Alaska governor's mansion, 60, 62–63
Alaska gubernatorial general
  election, 50–56
Alaska gubernatorial primary
  election, 41–50, 57–58

Alaska House of Representatives,
  61–62
Alaska Oil and Gas Conservation
  Commission, 43–44
Alaska Senate, 61–62, 242–245
Alaskan food crisis, 209–212
Alaskan Independence Party (AIP),
  166–168
Alaska's Clear and Equitable Share
  (ACES), 72–74
Albright, Madeleine, 201
Alcoholic Beverage Control Board,
  87
Alfalfa Club dinner, 201–202
Alfred P. Murrah Federal Building,
  166
Allen, Bill, 66
Allen, Mike, 178
Allers, Katy, 37
Anchorage Daily News, 48, 66–67, 159

Anderson, Tom, 44
ANWR. *See* Arctic National Wildlife
    Refuge
Arctic National Wildlife Refuge
    (ANWR), 92
Audette, Marc-Antoine, 185–188
Ayers, Bill, 154–155

Bailey, Frank, 83, 86–87
Baldwin, Alec, 170
Barnes, Fred, 179–180, 269–270
Bash, Dana, 178
Begich, Mark, 36, 236–238
Begich, Stephanie, 35–36
Berrier, John, 95
Biden, Joe, 93
    and debate, 139, 143, 145, 147, 149,
        150, 151
    and press, 124, 126, 171
Biegel, Linda Kellen, 240
Biegun, Steve, 114, 135–136, 185–188
Binkley, John, 42, 46, 55, 57–58
Bitney, John, 42, 44–45, 46, 48–50,
        55–56
    dismissal of, 77–81, 82, 83
    and Monegan, 88–89
    and Palin's resignation, 262
Blum, Dick, 201
Bradley, Jeb, 162–165
Branchflower, Stephen, 130, 158–159,
        160, 176, 189
Braun, Rebecca, 64–65
Bridge to Nowhere (Gravina Island
    Project), 109–110, 131
Brown, Ashley, 34
Buch, Bob, 63, 199
Buchanan, Brooke, 15
Buchanan, Pat, 113
Burch, Tory, 117
Burke, Eddie, 230, 257
Burke/Trig incident, 257–258
Bush, George W., 3, 4, 106, 114, 160,
        274
Bush Doctrine, 130

Cameron, Carl, 151, 194
Carlson, Dani, 53–54
Chao, Elaine, 201
Charlie (child with Down
    syndrome), 3–4
Chenault, Mike, 208, 209, 213, 248,
    249
Cheney, Dick, 114, 201
Cheney, Liz, 201
Clark, Christopher, 65–66, 67, 78, 79
    dismissal of, 81–83
Clinton, Bill, 97, 274
Clinton, Hillary, 108
Coale, John, 229, 251
Coghill, John, 71, 75
Colberg, Talis, 62, 245
Comella, Maria, 113–115, 181
Conservative Political Action
    Conference, 247
Conservatives4Palin.com, 255–256
Couric, Katie, 136–139, 139–143,
    195–196, 250, 268
Craighead, Shealah, 218
Crawford, Harry, 62, 204–205, 215
Crist, Charlie, 187, 201
Culvahouse, A. B., 97

Dahlstrom, Nancy, 55, 213, 261
Davis, Rick, 6, 9, 11, 12, 95
    and Alaskan Independence Party,
        166
    and Couric interviews, 139
    and debate, Palin/Biden, 146
    and e-mail/leak investigation,
        180–181
    and Michigan rally, 153
Davis, Scott, 221–222, 225, 226–228
Debate(s)
    gubernatorial, 52, 53–54
    Palin/Biden, 139, 143, 145–149,
        149–151
Delbridge, Rena, 234–237
Delgado, Bob, 97
Dew, Mike, 11, 13

Dial, Rodney, 86–87
Diamond, Bob, 201
Donahue, Jack, 157
Doogan, Mike, 74, 198, 204, 215
Dowd, Maureen, 149
Drake, Dwayne, 226
Duprey, Steve, 111, 164–165
Dyson, Fred, 63, 206

Eagleton, Tom, 115–116
Earmarks, 39, 85, 109, 110
Easterbrooks, Brad, 185
Edwards, Chris, 12, 134–35, 141–142
Edwards, John, 10
Egan, Dennis, 244
Elton, Kim, 242–243, 268
E-mail/leak investigation, 179–181
Embedded reporters, 125. See also
    Media
Erickson, Gregg, 72–73
Eskew, Tucker, 106–107, 142
    and Alaskan Independence Party,
        167
    and Gibson interview, 129
    and Sarkozy prank, 187
    and Vargas interview, 184
Etchart, Jeannie, 8–9, 127, 194–195
Eudy, Carla, 17–18
Exxon, 267–268
Exxon-Valdez case, 138

Failor, Ed, 273
Federal stimulus package, 214–215,
    253–255
Fedullo, Charles, 67, 68, 69–70
Feinstein, Diane, 201
Fellowship of Christian Athletes, 34–
    35
Ferraro, Geraldine, 108
Ferry, Christian, 97, 98
Fey, Tina, 131–132, 132–133, 137,
    169, 170, 275, 279
Fiorina, Carly, 132
Florida, 157, 272

Foster, Richard, 214
French, Hollis, 74, 130
Frist, Bill, 185
Fuhs, Paul, 42, 45–46
Fund-raising events, 156–158,
    251–252

Gallagher, Jerry, 248
Galvin, Pat, 64, 69
Gara, Les, 64, 120–121, 207, 213–214,
    255
George, Andy, 226
Gibson, Charlie, 128, 129, 130–131
Gingrich, Newt, 252, 272
Girdwood retreat, 199–201
Giuliani, Rudy, 113, 274
Glassner, Mike, 175
Goldsmith, Brian, 140
Graham, Franklin, 211
Graham, Lindsay, 9, 92
Gravina Island Project. See Bridge to
    Nowhere
Green, John, 129–130, 220
Green, Lyda, 70–71, 73
Greenspan, Alan, 201
Grussendorf, Tim, 244
Gun issue, 39, 63
Guttenberg, David, 62, 63–64, 215

Halcro, Andrew, 50, 51–53, 55, 89,
    163
Hamby, Peter, 178
Handlers, 250–251
Hannity, Sean, 103, 132–133
Harris, John, 80–81, 82, 205
Hasselbeck, Elisabeth, 177
Hayes, Lindsay, 5, 177
Healthcare, 265–266
Heath, Chuck, 24–29, 32, 34, 39, 47,
    118, 195, 279
Heath, Chuck, Jr., 23, 24
Heath, Heather, 23, 24
Heath, Molly, 33, 86
Heath, Sally, 24–29, 34, 35, 118, 195

Herron, Bob, 209
Hickel, Wally, 166
Hoffman, Lyman, 244
Holmes, Lindsay, 74, 204
Holtz-Eagin, Douglas, 136
Hostetter, Jordan, 174
Huckabee, Mike, 272, 274
Hume, Brit, 8, 180
Hurricane Gustav, 114

Ifill, Gwen, 149
Inaugural ball, 56–57
Iowa, 272–274
Irwin, Tom, 64
Isaacson, Walter, 201

Johansen, Kyle, 214, 215
Johnston, Levi, 98, 119–120, 229–231
Johnston, Mercede, 229–230
Johnston, Sherry, 229–230
Juneau, 59–61, 66

Kaplan, Rick, 140
Karzai, Hamid, 134
Kawasaki, Scott, 64
Kennedy, John F., 38
Kerttula, Beth, 243–244, 246
King, John, 178
King, Larry, 196
Kissinger, Henry, 134, 135
Kline, Lisa A., 21, 116–119, 158
Knowles, Tony, 50, 52, 53, 55, 70
Kohring, Heyde, 30
Kristol, Bill, 155–156, 179, 180, 270
KTUU, 38, 67

Large, Bill, 46–48
Larson, Chuck, 273–274
Larson, Jeff, 117
Lauer, Matt, 195
Leighow, Sharon, 56–57, 67–68, 80,
    241–242

Leno, Jay, 152
Letterman, David, 152, 256–257, 262
Lieberman, Joe, 9, 92–93, 100, 145
Loncar, Brad, 180
The Looming Tower, 127

Magazines, 127
Malek, Fred, 201–202, 252, 260, 261,
    275
Mansour, Rebecca, 255–256
Martin, Jonathan, 151
Mat-Su Valley Frontiersman
    questionnaire, 136–137
McAllister, Bill, 68–69, 82, 197–198,
    251–252
McBride, Rhonda, 67, 84–85,
    234–235
McCain, Cindy, 9, 13, 97, 99, 148
McCain, John, 15, 83, 173, 274
    and debate, Palin/Biden, 146
    and e-mail/leak investigation, 180,
        181–182
    and Malek dinner, 201
    and New Hampshire, 161–162
    and Palin, dinner invitation to, 7
    and Palin, Todd, 225
    and Palin as vice presidential
        candidate, announcement of,
        107
    and Palin's concession speech,
        9–10, 13, 14
    and post-campaign retreat, 195
    and press, 124, 125, 126, 171
    and running mate search, 91–94
    and Wright, 150, 155–156
McCain/Palin campaign
    and e-mail/leak investigation,
        179–181
    internal discord in, 172–174,
        178–182
    and Palin, Todd, 219–220
McConnell, Mitch, 201
McGuire, Lesil, 44, 247, 254, 277–278

McLeod, Andree, 239
McVeigh, Timothy, 166
Media, 54, 112. *See also* Embedded
    reporters; Press
Media Malpractice (film), 196–197
Michigan, 151–153, 272
Miller, Mike, 104
Millet, Charisse, 213, 214
Miss Alaska competition, 38
Mitchell, Andrea, 201, 202, 262
Monegan, Walt, 74, 83–89, 97,
    129–130, 189, 198–199, 210
    and Palin, Todd, 219
Moreno, Dave, 46
Munoz, Cathy, 61
Murkowski, Frank, 42, 43, 49–50, 55,
    63, 64, 208
    and McAllister, 68
    and press, 65
Murkowski, Lisa, 55, 85, 237

National Governors Association, 69,
    91–92, 247
National Republican Congressional
    Committee (NRCC), 251–252
National Republican Senatorial
    Committee (NRSC), 251–252
Natural gas pipeline, 64, 74–75, 95,
    120, 235, 238, 243, 267–268
Nebraska, 153–154
Neiwert, David, 165–166
Nelson, Joe, 244
New Hampshire, 161–165, 272,
    274–275
Newspaper/Magazine issue, 140,
    141, 195–196
Nixon, Richard, 275
Nizich, Mike, 85–86, 87–88, 95, 102,
    200–201, 210
Nobles, Bexie, 5, 6, 118, 194–195
    and Alaskan Independence Party,
    167
    and Sarkozy prank, 185, 186, 187

NRCC. *See* National Republican
    Congressional Committee
NRSC. *See* National Republican
    Senatorial Committee

Oakley, Susan, 32, 33
Obama, Barack, 38, 92, 202–203, 266,
    279
    and Alfalfa Club dinner, 201
    and convention speech, 101
    and Notre Dame commencement
    address, 248
    and Palin, attacks by, 120–121, 150,
    154–155, 155–156, 157, 161, 199
    and press, 124, 125, 126, 171
O'Callaghan, Ed, 198
Oil-tax reform, 72–73, 207, 243
Oklahoma City bombing, 166
Online donations, 108

Palin, Bristol (daughter), 224, 256
    and Johnston, Levi, 229
    and pregnancy, 97–98, 103,
    114–115, 229
    and Van Susteren interview, 229
Palin, J.D. (brother-in-law), 33
Palin, Piper (daughter), 16, 65–66,
    126, 222–223, 227, 241–242
Palin, Sarah
    and abortion issue, 39, 52–53, 160,
    161, 248
    and abortion-centric stump
    speech, 160
    and abuse of power, accusations
    of, 89, 158–160, 176–177, 189
    and acceptance speech, 105,
    107–109
    and announcement of candidacy,
    106–109
    and approval rating, 83, 139,
    199
    as beauty contestant, 38
    birth of, 27

Palin, Sarah (*continued*)
and Bitney, dismissal of, 77–81,
    82, 83
and Burke interview, 230
and Cameron interview, 151
character of, 19–20
as city councillor, 38–39
and Clark, dismissal of, 81–83
in college, 37–38
and Comella, dismissal of, 113–115
and communication skills, 51, 142
and concession speech, 3–6, 9–14
conservative values of, 33–34
and convention speech, 119–121
and Couric interviews, 136–139,
    139–143, 195–196, 250, 268
and debates, 52, 53–54, 139, 143,
    145–149, 149–151
early childhood of, 23–24
and election night, 15–18
in elementary school, 24
and End Times theology, 34
and energy policy, 70, 72–75
ethics complaints against, 239–241,
    261
and ethics crusade, 43–44, 67, 70–71
ethics investigation of, 112, 129–
    130, 158–160, 176–177, 189
and experience, 277–278
and farewell speech, 264–265
fighting instinct of, 231, 278–279
as fiscal conservative, 39, 62–63,
    71–72
and foreign policy experience, 134
and foreign travel, 26–27
and Gibson interview, 128, 129,
    130–131
and gun issue, 39, 63
and Hannity interview, 103,
    132–133, 171
and healthcare, 265–266
and high school basketball, 23–24,
    28, 29–32, 33, 34–37
and high school dating, 32–33

and high school grade point
    average of, 32
and high school track-and-field,
    28–29, 30
and infallibility syndrome, 238
and in-state duties, neglect of,
    204–215, 247–250, 252
and King interview, 196
and knowledge base, 103, 114,
    127, 132, 136, 279
and lack of cooperation, 163–165,
    167–168
and Lauer interview, 195
leadership style of, 69, 81
and lieutenant governor
    campaign, 42, 43
and magazines, 127
as maverick, 67, 94
as mayor, 39–40
and Mitchell interview, 262
and Monegan, dismissal of, 83–89,
    129–130, 158, 159
and newspaper/magazine issue,
    140, 141, 195–196
natural magnetism of, 64–65
polarizing effect of, 20
as potential running mate, 92,
    94–99, 108
and prayer, 148–149
and private jet, 63
and Real America speech, 276–277
as reformer, 43–44, 51
religious faith of, 33–35
and relocation of capital, 60–61
resignation of, as governor, 20,
    204, 259–265, 267
as rogue, 171–172, 173, 178–179,
    184
ruthless streak of, 22
and same-sex couples health
    benefits issue, 62
and self-preservation, 182
and sexual abuse issue, 84
sincerity of, 21–22

and son's service as protest
    rebuttal, 104
as sportscaster, 38
and Stambaugh, dismissal of, 40
and State of the State speech,
    202–204
and stump speech, 125, 129
and Supreme Court case issue, 138
and swearing-in ceremony, 56
and T-shirt issue, 41–46
and turkey pardon, 196
unveiling of, as vice presidential
    candidate, 99–106
and Van Susteren interview, 195,
    228–229
and Vargas interview, 183–184
and victim mentality, 172, 239
and victory speech, 1–3, 4, 5, 6
and wardrobe issue, 116–120, 158,
    175–176, 177–178, 179–180
and Williams interview, 172
and women's issues speech, 174
and Ziegler interview, 196–198
Palin, Todd (husband), 7–8, 32–33,
    46, 55, 96, 99, 217–220
and Alaskan Independence Party,
    166–168
and Bitney, 81
and ethics investigation, 176, 189
fighting instinct of, 231
and Letterman incident, 256
and McCain/Palin campaign, role
    in, 219–220
and Monegan, 219
personality of, 218–219, 220
and Tesoro Iron Dog race,
    220–229
and Troopergate, 85, 86, 87, 219
and wardrobe issue, 111, 118
and wife's resignation, 264
Palin, Track (son), 38, 103–104
Palin, Trig (son), 99–100, 161, 165,
    250, 257–258
Palin, Tripp (grandson), 230

Palin, Willow (daughter), 224, 256,
    257
Palin family
on news of mother as vice
    presidential candidate, 102–104
and wardrobe issue, 117–120
Parnell, Sean, 264
Paulsen, Kraig, 272–273
Pawlenty, Tim, 93, 98–99, 100, 105,
    272
Pennsylvania, 160–161
Perry, Kris, 7, 16, 83, 94–95, 96–97,
    98, 99, 101, 190, 194, 217, 241
and Alaskan Independence Party,
    167
and prayer, 148
Perry, Rick, 211, 248
Persily, Larry, 67, 69
Peters, Matt, 42
Petumenos, Tim, 176–177, 189
Poe, Bob, 51
Poehler, Amy, 131–132, 170
Powell, Colin, 100
Press, 64–69, 171–172, 174, 196–198,
    234–238. See also Media;
    Traveling press

Quayle, Dan, 10, 99, 268–269

Rallies, 127–128, 128–129. See also
    individual states
Ramras, Jay, 62, 73, 209–212
Reagan, Ronald, 52, 268, 269, 275
Recher, Jason, 10–12, 12–13, 13–14,
    15–18, 194–195
and Alaskan Independence Party,
    167
and Palin, Todd, 219
and Sarkozy prank, 186
and Saturday Night Live satire,
    169–170
Rodriguez, Alex, 256–257

Roe v. Wade, 138
Romney, Mitt, 93, 100, 105, 270–272, 276
Ross, Wayne Anthony, 245–247
Rove, Karl, 8
Ruaro, Randy, 210
Ruedrich, Randy, 43–46, 48, 67, 71, 208
   and Stevens, Ted, 236–238
Russia, 25, 131, 132, 138, 170

Salter, Mark, 5–6, 93, 97–99, 100–102, 107, 108
   and e-mail/leak investigation, 180
   and Palin's concession speech, 9, 12, 13
Same-sex couples health benefits issue, 62
Sarah Barracuda, 35
SarahPAC, 212, 251–253
Sarkozy prank, 185–188
Saturday Night Live satire, 25, 131–133, 137, 169–171
Scheffler, Steve, 273
Scheunemann, Randy, 136
   and debate, Palin/Biden, 145–146, 147, 150
   and e-mail/leak investigation, 179, 180–181
Schmidt, Steve, 17, 100–102, 103, 115, 116, 173, 197
   and Alaskan Independence Party, 166–168
   and Couric interviews, 139
   and debate, Palin/Biden, 146
   and e-mail/leak investigation, 180–181
   and Gibson interview, 129
   and Palin as potential running mate, 97–99
   and Palin's concession speech, 9, 10, 12, 13
   and Palin's knowledge base, 127
   and Palin's wardrobe, 180
   and potential running mates, 93–94
   and Sarkozy prank, 188
Schmitt, Tracey, 115, 132, 171–172, 176
Scully, Matthew, 100–102, 105, 109, 121, 202
   and Palin's abortion-centric stump speech, 160
   and Palin's concession and victory speeches, 3–4, 5–6, 11, 13
   and Palin's convention speech, 119
Seward, William, 252
Sexual abuse issue, 84
Smith, Andrew, 116, 171, 186
Smith, Ben, 178, 181
South Carolina, 275
Spank the Dog band, 41–42, 44–46
Stambaugh, Irl, 40
Stapleton, Meg, 67, 194, 198–199, 230, 231, 241
   and Burke/Trig incident, 257–258
   and Letterman incident, 257
   and NRSC/NRCC fundraiser, 250–252
Stedman, Bert, 206, 212, 247
Stevens, Ben, 61
Stevens, Gary, 200, 203
Stevens, Ted, 66, 182–183, 203, 236–238, 253
Stoltze, Bill, 51
Strutko, Wanda, 30
Sununu, John, 162–165
Supreme Court case issue, 138

Tallent, Becky, 146
Tasergate, 171
Teeguarden, Don, 29, 32, 33, 35, 36, 37
Tesoro Iron Dog race, 220–229, 239, 240
Thompson, Fred, 128–129
Tibbles, Mike, 78, 79, 81, 82
Time magazine, 262

Tracy, John, 67, 68
TransCanada, 74–75, 267–268
Traveling press, 123–127, 129, 133–
    134, 171–172. *See also* Press
Troopergate, 83, 85–89, 129–130,
    158–160, 171, 176–177, 189,
    198–199
  and Palin, Todd, 219
Truth Squad, 198–199
T-shirt issue, 41–46
Tucker, Nick, 210
Turkey pardon, 196
Twitter, 262–263
The Tyra Banks Show, 229–230

United Nations General Assembly,
    134–136
University of Hawaii, 37–38
University of Idaho, 38
Uribe, Alvaro, 134

Van Susteren, Greta, 195, 228–229
Vanderburgh County Right to Life
    Banquet, 248, 250
Vargas, Elizabeth, 183–184
VECO, 51, 66
Veghte, Ben, 118
Vetting process, 108

Wales, Dan, 37
Wallace, Cecil, 188
Wallace, Mark, 12, 145–146, 179, 180
Wallace, Nicolle, 12, 100–102
  and Alaskan Independence Party,
    166

and Couric interviews, 138
and Gibson interview, 129
and Palin's wardrobe, 116, 179–
    180
and Williams interview, 172
Wardrobe issue, 111, 116–120, 158,
    175–176, 177–178, 179–180
Wasilla, 24, 189–191
Wasilla Assembly of God, 34
Wasilla Bible Church, 34
Wasilla City Council, 38–39
Wasilla Multi-Use Sports Complex,
    39
Weinstein, Bob, 109–110
Weinstein, Jared, 106
Wendt, Greg, 111
White, Davis, 10–11, 12, 13, 17, 94–
    97, 98, 102
Wielechowski, Bill, 200
Wilke, Jim, 220, 223–224, 226
Williams, Brian, 172
Wilson, Peggy, 214
Woolson, Eric, 267
Wooten, Mike, 85–87, 88, 89, 158,
    171, 189
  and Palin, Todd, 219
  See also Troopergate
Wright, Jeremiah, 150, 155
Wright, Tom, 248–250

Yielding, Tom, 95–96, 102
Young, Don, 66

Ziegler, John, 196–198
Zuckman, Jill, 171

BARRY MORGENSTEIN

Shushannah Walshe was a producer at *Fox News* from 2001 until 2008. She was an embedded reporter on Mitt Romney's presidential campaign and also covered John McCain and Barack Obama before reporting on Sarah Palin's vice presidential campaign from start to finish.

Scott Conroy has worked as a *CBS News* and CBS News.com producer in New York and is currently a digital journalist based out of Chicago. He covered Mitt Romney's presidential campaign and Sarah Palin's vice presidential run as a *CBS News* embedded reporter.